NAKED THOUGHTS THAT ROAM ABOUT

John McGrath

John McGrath was born in Birkenhead, Cheshire, in 1935. After national service and Oxford University, he wrote and directed for theatre and television, as well as writing for cinema. Early work included *Z-Cars* for BBC-TV (1962), *Events While Guarding the Bofors Gun* (1966) and the screenplay for *Billion Dollar Brain* (1967). In 1971, together with Elizabeth MacLennan, he co-founded the 7:84 Theatre Company, which divided into Scottish and English companies in 1973 with McGrath remaining as Artistic Director of both. During his career McGrath wrote over 60 plays, including *Fish in the Sea* (1972), *The Cheviot, the Stag and the Black, Black Oil* (1973), *Blood Red Roses* (1980), *Border Warfare* (1989), *Watching for Dolphins* (1992) and, most recently, *HyperLynx* (2001). He was twice Visiting Fellow in Theatre at Cambridge University. His previous books include *A Good Night Out* (1981), *The Bone Won't Break* (1990) and *Six-Pack: Plays for Scotland* (1996).

McGrath founded Freeway Films in 1982, for which he produced, amongst others, *The Dressmaker* (1985), *Carrington* (1995), *Ma Vie en Rose* (1997) and *Aberdeen* (2002). He also founded Moonstone International Screen Labs to support and promote independent European filmmaking. He received Lifetime Achievement Awards from both BAFTA (in 1993) and the Writers' Guild of Great Britain (in 1997), as well as Honorary Doctorates from the University of Stirling and the University of London. He died in 2002.

Nadine Holdsworth

Nadine Holdsworth lectures in Theatre Studies at Warwick University, where she specialises in theatre that engages with the politics of class and nation. She completed her PhD on 7:84 England in 1995 and also catalogued the archive on 7:84 England at Cambridge University Library. She has subsequently written about 7:84, Theatre Workshop and Glasgow Unity in *New Theatre Quarterly* and the forthcoming *Cambridge History of British Theatre*.

John McGrath

NAKED THOUGHTS THAT ROAM ABOUT

Reflections on Theatre 1958–2001

edited by
Nadine Holdsworth

NICK HERN BOOKS
London

www.nickhernbooks.co.uk

A NICK HERN BOOK

Naked Thoughts That Roam About
first published in Great Britain in 2002 as a paperback original
by Nick Hern Books Limited, 14 Larden Road, London W3 7ST.

Lines on p. 244 from 'The Anachronistic Procession or Freedom
and Democracy' (translated by John Willett), from *Poems 1913-1956*
by Bertolt Brecht (Methuen Publishing Ltd), quoted with
permission of the publisher

British Library Cataloguing data for this book
is available from the British Library

ISBN
1 85459 239 4

Cover design: Ned Hoste, 2H

Typeset by Country Setting, Kingsdown, Kent CT14 8ES
Printed and bound in Great Britain by Biddles, Guildford

CONTENTS

CONTENTS

EDITOR'S ACKNOWLEDGEMENTS

For permission to quote from Brecht's poem 'The Anachronistic Procession or Freedom and Democracy' I would like to thank Methuen.

I would like to thank specific people and staff of the following organisations for taking the time to help me locate information, material and sources: Ann Beattie; David Bradby; Sarah Ferris; Anne Fleming; Emma Forbes; Richard Perkins; Cambridge University's Manuscripts Department; Glasgow University's Scottish Theatre Archive; The Scotsman Library; the National Museum of Scotland; the National Library of Scotland; Edinburgh City Council and Edinburgh International Festival. My gratitude is also due to Nick Hern and Caroline Downing for their patience and guidance in seeing this project through to publication.

I especially want to thank Elizabeth MacLennan for her warmth, encouragement and readiness to offer help whenever she could. I must also express my appreciation to Geoff Willcocks for his love, support and good-humoured acceptance that our study was to become a one-stop John McGrath archive.

Lastly, I must thank the late John McGrath, not only for his enthusiasm and commitment to this project, but also for his faith in the potential of theatre, socialism and humanity. He was, and will continue to be, a guiding light.

PREFACE

This book is by no means anything so portentous as my 'collected essays'. Rather it is an attempt at a 'documented account' of the arc – theatrical, political, social, literary – along which I have tried to steer my unruly creative life since I was ten. There is another book, about work in film and television, and maybe even another about Scotland, but this one is about theatre, my first love and discipline.

The 'documents' are pieces of all kinds I wrote at the time: sometimes with deep thought, sometimes against a deadline, sometimes in a rage or a passion. I stuck them all in a box and forgot about them, and then Nadine Holdsworth took them away and made sense of them. Then I could write the 'account' part, trying to be accurate and honest about my extremes and stupidities as well as explaining my motives and actions.

This 'documented account' of course leaves out several areas of work I never really documented properly; particularly in the development of my ideas on directing. A great deal of my writing styles sprang from my experience of directing – actors, design, lighting, audience relationships, comedy, variety and changes of mood. Another area which I regret not having documented better is that of music in theatre: its uses as an audience contact point – if it's the right music – as narrative, as emotional, as satirical, as comic, as pure enjoyment. But these 'Naked Thoughts' are enough for now, more than enough some will say.

I must thank a thousand people for their roles in this book, but first and foremost Nadine Holdsworth, whose hard work, patience, sweet temper and sense of humour have kept the whole thing on track for a long time. And then there are all the wild men and women we've worked with over the decades, many of whose ideas are in here, challenged in here, often un-recorded; my main gurus are Joan Littlewood, Alan Dossor, Colette King, George Devine, Anthony Page, Lindsay Anderson, Ariane Mnouchkine, Tumanashvili and the Film Actors Studio of Tbilisi, Richard Eyre and, I suppose, Bertolt Brecht (critically). I dare not even begin on a list of actors, musicians, choreographers, composers and technicians whose creative personalities have opened so many doors to my creative work. On the special level of design however I must thank Sean Kenny, Allan Ross, Jenny Tiramani and Pamela Howard for teaching me so much.

And two final lots of thanks: one to Nick Hern, long-suffering publisher, friend and critic, unfailing support. The other to Elizabeth MacLennan, partner, actor, mentor, strength, mother of our children – and to Finn, Danny and Kate, whose lives got tangled up in all this, and who survived as human beings and our, and each others', good friends.

JOHN MCGRATH
December 2001

INTRODUCTION

by Nadine Holdsworth

For over forty years John McGrath made a massive contribution to the cultural
industries as a writer, director and producer of theatre, television and film.
His multifaceted career encompassed journalism, theatre criticism, two
periods as a visiting Judith E. Wilson Fellow at Cambridge University and
committee membership of organisations such as the Screenwriter's Guild,
BAFTA, Channel Four, the Arts Council of England and contributions to
a think-tank of the European Commission. Just like his career, his interests
were wide-ranging within the broad arena of cultural politics, and he was
respected as a cultural commentator willing to debate the institutional
structures, internal organisations, conventions, subject matter and reception
of theatre, film and television in relation to their wider social, political,
economic, geographical and cultural contexts. If this book were to cover all
of McGrath's interventions into cultural politics it would necessitate several
volumes. Instead this book primarily traces the development of McGrath's
thinking on theatre by bringing together articles, interviews, lectures,
letters, internal policy documents and memos, many published here for the
first time, that range from his undergraduate days in the late 1950s to the
late 1990s. All confirm McGrath's engagement with the political intervention he could make as a theatre-maker in the local and national communities
his work reached – a concern that informed his challenge to the contexts in
which theatre takes place, his subject matter and experimentation with a
wide range of theatrical forms and techniques such as social realism, variety,
the rock concert, ceilidh, political pageant, monologue and carnival as a
means of investigating how an audience can best be engaged, entertained and
politicised. McGrath made a considerable contribution to the re-evaluation
of the ideological nature and social imperative of culture, and his theory and
practice has influenced community-based and political theatre companies
across the world. This volume provides further evidence of the particular
socialist vision offered by McGrath and how this permeated all aspects of
his long, fascinating career.

McGrath was born in Birkenhead, from where his family was evacuated
at the beginning of the Second World War to Buckley in North Wales. After
secondary education at Mold Grammar School he spent a year working
as a farm labourer and in a steam-laundry in Neston on the Wirral. He did
two years National Service as a gunner in the Royal Artillery in Germany,

followed by officer training and postings to Egypt, Jordan, Malta, Libya and Italy. National Service completed, McGrath took up a scholarship at St John's College, Oxford to read English Literature, after which he took a Diploma in Education. For a young man from a working-class, Irish Catholic background, experience of Army and Oxford life opened his eyes to the class privilege endemic to the social organisation of British society, knowledge that was to inform his advocacy of revolutionary socialism, as well as providing subject matter for several later plays. At Oxford McGrath also met Elizabeth MacLennan, with whom he had three children and who remained his partner and artistic collaborator for over forty years.

During McGrath's time at Oxford his questioning of the role and function of theatre began in a series of theatre reviews for *Cherwell* and articles for *Isis*. At a time when the British theatre scene was rapidly reinventing itself after the shock-waves created by John Osborne's *Look Back in Anger*, the visit of the Berliner Ensemble and the influence of European innovators such as Samuel Beckett and Eugene Ionesco, McGrath entered the debate on what contemporary theatre could and should be and how dramatists such as Brendan Behan, Arthur Miller and John Osborne were shaping up. These early pieces, included in this collection, signal the passionate commitment that remained central to McGrath's theory and practice. He calls for theatre to be a place where society debates itself and contributes to a climate of change in an acknowledged process of dialogue with the audience. At Oxford McGrath also began his practical engagement with theatre, directing productions of Molière's *Tartuffe* and Aristophanes' *The Birds*, which involved notable Oxford contemporaries such as Ken Loach, Ariane Mnouchkine and Dudley Moore and writing plays, including *Why the Chicken?*, which received a favourable review from Kenneth Tynan in *The Observer*, leading to a commission from the Royal Court and a job there as a play-reader.

Increasing frustration with the limited participation of the working class in theatre led McGrath to seek this audience within the fast developing popular medium of television. Working primarily for the BBC, he contributed to a variety of documentary, arts and drama-based programmes, but is perhaps best known as a co-originator, with Troy Kennedy Martin, of *Z-Cars* for which he wrote and directed several episodes, including the first one in 1962. This seminal television drama heralded a shift away from standard conventions of television and contributed to debates on the rejection of naturalism as the medium's dominant mode. Marking a radical departure from the sentimental depiction of the police evident in *Dixon of Dock Green*, *Z-Cars* sought to use the narrative of a police drama to document, through fast-paced, hard-hitting social realism, the factors influencing ordinary people's lives. Over time institutional pressures began to realign the form and content of the series to less controversial ground and McGrath was quick to publicly denounce these changes. Between 1967 and 1970, McGrath's screenwriting extended to the film industry: he adapted several novels into film scripts for *Billion Dollar Brain*, *The Virgin Soldiers* and *The Reckoning*. However, McGrath also returned to playwriting during this period and produced *Events While Guarding the Bofors Gun* (1966), *Bakke's Night of Fame* (1968), and *Random Happenings in the Hebrides* (1970). All three were performed in mainstream venues, the first two at the Hampstead Theatre Club and the latter at the Royal Lyceum in Edinburgh, but their preoccupation with post-war British imperialism, moral dilemmas and the importance of political commitment, foreshadowed later developments in McGrath's work.

Like many artists of his generation, McGrath was energised and politicised by the climate of national and international, socio-political protest during the late 1960s and by key political thinkers of the Left such as Antonio Gramsci, Rosa Luxemburg and Mao Tse Tung. He went to Paris during the uprisings of May 1968, an experience that strengthened his belief in, and commitment to, the formation of a vigorous counter-culture to inform and mobilise opposition against the class basis of British society. Returning from Paris, he contributed articles to the left-wing paper *Black Dwarf*, was a founding member of *7 Days* in 1971, added his voice to protests against the Apartheid regime in South Africa in *Anti-Apartheid News* and *Sechaba*. It was at this point in his career that McGrath took the unorthodox step of rejecting his established mainstream success in favour of actively seeking to communicate with working-class audiences. This step cannot be underestimated as McGrath established himself as a practitioner prepared to act on his convictions, someone willing to sacrifice both the credibility and the financial rewards of remaining in the mainstream in a determined effort to participate in the wider class struggle. Collaborating with Alan Dossor, he became closely involved with the Liverpool Everyman Theatre in developing, with an acknowledged debt to the work of Bertolt Brecht and Joan Littlewood, a regional theatre practice that took notice of the surrounding working-class community, its cultural traditions and entertainment values. For example, McGrath adapted Brecht's *The Caucasian Chalk Circle* to a Liverpool building site and reconfigured the prologue to take in a dispute regarding who had the moral right to the property: the workers who built it, the owners of the building firm or the owners of the land. *Soft or a Girl?* (1971) employed a rock concert format to develop a narrative around working-class identification, and in *Fish in the Sea* (1972) McGrath expanded this theme and the use of music to explore various manifestations of working-class consciousness and its disintegration due to the failings of the institutionalised labour movement, the impact of consumerist ethics, increasing individualism and the changing threat of global capitalism within multinational corporations. Both plays call for collective identification and activism and clearly mark the transition McGrath made to utilise his theatre practice to debate class-consciousness and political action.

In 1971, in a determined rejection of metropolitan-centred, bourgeois and universal concepts of culture, McGrath formed the 7:84 Theatre Company with Elizabeth MacLennan and David MacLennan. From the outset, 7:84, taking its name from a statistic that appeared in *The Economist* stating that 7% of the population of Britain owned 84% of the wealth, made its socialist orientation abundantly clear. The company aimed to attract a non-theatre-going audience to popular theatre concerned with the day-to-day realities of working-class life. To achieve this McGrath started from the basics: how do you get a non-theatre-going public to attend a theatre event? Firstly, the work needs to be taken out of the restrictive domain of the traditional theatre environment and resituated in familiar territory – the places where this target audience were already going to spend their hard-earned leisure time – working-men's clubs, trades union buildings, work-based social clubs and village halls. The company also needed to look at how an audience was attracted in the first place, through the nature and placing of marketing and publicity. Secondly, the work should draw on the local history, experience, political activity, struggles and contradictions in working-class attitudes and behaviour to ensure that the subject matter of the shows was relevant and accessible. Theatre would be used to represent the working class in ways excluded from bourgeois culture and media; the audience would be forced to confront their histories, failings and potential to generate socio-political change. Thirdly, by employing recognisable popular cultural forms such as variety, live music, stand-up comedy, satire, caricature and song to engage and entertain the audience. It is this three-pronged attack involving context, form and subject matter that characterises the sustained attempt by McGrath to use 7:84 to establish a dialogue with his target audience – a relationship fostered by conversations before and after performances to build the theatre company's knowledge of local history, experience and concerns.

It is important to appreciate that 7:84 functioned within a burgeoning enclave of left-wing theatre groups that emerged during the late 1960s and 1970s, including Red Ladder, General Will and Portable; in many ways 7:84 also paved the way for the formation of other companies such as Belt and Braces, Gay Sweatshop, Monstrous Regiment and Wildcat. In retrospect it is clear that this period provided an ideal context in which political theatre could flourish, as collective identification, ideological campaigns and opposition were commonplace across social, industrial and personal arenas. On the one hand, the student movement provided a protesting collective voice, there was a resurgence of class-based activism, increased trades union membership and industrial action; on the other, civil rights, feminist and gay liberation campaigns placed the personal firmly on the political agenda. Power relations were being fought on many fronts and theatre was no exception. The adoption of an increasingly liberal tone at the Arts Council also meant that groups like 7:84 received the finance to contribute to this process of interrogating society and presenting oppositional agendas.

Premiering at the Edinburgh Festival in 1971, *Trees in the Wind* was the first play of McGrath's staged by 7:84 alongside Trevor Griffiths's *Apricots and Thermidor*. McGrath's play examines the Chinese Cultural Revolution and addresses issues of human destruction, class affiliation and political action. In 1972, 7:84 produced McGrath's *Plugged into History, Underneath* and an adaptation of John Arden's *Serjeant Musgrave's Dance*, which toured with a new play by John Arden and Margaretta D'Arcy called *The Ballygombeen Bequest*. From the outset 7:84 experimented with collective working, experiencing the difficulties associated with 'ultra-democracy', personality clashes and different levels of political motivation, as is documented in several extracts in this collection.

In 1973 the company took the radical step of dividing into separate English and Scottish branches with McGrath remaining Artistic Director of both. 7:84 Scotland's first production, *The Cheviot, the Stag and the Black, Black Oil*, explores the intersection of class and national politics in the history of the Highlands, documenting the exploitation of its people and natural resources by ruling-class landowners and global capitalism from the clearances to the discovery of North Sea Oil. The employment of extensive research and the mediation between historical and contemporary events remained a characteristic of McGrath's writing from this point. *The Cheviot* was in tune with the Scottish psyche that was emerging in the wider context of national self-reflection, growing confidence and increasing political nationalism. It aimed to raise awareness, but also to entertain and to celebrate the popular cultural traditions and tales of resistance pertinent to the areas it toured to. With the decision to use the ceilidh form, and its use of unofficial histories, the Gaelic language, local stories, satire and music of the region, 7:84 succeeded in evoking a deeply ingrained cultural memory, a factor crucial to its lasting legacy. *The Cheviot* is widely acknowledged as one of the most successful radical theatre pieces Britain has ever produced and is credited with redefining the nature of Scottish theatre's subject matter, aesthetics, context of production and modes of reception. In terms of wider impact, the decision to tour remote villages in the Highlands revealed the existence of an audience denied access to theatre owing to their geographical location and contributed to a growing awareness of the social responsibility that arts organisations had to cater for such communities. The collective process of creation with a company of like-minded individuals, who researched, devised, performed and played in their own band, also signalled a new way of generating and executing material that influenced a new generation of theatre-makers across the world. On a local level, the result of this creative process initiated a relationship with Scottish audiences that flourished during McGrath's career. Alongside plays appealing to the Highland audiences, McGrath also set his sights on the industrial lowlands in a series of plays; *The Game's a Bogey* (1974), *Little Red Hen* (1975), *Out of Our Heads* (1975), *Joe's Drum* (1979) and *Blood Red Roses* (1980) that deal with such diverse themes as the history of Red Clydeside, industrial militancy and the position of women in Scottish society, alcohol abuse and the apathy evident in Scotland following the failed 1979 devolution vote.

In England, 7:84 continued to produce work throughout the 1970s and into the 1980s, although a degree of turbulence was caused by the perception that even though McGrath's creative energies were primarily focused in Scotland, he was unwilling to embrace contributions by other writers and directors. The reality was that Richard Eyre, Jim Sheridan, Pam Brighton, David Edgar, Claire Luckham, Barrie Keeffe, Trevor Griffiths, Margaretta D'Arcy, John Arden, Adrian Mitchell, John Burrows, Peter Cox and Steve Gooch all contributed to 7:84 England's output during this period. McGrath also wrote plays, with songs, for the company, including: *Lay Off* (1975), about multinationals, *Nightclass* (1981), which addresses the British constitution and a piece about the politics of Thatcherism called *Rejoice!* (1982). As with the work at the Everyman, these plays engaged a large and enthusiastic audience. However, this volume contains extracts from interviews which provide McGrath's open and honest critical assessment of both his own and other's input during this time, which clearly led to some of the difficulties experienced by 7:84 England.

One of the highlights of 7:84 Scotland's repertoire was the ambitious Clydebuilt Season of 1982, which aimed to retrieve a series of Scottish working-class plays from the first half of the twentieth century, which had been allowed to slide from public consciousness through a combination of apathy and cultural imperialism. This project revived interest in the work of Joe Corrie, Ewan MacColl and, perhaps most tellingly, Ena Lamont Stewart, whose play *Men Should Weep* (1947) was quickly recognised as a neglected classic. McGrath hoped that Clydebuilt would open up new opportunities for diversification into the classical tradition, and he conceived General Gathering as a parallel company to 7:84 Scotland, which would tour adaptations of classics for a popular Scottish audience. Unfortunately, despite widespread critical acclaim, the Clydebuilt Season had been a financial disaster, and artistic failure quickly followed with *Women in Power*, the first production by General Gathering. These factors contributed to the Scottish Arts Council's loss of faith in McGrath's judgement, a state of mistrust that was to characterise their relationship for many years to come.

The socio-political context of the mid-1980s brought devastating consequences for the alternative theatre movement that had been permitted to flourish throughout the 1970s period of cultural democratisation and decentralisation. Cultural plurality was replaced by faith in 'centres of excellence', and Thatcherite ethics of monetarism and the free market began to take hold across Britain's arts organisations, effectively invalidating projects like 7:84. Collectivism became subsumed by the power of the individual, epitomised by the Conservative government's determination to fragment the labour movement, disempowering activists by eroding the organisations that sustained them. As part of this ethos and process, the Arts Councils increasingly took on the role of policing oppositional cultural practice. The 1984 decision to cut 7:84 England as part of the Arts Council's so-called *Glory of the Garden* strategy, and the dismissal of the campaign against the cut, can be read as indicative of the all-pervasive right-wing ideology of the institutions that McGrath highlights in several documents in this collection. It is a tribute to the intervention made by 7:84 England that thousands of people wrote letters to the Arts Council and signed petitions in protest. Letters from leading theatre directors, playwrights, actors, politicians and trade unionists such as Richard Eyre, Joan Littlewood, David Edgar, Neil Kinnock, Arnold Wesker and Glenda Jackson, arrived together with those from audience members shocked by the implications of the cessation of a vital theatrical force in non-mainstream theatre – and one that had attracted an unusually large working-class audience.

As the decade progressed, McGrath came under increasing pressure to adhere to bureaucratic conformity in the running and organisation of 7:84 Scotland. In reality this meant an end to co-operative working and equal pay, as well as a threat to the company's tours to remote Highland venues. When the Arts Council demanded the imposition of an orthodox Management Team and Board of Directors, McGrath knew that the ethos which underpinned the company was under threat to the extent that he would have to resign. After resigning in 1988, McGrath responded by writing and directing two ambitious, large-scale epics of Scottish history, *Border Warfare* (1989) and *John Brown's Body* (1990). *Border Warfare* addresses the historical relationship between Scotland and England and the construction of Scottish national identity from the Dark Ages to the present day with tales of imperialism, invasion, manipulation, coercion, incorporation, complicity, treaties and corruption. The dialectical relationship between tyranny and liberty, subjugation and freedom, servitude and rebellion is placed in sharp focus, with the audience forced to rethink the consequences of history by the continual reminder that history is a dynamic process unmade and remade by human intervention. *John Brown's Body* explores the evolution of Scotland's industrial classes and the individual worker through developments in technology and capitalism from the onset of modernity to the free-market global economy of the multinationals. Within this framework, McGrath exposes the complex and contradictory nature of labour as alienating and dehumanising, whilst simultaneously signifying hope in the collective working and identification it engenders. Both plays, again with music, were staged as promenade pageant productions by Wildcat at the Tramway in

Glasgow, drawing on the political, social, cultural and economic resonance of the site – a disused repair depot and former transport museum – that embodied allusions to Glasgow's industrialisation, decline and reinvention as a European City of Culture in 1990. Theatrically, whilst drawing on the 7:84 trademarks of extensive research, satire, caricature, song, direct address, explanatory monologues and popular cultural references, both shows also exploited the carnivalesque forms McGrath first played with in *All the Fun of the Fair* (1985), the final show produced by 7:84 England. These works signal the influence of European directors such as Ariane Mnouchkine and Ronconi's Teatro Libero di Roma on McGrath's experimentation with carnivalesque forms as a means of literally and imaginatively liberating the body and mind of the audience. Drawing on Bakhtin's analysis of carnival and laughter, McGrath sought to emphasise the audience as a powerful collective force in their celebration of a temporary inversion of official culture and value-systems. Both productions also continued McGrath's creative exchange between theatre, film and television, a process begun in 1968 with the translation of *Bofors Gun* into a film script and consolidated by the reformulation of *The Cheviot* as a BBC2 'Play for Today' in 1974, which itself generated fervent debate on the possibility of transposing Brechtian epic techniques to the screen. *Border Warfare* and *John Brown's Body* were filmed by McGrath's own production company Freeway Films in co-production with Channel 4, following on from its earlier screenings of *Blood Red Roses* (1987) and *There is a Happy Land* (1988). This concern with translation from stage to other media was similarly evident in McGrath's adaptation of *Half the Picture*, a piece of documentary theatre tracing the 'Arms to Iraq' affair, which was originally performed at the Tricycle Theatre in London, and subsequently broadcast on BBC2 in 1994. McGrath also reinvented *Mairi Mhor* (1987), from a small-scale piece of theatre touring the Highlands, into a Gaelic-language film. McGrath continued to write for television (he was awarded a BAFTA for *The Long Roads* in 1993) and produced a number of films including *The Dressmaker* (1985), *Carrington* (1995), *Ma Vie en Rose* (1997), and *Aberdeen* (2002).

Alongside work in film and television, McGrath maintained his engagement in theatre. During the 1990s this ranged from the state of the nation play, *The Wicked Old Man* (1992), produced at the West Yorkshire Playhouse, to work with school children on a piece about the Declaration of Human Rights towards the end of the decade. Frequently his writing reached the public through Wildcat, who followed up *Border Warfare* and *John Brown's Body* with the first professional revival of *The Cheviot* in 1991, McGrath's adaptation of Neil Gunn's novel *The Silver Darlings* in 1994 and *A Satire of the Four Estaites* in 1996, a staging of his contemporising of Sir David Lindsay's sixteenth-century morality play, *Ane Satyre of the Thrie Estaitis*. McGrath continued to write, and tour on a modest budget, one-woman shows for

Elizabeth MacLennan that dealt with issues close to their hearts: the crisis in socialism and hope for the resurgence of political action in *Watching for Dolphins* (1992); human rights, events in Guatemala and the life of Rigoberta Menchu in *Reading Rigoberta* (1994); identity, migration and displacement in *The Last of the MacEachans* (1996), set in the rapidly changing environment of the contemporary Highlands; and, most recently, *HyperLynx* (2001), about anti-globalisation and the impact of 11 September 2001.

During his career, McGrath maintained his commitment to exploring the theory and practice of popular theatre. He engaged in fervent debates with other practitioners on the form, subject matter and potential efficacy of political theatre.

His 1981 publication *A Good Night Out* and *The Bone Won't Break* from 1990 both provide a call to arms by offering a heartfelt challenge to the inertia of mainstream theatre and its failure to stimulate and entertain the mass of the population thanks to its elitist attitudes and entrenchment in bourgeois practices. McGrath writes of the historical forces that have largely denied the right of working-class writers, performers, forms and stories to penetrate the major theatrical institutions and funding bodies. A hugely influential text, *A Good Night Out* situates 7:84's values and initial body of work in the wider context of developments in twentieth-century theatre inaugurated by, amongst others, the Blue Blouse Theatre Movement, Brecht, Littlewood and the Royal Court; as well as exploring the lineage of 7:84 from traditional working-class forms of pantomime, music hall and variety. He also secured notoriety by passionately arguing against misjudged notions of universal art and by attempting to define the nature of, and the characteristics central to, successful communication with working-class audiences. As McGrath was writing *A Good Night Out* in 1979, an increasingly right-wing climate was emerging, and in *The Bone Won't Break*, published almost a decade later, he tried to make retrospective sense of the devastating impact of this ideological shift on radical theatre practice – not only debating restrictions exerted by the state, but also exploring and celebrating the resistance evident in 7:84's work, alongside a worldwide popular theatre movement including Sistren, Het Werktheater and Ariane Mnouchkine's Théàtre du Soleil, that all demand new ways of looking at the world and its inhabitants. Later writings, often published for the first time in this book, reveal continuing themes on the politics of culture: the forms, uses and abuses of language; globalisation; national identity and localised cultural formations. The collection ends with a piece on theatre and the democratic process. Written in 1999, this lecture clearly articulated McGrath's hopes for theatre in the twenty-first century: for it to operate in public dialectical debate with the society from which it evolves, to ask difficult questions of the social processes that construct society and to provide a voice for oppositional opinion and the marginalized. Most striking is the through-line that can be traced from the first extract in this volume, *Notes on a Theatre* to the last (despite the fact they were written forty years apart), signalling McGrath's resolute faith in theatre's ability to contribute to humanity through its engagement with people, places and political processes – a commitment that is crucial to all of the articles, lectures, letters, memos and interviews which make up this book.

NAKED THOUGHTS

I was in a play when I was ten: The Wind of Heaven *by Emlyn Williams done by Buckley Amateur Dramatics. I was the wind. Later I got a speaking part in Williams's* The Corn Is Green *– but my lines were all in Welsh. I was attracted to the theatre. Nearly every Saturday afternoon I'd go into Liverpool, to the Playhouse, pay a tanner (2½p) to sit in the back row of the gods and watch actors with bright orange faces in Sherwood Anderson, Noël Coward, all of last year's West End hits. When I was 16 I worked on the railways for long enough to get a free ticket to Dover, then on to Paris, with twelve pounds in my pocket. It lasted a fortnight. I saw Louis Jouvet's last production: Sartre's* Le Diable et le Bon Dieu, *with the magnificent Pierre Brasseur, the brilliant Jean Vilar, the beautiful Maria Casarès. It was wonderful. The matinees at the Liverpool Playhouse weren't the same after that.*

Two years doing National Service put a halt to any such frivolous theatrical activities, but after that I went to Oxford, and began to think, and to write, about theatre:

NOTES ON A THEATRE[1]

England is lost, helpless and inefficient because of our Luddite treatment of Marx. We smashed the Spinning Jenny and we exported Marx. Now even the left in England pretends that Marxist thought never happened, because they are afraid of it. So are we all afraid of it. But we never made the leap past 1848, and so find ourselves using still the philosophical distaff and the economic spinning-wheel.

Having failed to *utilise* Marxist thought, we now are terrorised by it.

While the dread inevitable class war, now, by our imperialist blindness, also a race war and a colonial war as well, rages on outside, and the remorseless proletariat, whose image alters as it grows stronger and more effective, slowly comes to dominate two-thirds of the globe, while the American eagle retreats higher and higher up the mountain and grows more and more desperate for prey, while this our nation fumbles for a philosophy and this our culture cringes in terror before the knife, what can we do? Is it surprising that our moribund theatre is empty, and speechless?

There is only one thing it can do. It can try to affirm man's continuing humanity. It can be a place where human values remain uppermost.

In the rest of the capitalist world, the theatre is obsessively exploring the minutiae of decay and corruption. Here, that would be a betrayal. It happens here, of course, and the West End and all our theatrical 'minds' are busy at it, but it betrays our hope for the continuance of man.

Beckett is the most optimistic playwright of the Western World. His plays hold out more hope for man's future than all the others put together: for the others are dedicated to death. His are about death, but from time to time we are made aware that life goes on, and on. Not so with Albee or Miller or Williams or Rattigan or Cocteau. All aim point-blank at the human heart, and fumble at the trigger. It is a mark of their artistic failure that none of them has yet fired. Beckett has, and to his amazement the thing is still ticking. He is the last true genuine artist of capitalism.

All that is left for us is withdrawal and waiting. And that one joy, the obstinate tick of the shattered heart.

I do not believe that a serious artist can involve himself in the life of the community in this part of Europe today. He cannot identify himself with the cancer-riddled corpse of capitalism, nor feed upon it.

We must wait calmly, gently, and in silence if we hope to hear the faint ticking of the heart. Silence. Gentleness. Calm.

Are these theatrical qualities? When pure, they are. They are the basic qualities, because they open the door from the terror and confusion of everyday life into the place of waiting and feeling that the theatre must be.

And when the door is open? What is this faint ticking we are going to be able to hear? It is the voice of poetry, mostly. Through the years since 1790, the true voice of feeling in this country has been kept alive for the most part by the poets. This is possibly because they have been economically useless, therefore not hired by the community to pervert their true feelings, also possibly because of the extremely high standard of perception in the criticism of poetry throughout these years, through Coleridge, Arnold, Yeats, Leavis and Eliot to the new generation of Americans. So it is to the tradition of poetry we must turn firstly.

Also we must turn to the story-tellers of the past. Because the theatre must tell a story, even if it is most slender, it must be a story, not an amorphous collection of disparate experiences, which seems to me to be the inevitable cul-de-sac in which capitalist art will end in a fine frenzy of schizophrenic activity. So we must turn to the story-tellers of the past and ransack their collections for outlines that bear meaning to us now. And from these, and from our own deeper narrative springs, we must create new stories that speak clearly and truly.

The language of the human being alone in the universe is the language of myth, which has been locked for too long in the prison of quaintness and antiquarianism. We must let myth speak to us directly, meaningfully, immediately and alive – but not like the French botchers-up of Sophocles: Cocteau and Anouilh. Myth means something. It speaks of the profounder struggles of man to identify himself, to unravel his cosmic pain. That is why, in a time of crisis, we must listen to it. In our theatre, we must allow it to speak.

Thirdly we must turn to music. All art aspires to the condition of music, said the philosopher, little realising the sad implications of this remark, which are that bourgeois society puts all art to flight, and that music is fortunate in that it can fly further than anything else from the realities of decaying capitalism.

The reason we need music in our theatre is not because it can in itself express or articulate anything – it may be able to but that is another matter – and not because it can remove us faster and more effectively from our mercantile mentality of everyday, but because it can create within us a state of preparedness for another kind of mentality, for truth of a different order. And it is, in itself, a thing of freedom, a sea of allusion studded with archipelagos of the gentle moments of rest which we need in our theatre for the renewal of the human being, which it is sometimes impossible to do with words alone. So we must have music, our music.

And fourthly, we must have a new race of actors: out of their hearts must come the soft, barely audible tick of humanity, of true feeling. The myth must live again in them. The silence, the gentleness, the calm must be theirs. The renewal of the human, the re-affirmation of life, must come through them. As such they are no less than poets themselves, and must always have an elemental purity of spirit, a simple, good-faith, open-eyed relationship with reality, and an awareness of the meaning of what they are doing at all times. They are the messengers: they also inspire the message.

And do not let us insult them as human beings by asking them in our theatre to play elaborate games of make-believe. They must not pretend the audience is not there – they must acknowledge it. They must not pretend *they* are not there as *themselves* – they must assert it boldly. They must not pretend the characters they play are real, or the words spontaneous – they must give us their interpretation of both, but let the superstructure of meaning continue, unimpeded by their indulgence in play-acting. They must be men and women talking to men and women. This is the most difficult thing of all.

This kind of theatre is a theatre which recognises the realities of the global situation, and sees its position in this culture as being that of guardian of the eternal human questions, values and despairs. It is the only non-deceptive kind of theatre possible at this time. Its function is valuable. It will be charged with many irrelevant crimes, inevitably. But it is necessary that it should exist, somewhere, no matter how unpopular, if what man has learnt to be good is to survive the onslaught on this antiquated monument to evil, the Western Industrial Empire, and if we are to play any sort of meaningful role in the eternal revolution.

The stillness was somewhat shattered in my own productions: an Act of Le Diable
et le Bon Dieu *in my own translation and a rowdy riot of a production of
Molière's* Tartuffe. *I went to hundreds of shows, in Oxford and even in London,
reviewed for* Cherwell, *the student newspaper, and did classes with a wonderful
young woman who had trained as a drama teacher at Central School, then come
to Oxford, called Colette King. She is one of the best directors of my generation, but
refuses to work with professional actors. One day in my third year I bumped into
Colette in the street. She said she was looking for a play to do, so why didn't I write
one? So I did. Four days later I presented her with a brand new complete play,
which she directed beautifully. I stayed on for another year in Oxford to do teacher
training. During the first term of that year, autumn 1958, I directed a stage version
of Joyce's* Ulysses, *called* Bloomsday, *which began a lifelong devotion to Joyce,
and I wrote a series of pieces on contemporary writers for* Isis, *the undergraduate
magazine:*

BRENDAN BEHAN[2]

Writing about Brendan Behan is like trying to hold back a charging bull to
put a label round its neck: because there is such a rush of him, such an
indefinable animal strength in everything he writes, and because it is almost
as impossible. In a way this very impossibility is a relevant starting-point.
When Behan has written a play, we see not only a play, but also we are
treated to a series of sketches, on, off, or somewhere near the point of the
rest of it, and a bewildering flurry of brilliant ideas, some disappointingly
only half worked out, some thrillingly complete, some barely suggested, and
we are treated to an evening in which the verbal crust alone is enough and
more to dazzle and deceive.

Behan is a good writer, but the confusion of Behan the myth with Behan
the writer is easy to make. When, during a dress rehearsal of *The Hostage*
some member of the cast is rash enough to play the line 'Where's the
author?' to the wings, and a bellow comes from the back of the stalls, 'I'm
here, you blind bastard'; when the BBC bans him from its august corridors,
for one of the most honest, if alcoholic, interviews it has ever had the good
fortune to come across; when he suddenly comes on stage and does a jig in
the middle of another play; when the vast frame is as likely to make water
over a bus queue as it is to burst into song, there is every chance that the
great British public will place the real talent of the man in a capacity for
colourful living more than in a precise and vigorous skill with words.

The other basic fact about Behan is that he is serious. He is one of the
few really talented writers today who has had a vast experience of most kinds
of living in several countries, and who still continues to keep in touch with
his raw material. Because of this and an instinctive sensitivity to the feel of

the age he lives in, he writes about the things which really matter to people now. His subjects: the death penalty, the partition of Ireland and all that involves, the stupidity of war, and the 'ordinariness of people, which is an extraordinary thing at such times'. These are serious and central enough themes in themselves, but if we look again at the cooking of the pie, we shall see that he has much more to offer than that.

The Quare Fellow sets out to tell us that the hanging of a man is a horrible and disgusting thing, and it succeeds in dragging in front of the public that condoned this act the full horror of its effect on the people immediately concerned with it: the hangman who goes off and gets drunk, the curate who bravely comforts the prisoner until it is over, then faints away, the warders who have to hide their watches while looking after the condemned man, the coarseness and cruelty of the ones who joke about it, the sickness of the prisoners who really know what it means. But he also manages to convince us that, even in a prison, life is a good and exciting thing, that even though the drink is outside and the women beyond reach, the meths is sometimes available and the mots hang out the washing in the female prison – within view – once a week. All the seemingly irrelevant business, the satire on religion, the sadness of the songs, the miserable pleasure of the cigarette-end, the nasty competition of the warders, all these things are life, and they are interesting, if not good, at least they're evil, and worth a laugh if nothing else. It is a simple message, but the presentation is so vibrant with life that the death of the Quare Fellow seems not only a crime against his rights, but also a denial of our right to enjoy the play as we do unless we intend to do something about it. In fact it is a political play in the finest sense, for it is not content to demonstrate something – it makes each one of the audience feel it, personally.

The Hostage works in quite another way. The plum is a good dramatic line about an English soldier captured by the IRA, who will be killed as a reprisal if an IRA boy is hanged by the British in Belfast. He falls in love with an Irish girl who is in the house where he is kept, and eventually is killed by an absurd police raid on the house. But Behan refuses to let us be moved by his story. Throughout the play the action is stopped for a song, for a dance, for a few jokes, for an attack on English patriotism, for a laugh at the Catholic Church, for a discussion of the author's private morals – one expects to be asked on to the stage for a drink at any moment. But this is a sad story, a tragic story. Why must we laugh? And if we are to laugh, does this mean it's not really tragic, or serious? It seems that the style of this play carries an enormous weight of the meaning. It is shouting out to us, with vast Swiftian irony: 'No, don't be moved, don't think about the stupidity of war, dance and sing; don't worry if everything is thrown into confusion, if you call on somebody for a story, you'll forget; don't worry if the boy dies, ha ha, he'll just get up and sing a song.'

Any writer with this kind of sensibility, as well as the gifts of precision, vigour, theatrical skill, and – a point sadly neglected here – the sheer ability to entertain, must surely be one of the most important phenomena to appear in this country since the war – even if he did come first to blow it up.

ARTHUR MILLER[3]

Compared with Behan's bulging vitality, abounding humour, joy in people for their own sake, and intuitive contemporaneity, Miller's plays seem pale, thin, dry and dull. All, that is, except *Death of a Salesman*, which is the perennial exception.

But Miller has many fine qualities, and all his plays are inevitably (infuriatingly) good. Above all things Miller must be credited with a sense of social responsibility. He has always been aware of his plays as social documents, even when exploring the most private interests of his characters. But I find a curious deadness about Miller's social thought, a feeling that although the central situation (as in *The Crucible*) is overtly a social problem, the pressures of the work, the real forces which affect us in watching it, are the theatrical ones of screaming girls or iron bars.

It is very difficult to express the exact nature of dissatisfaction with Miller's social thought, but I know it is shared by many of his admirers. Perhaps just to say that it's corny is enough, but if we try to analyse further we might uncover some other interesting aspects of Miller's talent.

To begin with, it strikes me that Miller does not use his plays to explore social problems, to feel his way around them inside his characters. Rather he works out his problem intellectually, and planks it down in front of us wrapped up in theatre like a pound of lard in a Christmas wrapping. The real problems which engage his full attention in the writing of the plays seem to be purely theatrical ones. So it is not unlikely that the really exciting solutions are going to be theatrical ones.

Also the nature of his political thought contributes to the corny feeling. Although, as he says himself, no playwright ever said anything new about politics, one doubts whether any political playwright ever bothered to express again some things (e.g. the evil of witch-hunting, the consequences of grossly anti-social acts) which are not only constantly being emphasised in the press but also already firmly established as wrong in the minds of the audience.

Let us leave that and look briefly at his actual theatrical skill, which is prodigious. A long apprenticeship (over half a dozen plays lengthily worked out before *All My Sons*, his first success), an appetite for sheer hard work combined with the ability to apply his whole mind regularly over months to the same problem, a flair for the construction of a play, a ready command of the average spoken language, and the ability to heighten the language without undue embarrassment, all give Miller an almost hundred per cent certainty of putting over what he has to say efficiently and clearly.

But, and it is here that *Death of a Salesman* again demands exception, the willingness to submit the detailed build-up and exploration of each character to the demands of clarity of line, both narrative and symbolic, leaves one feeling slightly cheated. All too often one feels that what one took for a human being is in fact only a symbol of meaning. One takes them for human beings in the first place because of the proximity of the style and method of presentation to Ibsen, Miller's great master. It is because he has failed to explore and expand his style with sufficient unselfconscious daring that he has not moved away from Ibsen to his own particular theatrical genre.

In both political thought and theatrical expression Miller has shown a certain timidity, a reluctance to expand as violently as he ought to have.

But it is impossible to leave Miller without a word about the great exception. *Death of a Salesman* must surely be one of the finest, most genuinely moving, most deeply felt plays to have happened since the War. Willie Loman will not go unnoticed: he is a beautiful, real, sad creation, and it is in him, and his play, that Miller seems to have united all his talents, to have felt his theatre strongly enough to blend it in with the strength and complexity of real tragedy, and to have approached the inarticulate depths of creation where universal greatness operates. In *Death of a Salesman* the humanity is not a generalised, inhuman concept: it is there on the stage, meaningful to us in all its turnings. In this play Miller approaches wisdom. In the others he plays with cleverness.

JOHN OSBORNE[4]

John Osborne is the most grossly over-rated phenomenon since Ezra Pound. If we look back on his plays with a certain amount of perspective, it seems that there was one play, *Look Back in Anger*, which he really had to write, and which took many years to come out in its present form; and from then on it has been a question of contrivance. He is not really a writer at all – simply a small-minded actor with a big chip on his shoulder, knowledge of how to grab an audience, and a flair for publicity.

To begin with, that inarticulate raid on the already over-conscious: *The Entertainer*. What Olivier did with Archie Rice has got precious little to do with the permanent value of the play, but everything to do with its success. On re-reading some of the sentimental rubbish which Olivier turned into something real, by sheer genius, one feels that a kind of trick has been played on the emotions. Of all the sludgy, stock-response-baiting, unreal nonsense ever written, the speech of Archie's about the negress is about the phoniest. Admittedly Archie is drunk, but the mean-minded cleverness of 'beautiful fuss', the contrived picturesqueness of 'that old black bitch with her fat cheeks' gives this, the central speech of the play, a hollowness which does not derive from Archie's hollowness, but from his author's incoherent attempt to be tough, fashionable and sentimental all at the same time.

If we look at what the play is about we find an almost desperate attempt to be up-to-date. They are all there, the radical-minded girl, the brother killed in Suez, the crumbling old values, the fading mum, but the writing, the means of expressing these realities, it all belongs to the early days of the Fabian Society, and has nothing to do with the sensibility it expresses. The cloak of realism hides the characters, makes them unreal, and the corny old punch-line rings false.

> The bastards! The rotten bastards! They've killed him! They've killed Mick! Those bloody wogs – they've murdered him. Oh, the rotten bastards!

This, followed by a blues, is not the sort of thing that is central to the modern sensibility. If Mick had got up from the dead, as Behan's soldier gets up, and sung 'The bells of hell go ting-a-ling-a-ling, for you but not for me', the reality of the situation would be heightened, not diminished, and it would feel more like the nineteen-fifties than the eighteen-nineties.

George Dillon is one of his early plays, written in collaboration with Anthony Creighton. In it, he produced that talent for sharp, well-observed, racy dialogue which is his real strength. Osborne's main relevance to the world we live in is not in his own attitudes, but in his ability to caricature, or re-produce the caricature of others. He is not a serious artist creating drama from the tensions of his time in this play, he is simply writing good, competent satire, or comedy of manners, or both. The trouble with *George Dillon* is that the dialogue, which is good, does not have the brilliance to make it permanently good, nor a central situation strong enough to support it.

Something similar could be said about *Look Back in Anger*. While it has a fairly good 'theatrical' quality in the plot, the main incidents on the stage, Helena's arrival and departure, do not profoundly illustrate what the play is really about, nor are they particularly significant of anything. But in this play, written without collaboration, the pent-up fury against the destructive power of the English social structure today forces itself out, and gives a strong pressure of emotion to the play which drives it on in compelling style.

This play, again, is not conceived on any deep level of artistic creation. But it has the necessary power behind it, and the necessary social relevance, to make it what it is, the most popular play of our decade.

Looking at his work so far as a whole, one is struck by several features. The first is the fundamental earnestness with which the plays are written.

This is perhaps one of their main sources of weakness, for Osborne is often tempted to treat his characters as symbols as well as people which is both difficult to achieve and most frustrating to an audience if it is not achieved.

The second constant feature is the social attitude. 'They're all dead behind the eyes,' says Archie, and he is echoing Jimmy Porter and George Dillon. Now this is only partially true. Some people in England today are very much alive behind the eyes. After all, Shelagh Delaney's Salford people might well have gone to watch Archie perform, and they have more vitality, and are more important to us, than any sentimentally-viewed negress singing the blues.

Finally, Osborne lacks a centre. Both his lack of depth in character exploration and his inability to produce relevant plots show this. His is a peripheral talent, darting disconnected ideas and funny dialogue at us, but failing to get to the heart of the contemporary situation or sensibility. Nevertheless, it is a talent to be grateful for, since it at least makes people aware that contemporary life can be interesting in the theatre (he is rarely boring), and since he has achieved three plays at least in which some of the fatuities of the social order are vigorously pointed out.

IN CONCLUSION[5]

Balance is not easy; above all in the theatre. As one moves from disappointment to annoyance, from dissatisfaction to prejudice, from Stratford-on-Avon to Shaftesbury Avenue, it is too easy to lose sight of objectives in hasty condemnation, witty bitchery, morose prophecy. It is too easy to attack, mock, destroy; too difficult to understand, listen and forgive. It is incredibly difficult, in the face of the complications of theatrical management, polite finances, prejudices, personal intrigues and audience demands, to maintain a clear picture of what is necessary for real theatrical experience.

In the theatre the host of items of so-called interest faintly connected with the experience of theatre are dangerously near to being substituted for the experience itself. Theatre is not Art or beauty or fame or revolutionary economics or Freud or Jung or Adler or social usefulness or Rex Harrison's wages or Keith Michell's chest or Michael Hastings's age or Colin Wilson's father-in-law or Bert-Brecht-slept-here signs or Dylan's death or Ionesco's braces or fabulous first nights or good notices or bad photographs or Lawson's temperament or Olivier's car or Brando's shirts or Strasberg's daughter or even Miller's wife.

To begin with it is not limited by any consideration of religion, politics or theories of art. It is as likely to be found in fourteenth-century Holland as in seventeenth-century France, in modern America as in ancient Japan, advocating communism in Berlin or nihilism in Paris, in Calderón's Spain or in Sophocles' Athens, in Stanislavski's Art Theatre or in Molière's travelling theatre. It can be found in the conventions of naturalism, formalism, surrealism, in the widely different dramatic traditions of Aeschylus, Shakespeare, Racine, Congreve, Ibsen, Strindberg and Osborne. It has thrived among slaves, aristocrats, workers, scholars, in conditions of democracy, oligarchy, monarchy, Communism.

What limits the chances of real theatrical experience in England today? From the profession: self-aggrandisement, star-system, pandering to Aunt Edna's taste in high-life fantasy, stupid managements, spite, lack of co-operation, fear – of unemployment, of old age, of lack of ability – pretentiousness, deceit, pseudo-intellectualism, commercialism, as it is called, or the corruption of public taste in order to bolster private confidence and the personal bank balance.

The more serious challenge is very simply the failure of ability to experience in the audience. Ratiocinative rigor mortis, 'culture' calculations in place of feeling or response, contrived reaction and the national loss of a free imagination. The greatest danger to real theatrical experience is what can be called conceptual living – the failure to relax into life but to live at one remove, to live in a world of comment rather than in a world of response, of thought-out criticism instead of instinctive taste, a world in which one thinks 'Olivier is giving a good performance' and stays firmly in one's seat, watching, not participating, in which one thinks 'The author is witty' and laughs because everyone else laughs. This removal can be due to bad acting as well as to audience failure. It is also partly due to commercialism, which feeds its audiences on stars' private lives, amazing incomes, cleverness in tax-evasion, and tends to gloss over their acting ability. One produces the other, and that in turn encourages the first. A vicious circle.

Conceptual living is due to other things, which could begin to be remedied. The educational system to start with, in which teachers of considerably dead sensibility embalm the minds of their children with inane answers to stupid irrelevant questions in meaningless examinations. Evaluation, which presupposes actual experience of a work, is rarely called for. Description, cataloguing of feature, automatic approval is essential. The child does not need to like, or dislike, poetry or plays. He or she must be able to give false justification for an assumed approval, or supply a glib paraphrase of their more banal elements, or 'show knowledge' of the perverted Dane. That is how it starts. It goes on to the related habit of circumscribing the experience of the play (through dearth of imaginative response – result of education) with one's own narrow range of interests, and seeing the play as an oblique comment on pigeon-fancying, or to the equally devastating and more popular process of regarding works of literature as possessing no possible bearing on life 'as it is lived'.

The remedy? There's the rub. Influence politicians – to improve education, to support better theatre, to come to the theatre themselves. Influence managements – to sack half the profession and put on better plays? Probably not. To build or run a theatre in which the mature imagination is openly appealed to? In which star-system, Keith Michell's chest, Dylan's death and Brecht's love-life are of secondary interest? In which the real issues of contemporary living can be vitally presented and deeply felt, whether seen through the eyes of Beckett, Miller, Ionesco, Osborne or even those of an imaginative producer of Congreve?

We have the Royal Court. They have presented all the dramatists mentioned, with success, and have kept their doors open too. George Devine is a minor miracle. Unfortunately we need a major one. Nevertheless the Court has done a lot. It has been criticised, of course, mainly for refusing to limit itself with the current superficial idea of political commitment. Absurd. Of its nature it must remain available to all reasonable demands and opportunities, it must exclude as little as possible, it must not commit itself to a party line any more than it can commit itself to surrealist gaga or even sad old googoo.

We have Theatre Workshop. This fails to fulfil these functions simply because of its decision to stop touring and base itself in Stratford East, kidding itself that it attracts the working classes. Joan Littlewood and her company could move into town today, and start doing things *centrally*, to make the theatre a better place. So far, they haven't, for good reason – which is theatre's loss.

How, then, does all this affect me, as a putative playwright? First of all, let it be made quite clear that if a good play is written in England today it will be seen, thanks to those theatres we have mentioned. Therefore there is no justification at all for my crying shame at the theatre because it will not accept me. I have only myself to answer to. On the other hand, I am worried by the fact that the audiences will probably not pay any reasonable attention to the performances to which my writing has contributed, and I am also deeply concerned that, thanks to the state of the profession, there is every chance that the producer and cast will not be vitally interested either, but will simply use plays as opportunities to indulge their own egos. In none of the theatres mentioned however is this latter likely to take place, and since they are the only theatres for whom I am at all interested in writing in the first instance, I have not too much to worry about, except myself.

This, of course, is the great worry, but not to be treated as such. The most important thing to remember in the theatre, i.e. theatre seen as a means of communication, is very simply that there is no competition, there is no competition, there is no competition . . .

During that summer I had done some writing for an acting group at the Royal Court, run by Antony Page, and had met John Arden and Margaretta D'Arcy. I had to do a term's teaching practice in London, and while the Ardens were away

I stayed in their flat down Ladbroke Grove. In the summer I was back in sunny Oxford, and doing a huge production of Dudley Fitts's version of The Birds *by Aristophanes:*

LES BIRDS[6]

When Mike Simpson first suggested producing *The Birds* I groaned three times at memories of long-winded unfunny Greek jokes about seemingly hilarious characters about whom even the scholiasts hadn't got a clue. But on reading Dudley Fitts's new translation, which is brilliantly up-to-date in speech-rhythm, ideas and feeling, I began to see some hope after all, and when Simpson tentatively suggested setting one chorus to the *Blue Danube*, and we thought of Roland MacLeod and Jonathan Cecil in the lead, there was no holding back.

With the conception of MacLeod and Cecil playing vigorously in the music-hall-pantomime tradition, the rest became clear. Obviously it had to be in modern dress. After all, Aristophanes was taking the mickey out of the pretentious, pompous, affected, artificial, charlatan and just plain silly people he knew, and we didn't have to search far to find the modern equivalents. Apocalyptic poets, television dons, angry young men, prophetic tubthumpers, pompous policemen, self-important barristers, keen young things, and ranting priests simply demand the Aristophanic treatment.

And now the birds themselves. Choral speaking is out. I can't stick it – it reminds me of school competitions. But the birds also must be modern, cheerful, mickey-taking things, lively and likeable. So on they come, slinky birds, suave birds, singing birds ready to leap into a rock number, a Red Indian dance, a mass-meeting, a hymn of misery or a song of triumph.

For the music, I went, armed with a sheaf of ideas, to see Dudley Moore. Within three or four days tinkling on the piano, the ideas had been realised, magnified, increased and immeasurably added to. In the end, there weren't many kinds of music we *hadn't* parodied. Far from being set to a one-string lyre and a Sophoclean cymbal, the songs now come over hot and strong from three tenor saxes, two electric guitars, one bagpipes, Bryant Marriott's steaming Theban drum-kit, trumpets, trombones, and a swinging doublebass, not to mention Bert Chappell on the piano when Moore is playing the violin and Moore on the piano when Chappell is making the tea. Things were taking shape.

Sean Kenny produced a bundle of drawings for bird-costumes and masks. Slowly Kingfishers, Francolins, Egyptian Mallards, Hoopol-Hula Birds, Woodpeckers and Pseudo-Flamingos took shape. The human costumes, becoming more bizarre every day, caused a great deal of consternation to the shopkeepers of Oxford who *kept* getting asked for bright yellow trousers or violent purple jackets.

The cast is one of the strongest we have seen in Oxford, and certainly the most inventive; what Adrian Brine or Ken Loach can do with a grotesque character and a couple of pages of dialogue is worth watching. And the Birds themselves, all twenty of them, hurl themselves into their song-and-dance routines with alarming energy and feeling. But the greatest delight of the last few weeks has been watching Roland MacLeod and Jonathan Cecil bring to immediate life with infinite subtlety and humour the characters of Pisthetairos and Euelpides: they are the two best reasons for reviving Greek comedy I have come across.

The Birds *set off banks of rockets during the final rock number – my theatrical farewell to Oxford. But I had written another play for Colette King, this time to be done on the Fringe of the Edinburgh Festival. I described the play to Cathy Itzin:*

WHY THE CHICKEN?[7]

Why the Chicken? was about a group of kids in a New Town with nothing to do, who go off to a farmhouse, which they make their own. And it's about the relationship between this group of kids who've been dragged in from all over the place to this new town, and a girl, who is a social worker and supposed to be providing some kind of richness in the lives of these kids. She comes out to the farmhouse to find them. The plot was totally ludicrous, which didn't matter very much – fortunately! It was a clash really between working-class consciousness and living and feeling . . . and Oxford consciousness. I never worked that out, never articulated it, but that's what it was. And the working-class kids, interestingly, end up smashing up the youth club. I suppose that was how I felt about the Oxford consciousness, actually. Anyway, it had a lot of nice writing in it, and I began my life-long flow of monologues – characters just saying what they mean to the audience, rather than going through a whole naturalistic scene.

George Devine came and saw the show, liked it very much, but had reservations. And decided that he'd rather get me to write another play than do this one, which was fair enough. John Dexter read the play through the Court, worked on it with me, and helped me a lot in the revision of it. I was earning my living reading plays at the Court, which was a pretty miserable existence. Finally John got the play set up with Lionel Bart and Michael Codron, who were going to go into management together to encourage new writers. It's a long story, and all I can say is that it discouraged me from writing for the theatre for another three years. But during that time I met a number of very good actors – Terry Stamp and Michael Caine were in it, and Peter Gill was in it, who's a good director as well as being a lovely actor. But after John Dexter set it up, Lionel Bart decided he was going to direct it and forced Dexter out. He directed it quite well, in fact, until the point where Binky Beaumont came to Wimbledon where it was being tried out, to see it, and undermined his confidence in it. And at that point he decided to . . . make it acceptable for the West End. And from that moment onwards, which was just about the end of the first week of the run, the show just became more and more ludicrous, and the whole farcical West End pressure was on me. I stormed out, was dragged back, because all kinds of horrible things would happen to it if I didn't do them. Going back was a mistake – if you storm out, you should stay out. The show died by the time it hit Golders Green, after about eight weeks of screwed up life on the road. After having discovered what really goes on in the West End, what happens to a show before it hits the West End, the pressure and the evil that surrounds the whole business, I just stopped writing for the theatre.

This was the point at which I decided it was stupid trying to write for a Royal Court audience, or for a West End audience. It seemed to me perfectly obvious that all the people I knew and cared about at that time were watching television, so I thought, well, fuck it, I'll go and write for television, and try to use the popular medium in my own way, and contribute through that to people's lives.

But during this time I was still thinking and writing about theatre. The theatre magazine Encore *was in its prime. I wrote various pieces for it, including a review of David Campton's* A View from the Brink *that looked forward to much of my later work:*

A VIEW FROM THE BRINK[8]

A classroom in a primary school in Reading. Two naked bulbs. A stage covered with sleeping bags. Two hundred youth Protesters just arrived from Aldermaston on Good Friday. Two chairs, a table, a duffel-bag full of props, half-a-dozen dedicated actors from Oxford. Remove sleeping bags, point Protesting Youth vaguely at the stage, switch on bulbs, shove on actors, and begin the most exciting evening of theatre for a long time.

The three short plays by David Campton, grouped under the title *A View from the Brink*, produced by Michael Kustow, can only be reviewed as part of this occasion. Seen on their own they were exciting enough, derivative in manner from Ionesco and Joyce maybe, but meaningful and original in matter beyond doubt. Isolated from this context, the production and acting also call for a somewhat qualified appraisal – production a little slow, if highly inventive, a little centreless, if full of good moments, the acting lacking slightly in power and projection, if deeply felt – and highly competent.

Seen as a theatrical occasion, however, this evening was exhilarating to a degree. The complete and vociferous solidarity between audience and actors was overwhelming; the speed and clarity with which points were made by the performers and grasped by the brightest and youngest audience I have ever seen made one feel some faith in the future of the theatre; the exact balance between de-personalised caricature and emotional creation achieved by Roland MacLeod and Roger Smith, which suddenly gave a clue to the real English method of alienation, was stimulating, both immediately and in depth. Finally, the babble of comment from this young, footsore audience made one feel more certain than ever that the youth of England demand something to think about in the theatre and appreciate it when they get it.

I also wrote for Encore *a sub-Sartrian piece:*

POETIC AND DRAMATIC STRUCTURE[9]

By 'poetic' structure I suppose I imply that kind of structure in which the dramatist plays God and shows his characters to us as part of his divine plan. This may be done, as in Ionesco's plays, by flagrant caricature and submission of the will of the character to an over-riding symbolic structure. The teacher in *The Lesson*, for example, has no more chance of controlling his destiny than the symbolic rats' feet in 'The Hollow Men' have a chance of scampering off after a female rat and enjoying life for a change. The teacher is not human, he is an object in a pattern, a symbol in a planned relationship of symbols, a slave to a structure.

What, then, is this 'dramatic' structure, and where do we find it? Its first characteristic obviously is that the characters within it should be *free*. Free, that is, of conforming to a pre-conceived symbolic or poetic pattern; free to make their own choice when faced with a decision, free to act illogically, immorally, insanely, if they so wish, free to speak the words they wish to, free to do anything except renounce their freedom. And because they are free, they must be responsible for what they do. The characters, in fact, aspire to the conditions of humanity.

This whole conception of writing, however, raises three enormous problems. Firstly, if the characters are to be really free to go off in any direction, how is the play to come to any sort of *form* at all? And secondly, when the play does arrive at a form, this form in itself will be meaningful, and its meaning should be the author's meaning: how, then, is the author to arrive at a meaning for his form if it is in the hands of his characters? And, thirdly, one may ask, does not the author of this kind of play, in choosing his set of characters and putting them in an initial situation, make almost as much of a pre-conception as the author of a symbolic play?

To approach the question of arriving at a form, let us look at O'Neill's *Moon for the Misbegotten*, a play which becomes more and more fascinating, technically, the more one reads it. Here, the father's motives are with him from the start: Josie, and the farm. Similarly, Josie's chief motive – Tyrone – is with her too; and Tyrone's mother-seeking motive is more than permanent. The characters are strong, true and complex, the motives clear, and the situation – that Tyrone owns their farm and needs money – is powerful. Where they go from there is their business. Or is it? For somehow the play manages to maintain a good narrative line through it, and each act manages to be the right length, and each act manages to have a dramatic 'feel' about it, it goes up and down in an interesting way, the climaxes and the falls come pleasingly, the over-all shape of the play satisfies our demands for a well-constructed work – how is it that these supposedly 'free' characters just happen to choose to act quite by chance in this conveniently theatrical manner? All right, let's admit it. The freedom of these characters exists only in their author's imagination. And a powerful element in this imagination is the feeling for shape, for construction. Surely *his* feelings inhibit *their* freedom? The answer, I think, is that on this deep and complex level of creation, an extraordinary fusion takes place between the two, and it is part of the writer's job to make sure that he is sensitive to both.

To me, nothing is conclusive except that which is concluded – i.e. the past. Therefore it is impossible to begin writing this kind of play, which is an essay into the future for both author and audience, with any conclusive plan of meaning, for if the meaning is conclusive, the play will be an essay into the past.

To conclude I should like to point to some remarks of Camus, which are on a much grander scale, and which started off these marginal ramblings:

> In art, rebellion is consummated and perpetuated in the act of real creation, not in criticism or commentary. Revolution, in its turn, can only affirm itself in a civilisation and not in terror or tyranny. The two questions posed, henceforth, by our times to a society caught in a dilemma – Is creation possible? Is revolution possible? – are in reality only one question which concerns the renaissance of civilisation.

Dudley Moore had played a small part in my first play, and written brilliant music for The Birds *and had become a good friend. We decided to write a musical for the Royal Court:* Jack. *It began:*

When I was only seven years old
    My father went to war
He sent my mother no money so
    She turned into a whore

He lived the life that soldiers lead
    Before they go to hell
In Singapore and Tokyo
    And the Suez Canal as well.

When I was only ten years old
    My mother died of pox
They burnt her up in an oven
    And covered the ashes with rocks

They locked me up in this orphanage
    Here as you can see
And now I'm almost sixteen years
    They're going to set me free, me free, me free . . .

The Royal Court didn't like it much, and now I've lost it. As the Anglo-Saxons used to say, 'Lif bith laene' – Life is fleeting.

My work in television and film is a whole other book; throughout my time in the 'audio-visual' I constantly tried to find a way to reinvent the theatre in a way I could commit myself to, to find a way to the audience we were getting for Z-Cars, *and the television version of* Jack *I wrote with Troy Kennedy Martin called* Diary of a Young Man. *Eventually, after many good experiences writing and directing television, I simply stopped, took no more work. After many months not doing anything, I stayed in bed for a week and wrote a play:* Events While Guarding the Bofors Gun. *In this play seven men are assigned to guard an obsolete anti-aircraft gun in Germany during the bitterly cold winter of 1954. The story concerns the conflict between Lance-Bombardier Evans, whose plans for officer training would distance him from the working class, and the violent, self-destructuve working-class Irishman Gunner O'Rourke, who is intent on thwarting Evans and demonstrating the futility of their task. I sent it to the Royal Court who sat on it for a year, and, as far as I'm aware, still have not read it. George Devine was dead by then, and the theatre was run not for writers but by directors looking for vehicles for their own talents. Cathy Itzin again asked me:*

EVENTS WHILE GUARDING THE BOFORS GUN[10]

Itzin Bofors Gun *finally went on at Hampstead?*

In 1966. I just got fed up waiting for the Royal Court to read it, and talked to Ronald Eyre, and he said he would be interested in directing it, so I showed it to James Roose-Evans at Hampstead, and Ron came along and did it very well. The real conflict in *Bofors Gun* was between the way I felt then, in 1966, and the way I felt when I was in Germany, in the army in 1953 or 1954 – a kind of polarisation. It was all about the difference between Evans, who is climbing out of a working-class mentality into a middle-class one, with everything that that entails, and the total, life-destructive fanaticism of his desire to get out, get on, which is not simple. It's not a simple ambition syndrome, it's also connected with the homesickness within himself. It's very interesting, this homesickness thing, because very few people believe it or understand it, but in fact I think that homesickness is an emotion, an overwhelming, over-powering emotion – something you find in Anglo-Saxon poems, 'The Wanderer' or 'The Seafarer'. And nearly all Celtic literature has this really strong feeling, too.

Itzin *'Home' being anything from family to culture to nation?*

Yes, but particularly as it's experienced in exile. And I find it quite interesting that not many people today – or then – understood that. They thought it was just a trivial element in the whole show. But it's very much part of Evans's relationship with reality, his disorientation, the feeling of exile. And that's something that I found totally sympathetic. But it's also set off against his ambition, his efficiency, his cleverness, his . . . ruthlessness, really. So it's not really a one-to-one relationship, ambition versus anarchy, or whatever, but about two differences, two kinds of consciousness, one of which is going along with the rules of the game – not very good at them, but getting better all the time – and the other, the root-consciousness of the oppressed, who are driven to futile, alienated work, and who react quite understandably, with a kind of passionate abandon, abandonment of purpose, and fall back on to immediate, slightly irrational and self-destructive emotions.

Itzin *Having done that play, which was very successful, what was the next step?*

Well, Peggy Ramsay has been my agent since I began writing, and has really done an enormous amount just to help me keep going, and after she'd seen *Bofors Gun*, she sent me a novel which she thought would interest me, called *The Danish Gambit*, by an American writer called William Butler, and I found it very exciting, because it was a kind of continuation of the last duologue in *Bofors Gun*. The circumstances were totally different, but it was about a priest who was trying to convince a man in a death cell that he should live. I really was very excited about it, and adapted it, as a play. I called it *Bakke's Night of Fame* and again it was done by Ron Eyre at Hampstead. Butler's metaphysical gymnastics are amazing, and I liked them, liked being able to get those going in the theatre. Also the character of Bakke is an amazing creation – Butler's, not mine. It did well and it's been done in Germany endlessly. Been very useful as a way of keeping alive.

When I was in television I knew Ken Russell, and worked with him on some of his films, including one for Woodfall that never got made. He rang me up one day and asked me, would I like to do a spy film. By that time I was completely broke and heavily in debt, and the idea of doing a spy film appealed to me. And working with Ken. So I had a go at this one, which was *Billion Dollar Brain*. And that opened up yet another world of amazing people – but this time getting into the whole American film market machine. And during those years – 1967 to 1972 – I worked with and learned a lot from quite a lot of people – Fred Zinnemann, Carl Foreman, Harry Salzman.

Itzin *This involved spending time in America?*

I was in America a couple of times, but really the whole American film colony moved over here. It was like living in America. And it was useful, because having done *Billion Dollar Brain* and having done the first draft of *Virgin Soldiers*, I was qualified to write the screenplay for *Bofors Gun*, which I enjoyed doing. And then was asked to do another screenplay, which turned out to be *The Reckoning*. These mass entertainment media are not to be ignored, or you ignore them at your peril, because they contain within them the accumulation of fifty years' experience of mass entertainment. So you learn how it's done: you also learn why it's done. It's a real study of ideological penetration. I wouldn't have missed it for the world. Quite apart from the amazing array of characters who strut and fret on that particular stage, there is a lot to be learned from the technique of entertaining people from big movies.

Itzin *How does this period of movie work relate to the beginnings of your own discovery of a new form?*

Having gone through television and come out the other end, and then having gone through movies, I finally came to the conclusion that the mass media, at the moment, are so penetrated by the ruling class ideology, that to try to dedicate your whole life – as distinct from occasional forays and skirmishes – to fighting within them is going to drive you mad.

I had never lost touch with the theatre – mostly the London theatre. In 1967 I wrote three pieces for the New Statesman. *Actually I wrote four, one being a passionate denunciation of the irrelevance of the West End theatre to what was actually going on in the world, that was spiked by Nick Tomalin, Arts Editor, with the unforgettable phrase: 'We've asked you to write for the back of the paper, not the front'. The perfect expression of London Labour's fetish that theatre and the real world should never meet. They did however carry the other three:*

BLOODY MEN[11]

One of Shakepeare's grand designs in the English History plays was to show how unnatural rupture of the line of succession brings death and disaster to the entire country, stirs up the evil spirits, and continues to spread its poisonous effects until a new, purified dynasty is founded: one that led, flatteringly enough, down to Elizabeth I, who happened to be ruling England at that time.

Macbeth, as Peter Hall's production at Stratford clearly shows, is a sort of Scottish précis of this design, which serves to flatter the new monarch, James I, on his ancestry, and to distinguish his Christian sort of Scottishness from the pagan hooliganism that the average Englishman might have expected from someone north of the Border.

Within this design, Shakespeare has tried to show how Fate, in the shape of the Weird Sisters, can play some horrifying tricks on those not fortified against her by the rites of Mother Church. Macbeth is sucked into a Celtic maelstrom where witches, black power, blood and intransigent evil swirl him round to his death. Thus, although he tells us of his vaulting ambition, and although he is a fearsome fighter inured to bloodshed, his main crime is his imaginative contact with a pre-Christian underworld which unleashes the forces of destruction into an otherwise harmonious universe.

All this is made manifest in the Stratford production. One question remains. What on earth does all this have to do with us, now?

Peter Hall has chosen to see it as a play about the man and not the structure, about character and not forces, about being a Christian and not about Christianity. In so doing he in fact removes all relevance. Wrapped in a cocoon of bardolatry, verse-speaking, social acceptability and cosy bourgeois culturalism, this great play passes smugly by with nothing urgent, nothing new to say to anybody. Where Shakespeare tried to astound his audience with the stark bloody facts, here everything is muffled in a costly subsidised rug, set among Casa Pupo-inspired furnishings, tactfully lit, and beautifully spoken. Paul Scofield, an actor for whom I have the highest possible admiration, and whose presence in a play is in itself justification for going to see it, here resorts to vocal devices which his feelings reach out towards, but never quite touch. Nevertheless, his performance will never be other than conventionally theatrical unless it is given more meat. At the moment it seems to have been fed on sips of a poetical/metaphysical/literary-critical cocktail, which makes for interest but amazingly little involvement. It needs removing from the aura of self-congratulation ubiquitous in the Birmingham stockbroker belt, and harnessing in the service of a more passionately relevant conception of *Macbeth* in 1967.

PETER TERSON'S 'ZIGGER-ZAGGER'[12]

When I first read John Arden's *Live Like Pigs*, nine years ago this week, I could hardly stay in the house for excitement. Between scenes I stumbled aimlessly around in a high state of agitation, hands trembling, scalp tingling, like the gleeful baddie in a silent film discovering the hidden cache of gold. Suddenly the theatre was alive again, worth devoting one's life to. John Arden had seized the actual realities of this time and place, in all their depths and desperations and joys, had thrust them with immense theatrical vigour into the centre of the stage, and was blessed with the gift of language, the power of a poet, to help him. Gold indeed.

A comparable delirium possessed me the other evening while watching Peter Terson's *Zigger-Zagger*, performed by the National Youth Theatre. This time the source of excitement was more from the stage than from the page – the words were more ordinary, the scenes not so loaded – but from the moment the lights snapped on to the ranting, joyous crowd in the City End stand, to the final defiant chant with which we won a World Cup and lost a world – 'Clap, Clap, Clapclapclap, England!' – the theatrical vitality and originality of Terson's play and Michael Croft's production were never in question. Nor was the fact that here were a writer, a director and a cast giving us their own perceptions about an England they know all too intimately, trying desperately to astound us with the world we have chosen as ours.

The Sawney family in *Live Like Pigs* and the City End football crowd in this play have a great deal in common: poetry, music, violence, bloodshed, lust, language, laughter, uncontrollable feeling – a wild transcendental anarchy. Harry, our 'hero', is a boy who leaves school without the conventional benefits of 'A' levels, 'O' levels, or even ambition to help him. We are shown, in a series of strip-cartoon scenes played out in front of the crowded stand, how his pathetic teachers, rancid parents, bullying bureaucrats, exploiting bosses, insensate workmates, boot-licking vicars, and misguided magistrates conspire to present England as a moribund, not to say incurably evil place. The ever-present football crowd, by contrast, is flamboyantly alive, mystically united, rewarding in the way only a religion can be rewarding.

For 'football crowd', of course, one could read, equally validly, LSD, cannabis, gin, the whorehouse, art or any of the other devices by which the sensitive try to evade the oppressive reality created for them by their elders and betters. Some of the scenes are brilliantly theatrical – particularly the magnificent moment when the football chant rises like lust in a graveyard through the dreary school-song. Others are not so successful, some are cliché-ridden, but all serve to reveal that the Third World is here as much as it is in Asia and Africa; that the colonisers also colonised at home.

Peter Terson's Everyman, Harry (played with devastating insight by Nigel Humphreys), is not by any means a revolutionary, however. He is attracted, in the shifting sands of his adolescence, by the solidity of Les and Edna (his brother-in-law and sister), whose particular terra firma consists of satisfaction in the ownership of various possessions – their reward for obedience and smug obliviousness – in other words, for wilful self-deception, and cheerful bad faith. Harry is attracted to it, and finally, tragically, succumbs to it in a truly vicious scene where the author is clearly calling down a mighty curse on the persuasiveness of conformity and the ephemeral nature of youth's rebellion. It was difficult to tell whether there was more bad faith on the stage or in the auditorium at this point, considering that the whole venture was backed by the *Daily Mail* and applauded by the parents, teachers, bureaucrats, bosses, workmates, vicars and probably magistrates who made up the audience. One can only assume they were cheering the 'whole-heartedness' with which the 'youngsters' . . . 'threw themselves into it'.

But then this play is not simply making a social protest. There is anarchy and poetry and music and excitement in everyone, and this play demands attention because it puts us all back into closer contact with these feelings in ourselves, and renews us and purifies us in the way good theatre should.

Of Michael Croft's production I have nothing but admiration – for its energy, attack, canny handling of the company's necessarily limited resources, and above all, its conviction. I should point out that although the younger characters are beautifully played, notably by Nigel Humphreys, Anthony May as the Mephistophelean Zigger-Zagger, Andrea Addison as Edna and Jennifer Galloway as the glum maenad Sandra, one cannot expect, and does not get, more than an enthusiastic caricature of the 'grown-ups' from an under-twenty-one cast. Yet somehow, again as with John Arden, this play thrives on enthusiasm and conviction – qualities notably lacking in the posher theatres – and gives more joy and makes more contact in this shape than many a subsidised globule of smugness to be found elsewhere.

DAVID STOREY'S
'THE RESTORATION OF ARNOLD MIDDLETON'[13]

David Storey (like David Mercer, and Lawrence before him) is concerned with the beast beneath the skin of civilised man. Sometimes his beasts rampage, terrorising the neighbourhood, as in *This Sporting Life*. At others they lurk neglected until such time as they can no longer be evaded, then rise up and tear a man to pieces – as in *The Restoration of Arnold Middleton*.

Arnold himself is a schoolmaster, in a classical schizophrenic family situation. Being somewhat mother-obsessed, and having married his wife for maternal qualities which she refuses to display, he finds everything he needs in his mother-in-law, who is young enough to still be sexually viable, but old enough to be, as it were, his mother. As the three of them live together in one small house, the structure of interpersonal perceptions (and deceptions) becomes complex and frightening. He refuses to allow his wife to send her mother away (on grounds of human kindness – oh charity, your depths are murky!) – until, at the climax of the piece, in chagrin at his own mother not turning up to see them, goaded on by the inanities of the schoolmasterly world around him, he gets moody, drunk and sleeps with his mother-in-law. From this point onwards, temporary insanity sets in to express his inability to cope: it is only when the whole situation is destroyed by the removal of mother-in-law to a flatlet, that normality beckons and his wife takes him back to her bed.

It is unfortunate that the last part of this story is such a schematic affair, because in principle it explores a resolution – a restoration – comparatively new to the theatre: I suspect that if it had been handled at the same pace (in the writing) as the first two acts – had, in fact, been the two acts instead of one – David Storey would have had time to tease it out, give it the air of truth and humour, which makes the first parts of this play so memorable. Perhaps it is over-schematic because it owes too much to psychological theory: intellectual abstracts, however truthful, play havoc when allowed to creep in and dominate first-hand perception in a personal play.

O'Neill often found a fourth act useful, and there is indeed something of his genius in the grandeur of Storey's transmogrification of ordinary mortals with less poetry and more psychological awareness, less melodrama, and more wit. One can't help regretting that in the ten years since he wrote this play, David Storey has not written ten more.

Robert Kidd, who handled a similarly witty, gruesome chunk of drama, *When Did You Last See My Mother,* so admirably, here reveals a marvellous gift for making the commonplace theatrical and the rhythms of life worth waiting for through a thorough exploration of the text. Since its first presentation at the Royal Court, it has lost some subtlety and acquired more clarity – a danger sign; it has also lost Eileen Atkins, who made the wife a strong, original, twelve-tone sort of lady: June Barry, who now plays the part, gives us a sweet, ordinary and slightly dull person: possibly more accurate, but not so interesting. John Shepherd, who remains as Arnold Middleton, gives a performance teetering on the verge of self-indulgence, but still worth going a long way to see: febrile, discontented, constantly grasping at myths larger than himself, twittering, self-deceptive – the very mould of the young married – educated to expect more from life than he is emotionally equipped to extract from it, hollow, pained. Noel Dyson as mother-in-law mugs away at times appropriately, at others not, but can be forgiven all for the furtive delight she gets in being taken out to the pictures or being teased by Arnold.

All in all, *The Restoration of Arnold Middleton* is worth seeing. The beasts that lurk in Arnold are ashamed to show their heads for the same reasons that the British bulldog is ashamed to bite, the British lion to roar: guilt and lack of direction. The results in Arnold's life – bad faith, ignoble gestures, deceit, rash acts of aggression followed by temporary insanity – have their parallels in our public life. Arnold's constant reference to Robin Hood, heraldry and the many other myths of the late great Britain, indicate that Storey is not altogether unaware of the connections. *Arnold Middleton* has meaning on several levels, and remains a brilliant portrayal of a person: a considerable creation and a considerable play.

The Sixties were Swinging and so was I. Then along came 1968:

RANDOM HAPPENINGS IN THE HEBRIDES[14]

Itzin   *This was when you wrote* Random Happenings in the Hebrides?

Yes. That was a play for Richard Eyre, at the Lyceum in Edinburgh. Up till then, all the plays I'd written took place within a small group of people, all in the course of a day or even less. I felt the need to write more of a chronicle play. And *Random Happenings*, although it takes place all on one set, actually spans quite a number of years. [Set in the Hebrides between 1964 and 1970, *Random Happenings*, or *The Social Democrat and the Stormy Sea*, centres on four characters: Jimmy Litherland, a Labour politician, the alcoholic schoolteacher Aeneas McPhee, and his two troubled children, John James and Catriona. The play deals with human relationships, Hebridean life, labour relations and the failure of Labour politics to further the cause of socialism.]

Itzin   *How much of you is in that play? I mean emotionally, autobiographically?*

The play is about the whole complex issue of organised political activity, which is in conflict with the richness of experience. Jimmy became part of a purely party political machine – for getting votes, people into Parliament, power. He realised the conflict between that process and lived experience, indeed the people the machine represents. Jimmy realised that effective 'left' politics would have to make compromises, come into conflict with the realities of world politics, with the realities of the development of capitalism. He realised that local Labour politics would have to adopt tactics and a strategy which would apparently put it in conflict with its declared interests.

Itzin *The interesting thing in* Random Happenings *is that the great variety of individual needs creates a complexity which is almost impossible to sort out.*

Yes, there is a great complexity, and a parallel between Jimmy's sexual dilettantism and his political dilettantism, a sort of rootlessness about his behaviour which connects very much with a politician's rootless relationship with his electors. Because it is rootless – as soon as he goes to Westminster he is up-rooted, as soon as anybody adopts a political attitude towards reality they, in fact, are in danger of losing contact with that reality.

Itzin *Doesn't Jimmy discover this when he goes back, and settles for grass roots – but in an opting-out way?*

I don't think so. Do you know Neruda? In Neruda's later poems, there is a very strong feeling that actually to be involved – deeply – in the reality around you, is not to opt out of political action, but to get more involved in it, to be involved in a richer stream of political activity. Now this again is not a resolution, because at the end of the play the working class is still being ripped off. There has to be a struggle, there has to be a political organis-ation, has to be a very hard, bitter, disciplined fight against the powerful forces of capitalism. So that the conflict isn't resolved, because I don't think it's ever capable of being resolved. Both streams of human reality move forward together – they interact and they change emphasis. But that conflict between the density of experience and the urgency of simplified action seems to me to be the central conflict for anybody who wants to do anything in the world today.

I started to write in April 1968, and in May 1968 things started happening in Paris. And I went over and spent some time there.

We were incredibly moved and excited about the events in Paris. A meeting was held in Clive Goodwin's flat, the centre of left-wing literary activity, which raised a lot of money for two causes: for medical supplies for the students, and to help the Beaux-Arts to produce more posters. The problem was how to get the money to the right people in Paris. I'd just bought a huge Chevrolet Impala convertible, to signify the start of a family. I volunteered and Mo Teitelbaum volunteered to come with me. There were strikes, so the only way in to Paris was to airlift the car to Le Touquet and drive:

THE PERSONALITY OF A REVOLUTION[15]

The first signs of revolution: already, before the plane lands, we see the Stars and Stripes, the Union Jack and the Tricolore freshly laundered, aggressively reassuring the intrepid tourist that business is as usual.

Half an hour later, Route Nationale Number One, road from the Channel ports and the Belgium frontier: two gendarmes, two soldiers, working together, scrutinise cars, above all those with Paris number-plates. Their wireless crackles, but they have nothing to report.

France is very beautiful on a June evening.

We hit Paris. I worry about crossing the bridges, but there is no demonstration that night, they are free. On the way in to Paris, we have passed normally dreary factories now beautiful with red flags over locked gates, and magnificent posters. Now we go straight over the bridges to the Beaux-Arts, and everywhere in the Quartier are buildings with crowds around their gates and the red and the black flags defiant over their gates, high on their rooftops. Everywhere there are the posters, the wall-newspapers, the slogans, the jokes, the walls of Paris are alive, vibrant with passionate politics, with humour, rare graphic genius, the spirit of revolt, determined – funny, but determined. I jump startled: I cannot believe such a sentence would ever be written on a Western European wall: 'Down with the society of conspicuous consumption!' Clearly, this is an extraordinary revolution.

For the rest of my time in Paris, I was constantly startled, amazed, exhilarated, not so much by the power of the revolution, but altogether by its character. The world newspapers and their political pundits have all concentrated their hardened arteries on the question of power: the true genius of this revolution is that it is one which seeks to destroy power, to create a world where power is irrelevant, and to replace its operations with thought, humour, and, amazing to all the brain-washed, tolerance. It is aiming for a truly socialist world, where man is no longer distorted into filling a role in the power-game, but can be truly free to expand his humanity creatively for the good of all. And the splendour of the revolutionaries is that they are not theorists, either of policy or strategy: they fight their revolution in their streets, and they live their revolution in their lives.

Most of the people I met were painters, though I did spend a very happy hour with Jacques Prévert, and many hours in the Odéon, and at meetings of the 22 March movement, a grouping of Socialists, Maoists and anarchists. Three years later I looked back:

POWER TO THE IMAGINATION![16]
THEATRE AND REVOLUTION

I think the theatre within the four walls has obvious limitations and has to move into the streets and where people meet. I'm not ready yet to take the step, except that one of the great moments for me theatrically was the May–June events in Paris in 1968.

I spent most of the time I was there with Jean-Jacques Lebel who is the great Happenings man. Jean-Jacques literally created barricades and scenes of confrontation, and it was – though it sounds denigratory to say it – a form of theatre. The nightly confrontations with the CRS [Compagnies Républicaines de Sécurité] made one suddenly realise the tremendous dramatic impact of this. That is not to say it wasn't serious; it was immensely serious. But in Paris the street battles were theatre in the sense that they were more than themselves. There were 10 million people on strike throughout France. These battles were vital expressions of a total situation. Revolution cannot be reduced to theatre; but at times like this theatre can aspire to express revolution. The strength of these confrontations was the mobilisation of the workers in the factories. In the absence of such mobilisation, such actions become opportunistic charades.

Jean-Jacques thinks that what happens in the theatre is phoney: it must happen in life. I'm not with that yet. I suppose it's because I'm more firmly rooted in English literary history and the values of the past and I'm apt to move forward with a certain amount of security. At the same time I can see that as the thing against which I measure what I'm doing in small halls round the country. I think it's true that naturalistic theatre is restricted to showing failures in movements towards change and when it gets involved in things like the Russian Revolution you end up with rather banal shows. Stanislavski was incapable of producing anything of interest about the revolution. It took a Meyerhold and a Mayakovsky, a poet, not a naturalist by any means. What Meyerhold was doing, as far as one can see, was using the theatre as a building with some people in it to present new forms of ritual. In the same way Mayakovsky was using the visual elements of theatre, incorporating a sort of futuristic style, and his own highly charged verbal style, to present images of a transforming society.

THE PROBLEMS OF CONTEMPORARY FORM

Most participatory theatre is embarrassing, shambolic, gauche, and disastrous. An audience in a theatre is a very arbitrary, random collection of people, and to try and mobilise them as a unified force is a completely contradictory thing to try to do. In the streets it's the same. As an audience you get characterised by people you don't know. I think that one has to get to a point where there are actual social forces in society prepared to move before you get people actually unifying in the required way. One of the strengths of the Paris thing was that there were these forces, combined with the imaginative drive coming from people like Jean-Jacques Lebel, who led the taking of the Odéon. What revolutionary group would think of that in England? They'd close it down as bourgeois; or they'd use it for boring sloganeering, instead of creating a continuous debate for six weeks, most of it at a very high level. This kind of thing has its own built-in danger, though, for what actually happened at the Odéon, as a concomitant of this great anarchic energy, was that the place began to get rather dangerous and criminal elements and kids who were tripping out came in. So one has to have a political structure – which was lacking – along with this imaginative drive. I'm not anarchist – I just like anarchist energy! Political structure is absolutely vital.

Inevitably, on returning to London, I was disappointed at the rather pathetic response in England to the earth-shattering events in Paris. Although tens of thousands could be mobilised by the Vietnam Solidarity Campaign, our own revolution, it seemed, was restricted to a few tame speeches in the LSE [London School of Economics] and a series of opportunistic follow-up meetings manipulated by the Socialist Labour League.

However, the after-shocks of May '68 went on for ten or twelve years, right up to Thatcher. For me, it radically changed my approach to audience in the theatre: just as I had gone into Z-Cars to find the people I grew up with, so now I resolved to find that audience. It began with a reappraisal of Joan Littlewood and her company. She began with Ewan MacColl in a theatre group in Salford called The Red Megaphones, then toured the industrial areas of Britain – the Central Belt of Scotland, the North of England and South Wales in particular – for many years, playing to working-class audiences. She settled, against MacColl's wishes, in the Theatre Royal, Stratford, in the East End of London:

JOAN LITTLEWOOD[17]

From the mid-50s to the early 60s, she and her company created theatre with an astonishing variety, with tremendous popular appeal, and ultimately with such great commercial success that it destroyed itself. Productions like Behan's *The Quare Fellow* and *The Hostage*, Shelagh Delaney's *A Taste of Honey*, and *Sparrers Can't Sing, Fings Ain't Wot They Used To Be*, and *Oh What a Lovely War* crashed and exploded onto the stages at Stratford, and left audiences reeling with delight and great joy, and young writers and directors breathless with the possibilities of our theatre.

By some strange chance I happened to be at the dress rehearsal of *The Hostage*, with Brendan Behan shouting friendly drunken abuse at the actors through the second half, and them giving back as good as they got, and Joan charging around muttering, unable to sit still for very long. What was happening on the stage, in the pub down Angel Lane, in the street outside the door, all seemed to be a piece of the same universe. This group of people were telling a story – they were mediating contemporary reality, but in a way that the Royal Court or the West End or the repertory theatres had not dreamt of: they were telling it the way the working class saw it, and in a way that the working class could enjoy, and, what is more, *did* enjoy.

There is a moral tale going round, which Tynan falls victim to, which says that the working class rejected Joan Littlewood's work, that her theatre was full of trendies from the West End. Now while it is true that in the mid-50s the Theatre Royal was *not* crowded with merry Cockneys, and that Rolls-Royces *were* to be seen outside the door – mostly those of West End managers come to rip off the show – this is not the whole story. Their work touring round the Manchester area gave her, and her company, a real basis for creating theatre for popular audiences. Joan and the company who worked with her had worked hard and learnt the cruel way about entertaining the working class before Brendan Behan blew in with his wonderful piles of paper – his laughs and songs and his sentiment and his rebelliousness – with his exploration and illumination of the life of Dublin. Avis Bunnage, who first played the mother in *A Taste of Honey*, had toured with Theatre Workshop for years before Shelagh Delaney appeared with the play – and Avis was able to get to work with Joan on that part in a way that brilliantly conned the audience up to the point where they realised they were being conned, then fell apart to reveal another whole layer of human being underneath. Ken Tynan complained that he couldn't understand why the mother kept delivering her lines to the audience! Not only was she the kind of woman who buttonholed every passing person, but also that *kind* of woman was the basis of a whole line of Lancashire comic ladies – ending up with Hilda Baker – who played the variety halls, the pantos, the summer seasons and the clubs. The way Joan directed that character came straight from that line.

David Edgar, in his laconic dismissal of an entire cultural tradition, says: 'It is interesting that they [some groups and companies] have achieved most when they have employed forms actually peripheral to the urban British working class. Joan Littlewood's *Oh What a Lovely War*, for example, used the Pierrot show (a basically Italian form, translated into British seaside entertainment).' Now there are many things to be said about this. First, the Pierrot show at the seaside in the 20s and 30s was a totally British working-class form, well-known and loved by the mums and dads of the 1950s. Secondly, the style of presentation, the construction, the relationship between those actors and the audience, the way of singing the war songs, the degree of sentiment and the mix-in of comedy in some of the cameos, all these and much more, owed everything to music hall, variety and ENSA-show forms, not one of them 'peripheral to the urban working class'. And the urban working class came to see the show, and loved it.

What was striking about *Oh What a Lovely War* was the way Joan and the company had worked together with great confidence in a style that had developed from these popular forms, and were able to use them and the language they created to go beyond a mere imitation of a Pierrot show, or a collection of variety tricks. Because the subject of the show, the unspeakable waste of so many human lives to help the ruling classes of Europe to settle a quarrel over exploiting and killing ever more human beings – this subject would exert an immense pressure on *whatever* form were to be employed. In this instance, it forced Joan and the company to create an immensely powerful piece of theatre. If you want to see how to make a disgusting mess of the same material, go and see Richard Attenborough's film of the same name. See what some truly bourgeois confusion, and a great deal of American money, can do to destroy something strong and valuable.

But *Oh What a Lovely War* had an extraordinary effect on British theatre. In the 1960s it was performed and loved in almost every repertory in the country. A new generation of young actors playing in it sang the songs, and heard how Joan's actors had worked on it. The fame of Theatre Workshop spread, and with it a whole set of attitudes to making theatre.

I joined the Editorial Board of The Black Dwarf, *sustained by Clive Goodwin, edited by Anthony Barnett, and I contributed a lot of effort and articles and a poem, which Tariq Ali liked, but published with the pages in the wrong order so it made no sense. In the heat of the moment I wrote a poem for The Mexico Olympics (film department) for a John Irvin documentary that won a gold medal:*

GIVE US NO FRONTIERS

Give us no frontiers.
You are the foreigners,
You who draw lines on maps,
Invoke old wars and bent alliances
To keep us in, to keep us out.
Gagarin flew above the air,
And down fell the walls of Jericho
And out we poured in all directions.
And lo we had the gift of tongues,

And the earth was no longer divided
And round fat babies rolled over and over
Bowling about the surface of the globe, laughing,
And grave young men with long-eyed girls
Walked hand in hand
Past customs men who rubbed their eyes
And fled,
And mild apprentices conspired
In a general passport burning,
And the elder statesmen erected barricades
At their own garden gates,
And prepared to defend themselves
Against the freely migrating hordes –
Mexicans, Germans, Red Chinese –
All taking transworld nature rambles –
But they were disappointed:
We just ignored them,
Left them to their own futility,
To demarcate the bed space
Between themselves and their wives,
Unbelievably unemployed.

And as the rambling crowds
Walked hand in hand
Savouring our beautiful earth –
Poles in Peru, Tibetans in Manchester –
They began to sing
In many languages,
A song with a thousand tunes,
And the planet earth blushed,
And jumped,
And shook off into outer space
Every man, every building, every single thing
That did not sing,
And every Customs shed
Became a star
And every frontier post
A meteorite
And every barrier
Between man and man
A receding speck in the astronomer's eye,
Bound for the edges
Of the infinite universe –

At the same time I wrote a punitive review of Arnold Wesker's The Friends *which upset Arnold's self-image considerably. Two days after sending in the reviews I rang Anthony Barnett to ask him not to carry it, but he insisted, to my dismay. Here it is, with Arnold's characteristic response (the correspondence did, however, go on):*

FRIENDS AND ENEMIES[18]

Arnold Wesker's tremulous flirtation with 'progressive' ideas and his disgruntlement with the cultural level of the British working class in his early plays summed up the attitudes of many 'intellectuals' in the late fifties and early sixties; for this reason the plays are at the very least of historical value. Similarly his Centre 42 efforts symbolised the crusading optimism of the mid-sixties. But both the early plays and Centre 42 contained features which prefigure startlingly the ideological bankruptcy of his latest play *The Friends*, and the sad fate of its venue – The Round House.

Wesker's *Trilogy* made a minimal, possibly irrelevant, demand for articulacy and the values of a good liberal education to be brought to the working class. It displays a lamentable ignorance of the strengths and values of the working class itself. This has blossomed into the formulation, in *The Friends*, of the appallingly ill-conceived question: How can we respect and look for guidance to the virtues of the proletariat, when the British working class is so corrupt and backward? This formulation is presented as a paradox justifying bemused inaction, and by no means as a dialectical opposition leading to action.

Perhaps Wesker's bemused inaction comes mainly from the naive opposition, first articulated in *I'm Talking About Jerusalem*, of romantic, nineteenth-century pre-Marxist utopian socialism, to the twentieth-century capitalist rat-race. Wesker's admiration for hand craftsmanship and the rural utopia will of course lead him to disappointment and bitterness: without a trace of Marxist – let alone Leninist – thought in his approach, Wesker is unable to see any way to act. Given his objectively fallacious assessment of the working class, it is hardly surprising that, in *The Friends*, the portrait of Lenin on the wall remains little more than a decoration.

Another source of Wesker's disillusionment is clearly the failure of Centre 42. Its creation, the Roundhouse, now operates on a virulently commercial basis under a management which clearly puts business before any form of political commitment. The Trades Unions have failed to provide enough money to keep the local Centre 42 'festivals' going, and the people of Wellingborough are now mercifully free to drink their pints without hectoring folk singers thrusting a supposedly superior form of culture in their faces. Wesker's crusade for Centre 42 to bring *culture* as he understood it – Stravinsky, Ewan MacColl, Royal Court plays, his own plays even – *to* the working class, rest on a completely false analysis. The idea, which he shares with Roger Planchon in France, that culture is a product to be sold by culturally-conscious (therefore superior) artists and intellectuals to culturally starved (therefore inferior) workers, is based on the bourgeois concept of culture. While it is possible that the cultural forms so far developed by an urban proletariat cynically fed on escapist rubbish under capitalism are not, as yet, either matured or even viable, it is no way to improve matters by thrusting alien art forms, the product of the class-enemy, at a backward proletariat and expecting them to like it, learn from it, and pay for it through their unions. If Wesker had concentrated on bringing a truly socialist consciousness to bear on the mass forms of television and film, on the media which the working class really use, if he had tried to make the theatre he presented relate directly to the conflicts within the working class, or to illuminate the history of the working class, or if he had at least attempted to break down the bourgeois forms and mystique of the theatre – he would have been somewhat more convincing in his concern for the cultural well-being of the proletariat.

It is interesting and not altogether surprising that Wesker's bourgeois-cultural elitist ideas have found a warm welcome within the 'Arts' machinery of the Labour Party establishment. He could, indeed, be the somewhat verbose laureate of Wilsonian politics.

The logical culmination of his history of mistakes and confusions is, indeed, *The Friends*. The form is unmistakably that of bourgeois theatre. The friends are a group of ultra-sentimental interior designers, one of whom, a so-called *revolutionary*, dies of cancer on stage through the first act. Wesker exploits sickeningly the 'I want to live' theme through Act One and the 'What does it all mean?' theme through Act Two. He presents all his characters to us not for our judgement but for our sympathy. The effect is the classical one of bourgeois theatre: to reassure the middle classes that humanity is all one, we are all mortal, and the differences between us are not really so important. The British working class are dismissed as corrupt and backward, and the formulation already mentioned used to discourage any thought of revolutionary social action.

The characters are allowed to swim about in a syrupy mixture of despair and sympathy, fondling their own and each other's psyches until they throb and waving their 'North Country' backgrounds like distress flags until one wishes they would drown.

Wesker and his people are stuck in the sad attitudes of an Aldermaston marcher's reunion rally; Wesker may well outdo Tiny Tim himself in hard-line nostalgia, albeit for a different decade.

What he must not do is, by left-wing posturing, to confuse anybody, including himself, into thinking that he is in any way socialist, or that this play relates in any way to any possible form of socialist theatre.

18 June 1970

Dear John

You telephoned to warn me that you'd written an attacking review of *The Friends* for *The Black Dwarf*. *The Black Dwarf* had always given me the impression that, one day, *Gauleiter*-fashion, it was going to draw up a list of people it didn't like and urge its readers to stone them. The last sentence of your article still confirms this. In old-style Stalinist decree-making you have passed judgement on me for your public. 'What he must not do is to confuse anybody, including himself, into thinking that he is in any way socialist or that his play relates in any way to any possible form of socialist theatre.' What he *must* not do! Must I not? You write as though Lukacs, Fisher and Berger had not existed.

But worse, you write irresponsibly (we'll ignore the almost foaming venom). I said on the phone you were a silly boy to write the article because, as I'd guessed, you'd not read the play and had only seen it once; and this irresponsibility is typical of the entire article which is full of sheer mistakes all of which could have been cleared up in a brief talk. Examples:

1. The Roundhouse's activities have nothing to do with Centre Fortytwo; Fortytwo has not operated since 1962. Nor did Centre Fortytwo fail and leave the people of Wellingborough 'mercifully free to drink their pints'; the people of Wellingborough and many other working-class areas wanted more festivals but we refused because we didn't have enough money to do it properly. Fortytwo failed to raise money from the Labour Movement and the Arts Council – with Jennie Lee at its head. I don't understand what warm welcome 'from within the arts machinery of the Labour Party establishment' you are talking about – we were rejected by them, almost totally. Victor Feather's words to me in 1965 were 'I've been instructed by the General Council of the TUC to tell you that you need feel no obligation (or responsibility) to them and that they feel none towards you or Centre Fortytwo'. Jennie Lee's words to Fortytwo in 1968 were: 'Arnold must realise that what he wanted to do is now superseded by the work that I've been doing and he must reduce the scope of his aims accordingly.' 'Laureate of Wilsonian politics' indeed!

2. My play, *I'm Talking About Jerusalem* does not oppose 20th-century capitalism with the handicrafts movement; on the contrary, it shows the characters failing, inevitably. The play is a statement to socialists that though industry is a fact in society yet man in relationship to his work must be a real socialist's consideration.

3. The character in *The Friends* dies of leukaemia, not cancer; you just didn't listen – to any of it.

All your points are typical of spit-and-run fringe left-wing polemics. You do not quote from *The Friends* to prove your points nor tell us its real story; look at the sneering, could-mean-anything words you use, so typical of the over-night theatre reviewing we are all supposed to deplore. 'Wesker's *Trilogy* made a minimal, possibly irrelevant, demand for articulacy and the values of a good liberal education to be brought to the working class.' But you offer no evidence; it's just a superficial reading of the plays. After all, how must we view *your* university education (which I didn't have)? Could that not be seen as a liberal education and could we not say your criticisms of me are due to that liberal education? It is all such unworthy, childish, simplistic labelling.

You then, as a writer of TV plays and serials reaching millions, suggest I have no right to want my theatre plays to be seen by as many as possible: What hysteria are you afflicted with for God's sake that you presume your work is more 'a truly socialist consciousness' than mine? If it is, where is your audience? And why has the right to be spoken to in a friendly tone of voice been denied to me? What terrible crime have you black gnomes decided me guilty of that you withdraw comradely words of advice and inflict, rather, the lash of vitriolic and self-righteous condemnation? And if I am not a socialist why did you send me your last play about Winstanley to read?

I cannot answer your analysis of *The Friends* because you don't make one. You devote less than a quarter of your article to the play and spend the rest attacking me and my past work and activities. It's as though you'd waited ages for an opportunity to get a lot of personal resentment off your chest; or did you interpret references in the play to 'those endless dreary episodes about ordinary life on the telly' as an attack on your contribution to the *Z-Cars* series? Now you've done it I hope you feel better.

I have only one observation to make in direct reply to one of your state-ments. You say that the wish of Planchon and myself to find wider audiences for the arts is based on 'the bourgeois concept of culture' and that we are 'culturally-conscious (therefore superior) artists and intellectuals' who must impose on those otherwise happy, pint-drinking 'culturally starved (there-fore inferior) workers.' In this instance your choice of language is similar to that in a pamphlet called 'Patronage for the Arts': 'A large section of the population is completely indifferent to anything that comes under the general heading of culture and they have every right to stay in this state of non-grace.' It is not coincidence that the tone is the same. Both you and they inherit the same ruling-class attitude – a peculiarly English sneer at the notion that the working class could or should ever be interested in more than pint drinking . . . In fact you and they are repeating the ancient ruling-class arguments that the workers are best left happy and undisturbed. Dear John, mind your own business; you suffer from bourgeois guilt which I don't want imposed on me as one who comes from the working class. I'm capable of knowing when I'm being contaminated . . . .

I thought, after the Krushchev revolutions that articles such as yours could never be written again – they contain such stale jargon and jaded spites. I've argued against them again and again and if I'm tired I hope you'll have enough charity to understand and forgive me for quoting a passage from a lecture I gave way back in the 'distant' days of 1966. In defence of Fortytwo's ideas I said: 'And to those artists and intellectuals who would accuse us of self-righteousness and priggishness I would say this: why do you imagine when we point to the humanising qualities of great art that we must be implying that our own humanity is complete? Why, when we refer to the crippling effect upon society that indifference to art creates, do you imagine that we are not aware of the cripple within ourselves? There is no logic in this, you only sneer at our enthusiasm as a convenience to hide your own miserable contempt. You would like to appear the guardian of the people's right to pursue whatever they care to pursue in that state of 'non-grace'. But all you are doing is justifying the bother you do not care to take to ensure that every man enjoys the knowledge you enjoy . . . '

I repeat the accusation Simone made in *The Friends*: you and *The Black Dwarf* are the real counter-revolutionaries for you stir up that to which you have given only the most superficial considerations. 'In your haste to mobilise support you've given blessings and applause to the most bigoted, the most loud mouthed, the most reactionary instincts in the people . . . And now, I will neither wear cloth caps nor walk in rags nor dress in battledress to prove I share his cause; nor will I share his tastes and claim the values of his class to prove I too stand for liberty and love and the sharing between all men of the good things this good earth and man's ingenuity can give. Now shoot me for that!'

Indeed, you can shoot me for that, John; and against the wall I would still declare *you* to be the counter-revolutionary because *I've* always spoken about what the working man *could* be and felt anger that he's abused for what he *is*; and in doing this it was necessary to tell him what he *is as I know him from experience*. He's *my* class and *my* background and therefore what I say I say from love and a concern for wasted lives. You might want him to remain only a happy 'pint-drinker' but I say you are patronising and insulting to do so. He is capable of infinitely more and within him is a spirit which I want to see as other than the sour, doctrinaire and uncharitable spirit such as emanates from your article. That's what my revolution is about.

When you think and write responsibly about my play then I'll defend it in full. Meanwhile, as you put it in your headline over Peter Weiss's letter to the Russians in defence of his play on Trotsky – 'Lay down the ice-axe, comrade'; though I'm very disinclined to call you 'Comrade' for I think you to be treacherous and dangerous to progress for the silly confusions you perpetrate with your old-fashioned, Stalinist jargon.

Yours

Arnold

To be fair to Arnold, I do wince at the tone of the review, and did so two days after I wrote it; it is the tone of the students of Paris in full flight, of Alain Geismar, even of Sartre at that time. I do not apologise for it, but I am sorry it was turned on such a nice, kind friend as Arnold Wesker. Yet I still believe what it is basically saying to be true.

There were many other parts of the world where things were going badly for people. I wrote several articles supporting the dissidents in Moscow and Leningrad, who were bravely trying to assert the right to free speech. I went to Algiers (and was nearly barred from entry, as the revolutionary government didn't approve of the length of my hair!). In Algiers, I did an interview with Eldridge Cleaver for The Black Dwarf, *which Cathy Cleaver actually approved of, and which was later carried in* Les Temps Modernes. *Of course I protested in Grosvenor Square against US slaughter in Vietnam, and sat down at Tariq Ali's behest in the middle of Oxford Street. But nowhere were things so rough as they were for the blacks and their allies in South Africa. I encouraged writers I knew to donate manuscripts to the Manuscript Collection, to be sold to buy guns for the ANC [African National Congress]. I helped organise, with the Anti-Apartheid office, the Playwrights' Boycott of South Africa, as requested by Mandela and the ANC. However, some of our 'intellectuals' thought they knew better than the ANC what was good for South Africa. I took Tom Stoppard to lunch, and he flatly refused to stop his plays being done in front of segregated audiences there. He, and Arnold Wesker, argued that their plays would somehow bring the South African Apartheid government to sweet liberal attitudes. I pointed out that if they were likely to have any effect whatsoever, they would be instantly banned, and wrote a piece for the* Anti-Apartheid News:

ANTI-APARTHEID STAND[19]

In 1963, a great many British playwrights, along with singers, actors, film stars, sportsmen and journalists, pledged themselves to express their utter rejection of apartheid by refusing to allow their work to be shown in South Africa before segregated audiences.

It was a specific gesture designed for this specific purpose, and relied for its effect on the solidarity of its supporters. No one expected the South African government to fall, nor to change its policies: there would have to be other action to bring that about. This was a small way of endorsing the United Nations' call for economic sanctions against the regime, and of giving moral support to those inside and outside South Africa who were fighting in more positive ways for change.

A few months ago the theatrical managements of South Africa decided to have a go at changing the minds of the playwrights. They met, discussed the situation, and sent one of their members to New York and to London to see what he could do.

In New York an agent from a large theatrical agency called a meeting of the leading Broadway playwrights, most of whom, it appears, were not convinced. The ban was to remain.

In London, Lord Willis was persuaded to issue a statement to all members of the League of Dramatists, and other playwrights, asking: Is it time for dramatists to reconsider their attitude? It suggested that the ban is not having any 'real political effect', and goes on to use the very words of Sir Alec Douglas-Home over the Rhodesian sanctions policy: 'It is actually doing harm to the people we most want to help'.

He proposes, with the support of Arnold Wesker, that we should lift the ban immediately, allow our plays to be performed in South Africa before segregated audiences, and donate whatever royalties we earn to one of the coloured artists associations in South Africa – 'by this means practical help will be given to non-European artists and audiences.' He insists that such a policy 'would by no means imply a change of attitude on our part towards apartheid, or any support for it.'

A great many of us felt the arguments used were wrong, and fourteen of us signed a letter to *The Times* rejecting them utterly. These fourteen were: John Arden, John Bowen, Margaretta D'Arcy, John Hopkins, Evan Jones, Doris Lessing, Henry Livings, John McGrath, Troy Kennedy Martin, David Mercer, John Mortimer, Edna O'Brien, John Osborne, Harold Pinter and Robert Shaw.

The arguments which followed the publication of this letter – carried on in the columns of *The Times*, on television and in private – indicated a fairly deep division of thought between two sides, deeper than a mere disagreement over tactics.

Whereas the arguments of Lord Willis, Frank Marcus, Laurens Van der Post, Terence Frisby and others seemed to concentrate on bringing spiritual comfort and support to the white liberals in South Africa, and bestowing charity in a somewhat eighteenth-century manner on those coloured people who wished to *better themselves within the existing society*, it was quite clear that all the fourteen signatories of the original letter, plus Robert Bolt who wrote in later, and many others besides, wished all their spiritual comforts and practical financial support to go to those coloured South Africans who were preparing to change the status quo in their country in the only truly practical way left – by force of arms.

Those who wanted the ban lifted assured us that they did want change – but seemed to think it would somehow be brought about by the 'free flow of ideas' (or at least, those ideas the Nationalist government would allow to flow so freely), by the coloured man 'showing he was as cultured as the white man' by the normal processes of forming a climate of opinion within a parliamentary democracy.

When David Mercer suggested that in this situation guns were in fact more persuasive than plays, a howl of outrage arose from those who had been taught in school that the pen is mightier than the sword. Laurens Van der Post waxed eloquent on the subject: 'For me, art in its first and most important value, is utterly a-political, and reaches before and beyond and deeper than any political consideration. I believe that its main concern ultimately is to increase human awareness.' And he abused the signatories of the original letter roundly for offering to put their works at the service of the disenfranchised, the humiliated, the beaten, the tortured, of those who will be refused admission.

If the white liberal friends of Mr Van der Post really want their evil society to change, they must be prepared to make some sacrifices. They can always *read* new English plays: no one is denying them the intellectual succour, merely the public segregation, to which none of us will subscribe.

Throughout Britain, Europe, throughout the world, there is indeed a growing human awareness. An awareness that the old arguments of liberalism and gradualism and wait-and-see and be-good-children-and-things-will-get-better are utterly bankrupt; they are the last resorts of the weak-minded optimists who cannot face the realities of the world; they are the fantasies which populate the imagination of the frightened imperialist. The banning of our plays before segregated audiences, in South Africa or anywhere in the world, is a minute gesture of solidarity with those who are prepared to act, not talk, fight, not be enslaved, to stand up and demand freedom, not lie down and grovel.

Lord Willis and the South African theatre managers argue that because films of our plays can be shown in South Africa, we are wasting our time: we reply – No: rather let us try to have our films *also* withdrawn from exhibition before segregated audiences. The first step in this direction is a motion before the Screenwriters Guild of Great Britain, as obviously this cannot be an individual effort, it must be a corporate one. The next step will be to contact the other film unions here and in America to get their support. We cannot just give up.

Lord Willis is a Labour peer, and his arguments and those of his supporters have the comfortable, defeated sound of Harold Wilson on Rhodesia. The sanctions are not working – fine, let's think of good reasons for giving up, covering up, forgetting them: this is the tone one detects beneath all the rhetoric about art and literature.

Let us hope that this attitude will not prevail, or the world will become sadder and sicker every day.

My intense political conviction at this time is perhaps best experienced in a short poem I wrote:

THE WRITING ON THE WALL

Is the writing on the wall
In letters of arrogant red
Twelve feet high
Perhaps, you think, a little overstated?

Look to the foundations of the wall itself;
The bricks are crumbling.
Soon all that will hold it together
Will be the red paint.

The red paint did, indeed, hold the wall together. De Gaulle was re-elected with a huge majority. Despair and several suicides followed among my friends in France. But we worked on.

All of which brings me to the Liverpool Everyman:

THE LIVERPOOL EVERYMAN[20]

I should like now to trace a personal, verging on the megalomaniac, sequence of events. Some time in 1968 or 1969 I was in Liverpool staying with my family. A friend was coming up from London to see a new play at the Everyman theatre, so I said I'd be interested to go along as well, as I'd heard about this place but not been there. I arrived in Hope Street, and we went into this ex-cinema, ex-church hall, and sat with a very few people and watched a highly pretentious piece of avant-garde whimsy, the hero of which was a pair of Siamese twins dressed in green and purple satin. By the interval I could bear it no longer: I asked my friend if she had in fact been to Liverpool before, to which she replied that she had, but only to sit in theatres and watch other equally awful plays. I suggested that a trip to stand and stare at the dock wall might prove more entertaining, and she, being a metropolitan lady of the theatre, agreed with a certain amount of caution. We escaped from the Everyman, and I vowed never to return. I was shocked, and appalled, that a second theatre in Liverpool should be created merely to extend the whimsical experimental department of cosmopolitan bourgeois high culture. This was, after all, Liverpool, where the dialogue in the street is matched only in Dublin, and where the Liverpool poets were already dragging in large audiences for their poetry readings.

However, there it was, and what could be done about it? About a year later, in autumn 1969, I was back in Liverpool, and noticed that the Everyman was doing a play about Bessie Braddock, the famous, or infamous, or anyway large, Labour MP and personality of the 1940s and 1950s. This seemed a bit more to the point, and at least something to do with Liverpool. I broke my vow and went. I found that a new director had taken over, a man from Hull with a degree in Drama from Bristol University called Alan Dossor: he had an immense admiration for Joan Littlewood, had studied her work and her audiences, had done some time with Peter Cheeseman at Stoke, and started directing at Nottingham Playhouse under John Neville. He had assembled a company of excellent young actors, who worked in the inventive, confident, audience-grabbing way of Theatre Workshop, and the story was told with a certain amount of pace and variety. There was not much music, however, and the writing was not very sharp in the way Scouse can be. However, in subject, style and attack, Alan was obviously going somewhere positive. I met him, and decided to try to work with him to fill this theatre: the Braddock show was playing to only 30%, a hangover from the Siamese twins era – I felt this was wrong.

The first thing I wrote for them was a group of five short plays called *Unruly Elements*. Four of them were set in Liverpool, and were mostly comic, linked by a series of authoritarian figures talking semi-comprehensible gibberish to the audience. The sets of each play were different, but the permanent framework was a group of standing or hanging giant blown-up objects, like a four-foot toothbrush or a six-foot-high packet of cigarettes.

The audience figures went up to 75%, and the audience responded to the jokes, the presence of recognizable local people and problems on the stage, and the style of the pieces, which varied a little, but which was on the whole full of verbal attack, not at all naturalistic in its pacing, articulacy, or compression. The plays, and the actors and director, created a sense of excitement about the theatre within the community and, encouraged by a determined publicity campaign, by the price of the tickets, by the informality, lack of middle-class bullshit about the theatre, and by the fact that you could get a decent pint of ale before, during and after the show, some young working-class blokes came with their wives for a night out. They enjoyed themselves and sent their friends. As the theatre is near the university, quite a few students from there and the Poly began to take an interest. Oddly enough, very few of the regular 'theatre goers' of Liverpool ever came: they had the Playhouse in the centre of town with plays from the West End, and occasionally from the Royal Court, to go and see.

After *Unruly Elements*, Alan tried to mount a show based on Brecht's *The Private Life of the Master Race*, with several writers contributing short scenes about contemporary living. It was interesting in that a whole jumble of styles emerged from the writers, and we could see what was working with the audience, and guess why. But all the time I was quite sure that the thing to do was to fill the theatre, and I knew that then we could really move, and take the audience with us.

The rock concert is one form of entertainment that had fascinated me, partly because I like a lot of that kind of music, partly because the Beatles, Loving Spoonful and the folk-rock groups had developed lyrics which were literate and worth listening to, and partly because the UFO groups like Pink Floyd had established a whole rather twee performance, or acting level, during and between their numbers. Alan Dossor asked me to write another show, and I suggested a musical in the form of a rock concert, with the actors performing a story and a band performing a series of numbers, the whole set in Liverpool, with the central story involving a Liverpool girl who goes to university and feels she is leaving her class behind, and the working-class boyfriend who couldn't make it to university, but who gets off with a cute middle-class girl he meets while driving his delivery van. And their mums and dads. We found a local band – ex-folk, gone electric, now playing heavy beat in a disco in Seacombe and hating it – who were delighted to come in and write the tunes and perform.

Needless to say, this simple form-concept developed in the writing. The whole thing started off with the two dads in 1940, fire-watching over Liverpool during the blitz, singing Flanagan and Allen numbers, then having a horrifying vision of their children and even worse themselves in the future – thirty years ahead. But this served to introduce another sequence of popular songs, and to give an overview from time to time; the main action went on loosely in the shape of a rock concert, with scenes.

What was really interesting and exciting was that *Soft or a Girl* was one of the most successful shows ever on Merseyside. The working class, young and old, flocked to the Everyman. We played to 109% capacity, which is really quite full, for the three weeks scheduled, and then came back for another three weeks, and could have gone on for another three. That audience did stay. Alan, as director, found ways to present Shakespeare and other new writers, and Brecht, that kept faith with that audience's expectations.

In 1972 I was in the Fisher-Bendix factory while it was being occupied by the workforce. Almost every worker there that I spoke to had been to the Everyman, and was going to keep on going. And the work at the Everyman was getting better, livelier and more like real theatre than anything I had seen at the Royal Court or the Old Vic.

Altogether I had thirteen plays presented at the Everyman in the four years from 1969 to 1973. Perhaps the high point of my involvement in Liverpool was Fish in the Sea, *which was later revived by 7:84 [the theatre company McGrath founded in 1971 with Elizabeth MacLennan and David MacLennan].*

FISH IN THE SEA[21]

Fish in the Sea was written for late 1972. I wanted to build on the work of *Soft or a Girl* in terms of music, to appeal to the same audience, but to present them with something more difficult, more challenging.

During 1971–72, apart from working with 7:84 and the Everyman, I had been working on a socialist weekly magazine called *7 Days*. Amongst other jobs, I had covered several factory occupations for them notably at Mold in Flintshire and Fisher-Bendix in Kirkby. 7:84 had also taken a show to an occupied engineering factory in Glasgow. It was this Glasgow occupation which most related to the occupation in the play, re-set fictionally in Liverpool. (It is certainly not meant to be a reconstruction of what happened at Fisher-Bendix, which is a whole Wagnerian cycle in itself.)

The main elements I wanted to set in some form of dialectical motion were – the need for militant organisation by the working class; the anarchistic, anti-organisational violence of the frustrated working-class individual in search of self-fulfilment here and now; the backwardness of some elements of working-class living: attitudes to women, to socialist theory, to sexual oppression, poetry, myth, etc.; the connections between this backwardness and Christianity; the shallow optimism of the demagogic left, self-appointed leaders of the working class; and the intimate realities of growing up and living in a working-class home on Merseyside.

To me, these were the main elements of working-class Liverpool, and the conflicts between them are at the centre of the play. Ultimately the play is trying to do two things: one is to analyse and set in motion these elements. The other is to call for more maturity, and more determination, from the working class, its allies, and the socialist movement in Britain.

The title is taken from Mao's analogy of the Party or Front as the head and body of a fish, and the population as the water through which it moves. Brigadier Frank Kitson, the British Army 'counter-insurgency' expert, takes up this analogy in his book *Low Intensity Operations: Subversion, Insurgency and Peace-Keeping* (1971):

> If the fish has got to be destroyed, it can be attacked directly by rod or net . . . But if rod and net cannot succeed by themselves, it may be necessary to do something to the water which will force the fish into a position where it can be caught. Conceivably it might be necessary to kill the fish by polluting the water . . . The first aim of those involved in counter-subversion is to gain control of the people, because in most cases this is a necessary prelude to destroying the enemy's forces – and in any case it is the ultimate reason for doing so.

I mentioned 7 Days: *it had arisen from the ashes of* The Black Dwarf. *After eighteen months of collective discussion, endless papers, memos, dummies, after Anthony Barnett and I had wasted day after day trying to raise money from rich lefties (a soul-destroying task), finally it emerged as a rather boring photo-magazine. I was in Liverpool rehearsing when the first three or four issues came out, and I grew more and more appalled. I tried to inject news and documents from the ongoing class struggles into the magazine, and wrote a memo to the Editorial Collective.*

7 DAYS[22]

The source of the troubles is a failure to come to terms with the fact that 7 *Days* has no direct political purpose: from this failure comes (in no particular order):

1. Breakdown of democratic structure. Because no one is responsible to any large group or body of opinion, and because the collective has no adequate discussion either before or after publication or any system of checking material before it goes in, a situation has been created in which individualism is unchecked and 'flair' is being substituted for hard political discussion. Our sources of material have no organic connection with the paper and staff feel unsure as to exactly who they are working for.

The root of this whole structural problem is that a Marxist newspaper must lead through from reporting of action to further action. At the moment the paper is in danger of serving as a cover-up for idealism, with concomitant indulgence of bourgeois flippancy in tone and bourgeois irresponsibility in organization.

2. The characteristic *tone* of the paper is one of distance, cool, lack of passion, lack of involvement, lack of feeling of comradeship with others involved in action.

3. Closely allied to this are certain other features:

(i) Arrogance. A form of intellectual superiority to the people we are writing about. We do not compare our opinion with theirs. We ride over them, often unconsciously.

(ii) Failure of experience. Very characteristic of the paper is a sensation that the writer has no, or not enough, actual lived *experience* of what is being written about – this allied with intellectual arrogance is a disastrous combination.

(iii) We make massive assumptions about (a) the level and (b) the knowledge that our readers possess – we don't seem to care *who* the articles reach, as long as they please a small coterie of acquaintances.

(iv) A tone of superiority allied to truculence, stemming from social privilege allied to frustrated political ambition.

(v) Certain individual contributions of great brilliance, clarity and perception.

4. Almost all articles are far too long, do not contain enough information, and are generally 80% comment, 10% necessary fact and 10% unnecessary fact.

5. Inertia of lay-out, presentation, and division of the paper. Because we are not trying to cause a specific group of people to read, think and *act* we lay an even emphasis throughout, we neutralise vital mobilising material by not spreading it, and blow up trivial pseudo-academic chatter into cover-story material under the misapprehension that it will 'appeal' to 'our readers'. We have created ghettoes for culture, life, and special features when they should be fighting for their place in the paper.

6. Closed doors. Although there is clearly no conscious desire to do so, we have, by our style and actions, closed the doors firmly in the face of the bulk of our best friends.

7. Finally, the content of the paper. a) A balance between what the readership wants, and what we feel should be thrust upon it, i.e. our actual ideological intervention – is impossible. We don't know our readers' wants, we make token sporadic interventions here, there and everywhere, and the actual level of the interventions is erratic, frequently dogmatic, sometimes over-academic and sometimes politically wrong. b) We do not seem to be able to report on the experiential level, but always on the sociological or abstract-cultural, so we lack the ability to intervene in the lives of our readers *as they are lived*. c) The preponderance of comment over interview, fact, document, speech, poem, manifesto, extract, statement, etc., means that we place ourselves in the position of arbiters, judges, gurus, inexpert management consultants, etc. Instead of creators of a much-needed line of communication between the pressure of events, the urgency of ideas and those readers who will want to or even need to respond to these events and ideas with their own events and ideas – the paper must be an instrument of this dialectic, not an applicator of principles. We have no concept of putting ourselves at the service of, available to, at the disposition of these forces in society, primarily that of the conscious working class, secondarily that of the class-conscious intellectual, which will create a movement, a momentum, towards revolutionary change, the overthrow of capitalism, and the beginning of the new dialectic of socialist society in this country.

We have a going concern, an established weekly magazine, which is known, and has been bought in quantities. We are not satisfied with it. Let us make our own cultural revolution, now, and see if we can survive it; rather than go down with a dull thud and screw up the chances of the left having a good magazine in this country for the next ten years – which would be – will be, if we do it – criminal.

It was in one of the interminable collective meetings before the launch of 7 Days *that Clive Goodwin had suggested calling the paper 7:84. The most recent survey showed that 7% of the population of Great Britain owned 84% of the wealth. This did not include the houses people lived in, but did include land, assets and capital. It was nothing to do with wages, all about structures of society. The collective, in its wisdom, rejected it. When I finally got a theatre company together, in the summer of 1971, I remembered it, and that's how the company was named.*

Trevor Griffiths rang me to ask if I could help him find a venue on the Edinburgh Festival Fringe for two short plays which he wanted put on as a late evening show. At the time I was brooding on a full-length play which could go well on the Fringe, so we agreed to find a hall we could share. We drove up to Scotland together, and thanks to Ricki di Marco and Sandy Neilson we ended up with the Cranston Street Hall. We were in business.

THE ORIGINS OF 7:84 [23]

Barker   *When did the idea of starting this company arise and why?*

Since the beginning of the 1960s I and my wife, Elizabeth MacLennan, had been talking with quite a lot of people about the idea of starting a theatre company because we found it increasingly difficult to do what we wanted to do in commercial theatre. After several attempts to get a company together during 1968-69, the fringe began to blossom and touring circuits emerged. Also, the Arts Council began their policy of giving some support to those fringe activities and it became possible to tour a play for long enough to cover the costs, roughly speaking.

In 1970 it became clear that there was the possibility of starting a theatre company that would not need to have a building. At first we'd been working under the assumption that we would have to have a base, a theatre or a hall, that we would operate out of. But we didn't see our job connected specifically with one small area or community. We wanted to be able to tour plays which had a very strong and immediate contemporary connection, that would raise a socialist perspective on contemporary events, that would entertain people and would notably appeal to the working class and the supporters of the working class, who can be found amongst students and amongst the intellectual circles who hover, one foot in the middle class and one foot in a general liberal movement. We wanted to present those plays in a way that would serve as an agitational injection into a community rather than as an ongoing, every day, involvement with a community. So in 1971 we decided, more or less on the spur of the moment, as a lot of these things happen, to start the company. I wanted to write a play called *Trees in the Wind* and we decided, towards the end of June or the beginning of July, that we would open on the fringe of the Edinburgh Festival. Within six weeks we managed to get the people together, the play written, the hall and the staging organised and to open the play.

The people we recruited were a very good cross-section of the kind of actors that we were after. Elizabeth had obviously been talking about this idea with me for a long time; she had been working mostly in television and film, before that in Reps and she had recently received great notices for a West End show. Victor Henry is somebody that I'd first met through Ken Loach. Victor played the lead in a series of television plays that I wrote with Troy Kennedy Martin, and we'd got very close on an artistic level. He was obviously somebody who was bursting out of the seams of commercial theatre. I'd done a lot of work at the Everyman Theatre where Gillian Hannah had been for three years and she felt that it was time to move on. The other was Deborah Norton, who was excited by the play and what we were trying to do. When we were on in Edinburgh, several people came up and asked us to bring the play to their University or club. The play was reviewed nationally and people began to know about it and to know about 7:84. After the Edinburgh Festival we toured for six weeks doing mostly one-night stands or two nights around the circuit. It seemed important that we continue in operation, even though we soon realised that we wanted to reach out beyond the audiences we were getting, to people who wouldn't go to any of these places. It was very important that we continue playing those places as a means of staying alive; also, because they were very lively, we didn't want to pour cold water on the audiences who did come.

The other important thing was that we had as a conscious policy that we would recruit a lot of different people for each show and different directors, with the aim of establishing a more permanent company, which would stay together after the first year of operation. Also, this policy was semi-thrust upon us because in between shows we couldn't afford to pay people so they had to go off and get other work, and this meant that when we were ready to do the next show they were often in the middle of rehearsals for something else. David [MacLennan, Elizabeth's brother] remained constantly looking after the whole organisation of the tour, the stage, lighting, transport and keeping contacts alive within the places that we went to and building up potential audiences in those areas. Elizabeth MacLennan was constantly with the company, Gillian Hannah stayed for the first year and Gavin Richards came for the third production and remained with the company for quite a time.

We were beginning to build a nucleus of people and getting good reactions from audiences, on the whole. In particular we were getting the kind of reaction I was very anxious that we should get in the area of extending the audience. For example we played in Cardiff and it was obviously an audience of people interested in theatre, but somehow one or two people who had a wider political interest, because it was a play about Gramsci, also came to see the show. Karl Francis, now a film-maker, came up to us afterwards and said, 'Look, you should be doing this in the valleys. The next time you come, let us know and we will arrange gigs for you in the mining valleys and in miners' halls.' That was exactly the kind of response we were hoping for during this year and it happened a lot. We managed to build a network of contacts which was broader than the arts theatres, with a view to future development.

We did *Trees in the Wind* about three girls sharing a flat: each had different attitudes towards society, they all had a concern, and in the broad sense a left-wing concern, for the future of the society they lived in. Each one had a sharply different attitude to the way in which this concern should express itself. One character was practical and functional, she was doing psychiatric social work and believed that the thing to do was to make everybody feel better. Another character had a strongly feminist attitude; as far as she was concerned it was latent male chauvinism and the masculine drive to destruction and aggression that was destroying the world. And the third one was involved in a Marxist-Leninist political organisation. In amongst these three we put a catalyst who attacked each one in turn and tried to destroy them, creating a dialectic between his ironical stance of deciding to be a capitalist and demanding to know from them why he shouldn't be. The resolution, or the temporary resolution of the play, was a unification of all of their concerns in a quotation from Mao about how opposites work on each other. What the play was saying was that although the movement is broad and has got many conflicting positions inside it and although some are wrong, some are mistaken, some are backward, some are progressive, some are ineffective, some are backing up the system as it stands, in part the overriding thing is that the movement goes forward and the dialectic goes on as strongly as possible within the movement towards a socialist future. This dialectical process has been constant in, I think, all of the shows that we've done. There has always been this element of contradiction and counter-contradiction embodied in the shows. One of the most important things, which is unwritten and unformulated, is that we do not present propaganda. We don't hammer people with the results of thinking, we always involve the audience in the dialectical process of experiencing life as it is now and the contradictions as they are now. In this way we try not to do a liberal presentation of both sides of the picture, but to show the forces that work in society in the way that *Trees in the Wind* showed the forces that work within the left-wing movement.

Then we did four short plays of mine under the title *Plugged Into History* and then a play of Trevor Griffiths' called *Occupations* and a third play of mine called *Underneath,* which was really a very seminal play, although it wasn't altogether a triumph on its own. *Underneath* was about building bridges. There were two plays within it: one was about the attitudes of the designer of the bridges, who believed that scientific progress could only be made at the risk of lives, that you could only move forward in this massive area of human development, construction engineering, by taking risks; and the other half of the play was concerned with the life of a man and his family, a man who built bridges, who actually went out on the bridge and was killed. One of the things that happened while we were in rehearsal with *Underneath,* was that Dave and I rushed out to a music shop in Brighton and bought a collection of musical instruments, microphones, speakers and amplifiers. With *Underneath* I wanted the company to develop into a more musical entity using the rather motley assortment of instruments that we had got together to tootle on. We began our involvement with songs and music from that fairly curious beginning into the much more serious developments in the second and third year of the company.

Barker *Now that you have got the beginnings of an established company, do you do any training work?*

With *Trees in the Wind* we did one or two interesting sessions on the idea of having three people simultaneously improvising in three different corners of the room and explored what this style demands. It is not naturalistic absorption in what you are doing yourself, but listening (almost like instrumentalists in an orchestra) to yourself and to the rest of the orchestra and to the overall thing. The idea of this was to get away from the old system of being on stage at the same time as somebody else – which was that you did something naturalistically only you toned it down – to get to the level of music that some of the more complex Stockhausen pieces have where you have four or six loudspeakers in a hall, each one carrying a different message, each one doing a different thing, but all of them related to each other and the experience. The electronic music concerts that I had been to in London were packed with a very young, very interesting audience, and they were enjoying the experience of multi-level communication and this is what we were trying to get with the actors. In *Trees in the Wind* we tried to open up the theatre by putting the audience in the centre and having three sets of action going on around them.

Since then we've experimented with the style, that we developed in *Plugged Into History,* of heightened naturalism, whereby the actor is in a naturalistic situation but speaking with far more directness and articulacy than one normally expects a person to have in such a situation. The overriding medium that made this articulacy acceptable to an audience was comedy. You establish a level of comedy, of heightened verbal wit and heightened verbal comedy, which replaces the relationship between the actor and the audience in a naturalistic situation, which is one of simple belief or disbelief with a different medium of communication. The verbal level of play with words and comedy and ideas works so that you are able to introduce through the verbal level an ideological level, or an ideas level, and still remain in a recognisable situation.

Barker   *How did you finance the company?*

When we began I'd been fortunate. I'd just written a film, it was about the sixth or seventh film that I'd written, but this one happened to be quite well paid and I happened to have some money in the bank. That was a financial springboard but obviously that couldn't go on for very long, so we app-roached the Arts Council touring section. They were very sympathetic, they were encouraging companies to tour outside London. So we began with a very small grant for the first tour, and we've existed ever since then on the basis of a grant towards a tour not on a grant to the company. The result is that in between tours we don't have any money coming in. This has been a constant difficulty. We've been fortunate in that as we've gone on we have managed to maintain an increasing grant from tour to tour from the Arts Council. It's always a guarantee against loss, not a direct grant. Apart from the box office and the Arts Council, the other source is guarantees from the organisations that run halls or theatres, which vary enormously. We can't think, at the moment, in terms of a year's work, we have to think in terms of a production. We have to balance what we get in from the tour and the Arts Council, with all the expenditure of rehearsal, production costs, touring costs, accommodation, office costs and all the wages. We've actually managed to balance just about every time, in fact when it comes to things like buying vans, we got a small capital grant from the Arts Council for the first one and ever since then I've had to go off and do another film, write a television play or something, to get the cash. In fact it's been necessary to subsidise 7:84 partly by other work and in Dave's case working for weeks and weeks for no money at all. I think the answer to this is to have an annual grant – the Arts Council has been reluctant to put us on this basis. It's a form of keeping an eye on what we are doing.

Barker   *What about the second year?*

In the first year we had established that the company existed, that it did good work, that it had high standards of acting and efficiency, that its political stand was clear, that we had an audience who wanted us, that we'd built up the contacts and people wanted us to come back, and that there was a growing group of people who were interested in working with us and that they were the right kind of people.

At the end of the first year I set in motion what I wanted to do, which was to devolve the decision-making process into a more collective decision-making process. In the first year if the company was to continue it had to have a push and an organisation, a centralisation. But from the beginning we wanted to devolve power as much as possible. I tried to do this by creating a collective machinery where discussions took place on all major decisions, where the power to take other decisions was delegated by the collective to individuals who were responsible to the collective for what they did. With the next shows, which were John Arden and Margaretta D'Arcy's *The Ballygombeen Bequest* and *Serjeant Musgrave Dances On* (which was an adaptation I had done, at John Arden's suggestion, of *Serjeant Musgrave's Dance*), we put this into motion and we got together a much larger company than we had before. *The Ballygombeen Bequest* developed what we had begun, tentatively, in *Underneath*. There were a lot more songs, there was a lot more direct address to the audience, it was a more free-and-easy structure. The musical involvement of the actors, in not only singing but in playing, was much greater, and the style, the connection between the actor and the audience, was beginning to be even more direct. It's got a tremendous mixture of styles, which still retains a political logic and human logic and vitality. It was a great play to do.

I had been asking John and Margaretta for a play for some time. I had known them for sixteen years, and they were two of the people we had been talking to about starting a company. They were interested and they sent us *Ballygombeen*. Gavin Richards, who was acting in the company, who I don't think had directed very much before, seemed to me to be the right person to bring out the qualities in the play. He did a very good job on it and a particularly good job on liberating the actors from their preconceptions of acting. It was a painful process in some cases because Gavin was throwing them more and more back on themselves as people, insisting that it's what you want to say, through the play and through the character, that is important. This was very fruitful in the long run and some of the actors have never been the same since.

That production went very well, aroused a great deal of comment and got us into a certain amount of trouble, through threats of litigation and so on.

Then we rehearsed *Serjeant Musgrave Dances On* and we toured those two plays together. *Serjeant Musgrave Dances On* was directed by Richard Eyre, with Gavin as Musgrave. Richard required a very high standard of acting discipline within the company, which was good. The opening up of the third act of that adaptation, when the audience is very intimately involved in what is going on, was probably a stage further in the development of our relationships with and direct political challenge to an audience. At this time we thought that the company would stay together and continue to develop excitingly along these lines. Sadly, we found that the end of the tour was probably the most disappointing period in the history of 7:84. The tour finished about the middle of December, and we had actually started rehearsal on *Ballygombeen* in July. Everybody was pretty exhausted by this very hard and demanding life. We didn't have money to put people in decent hotels or even decent digs. People were in pretty trying circumstances, always sharing rooms, sometimes pretty grotty rooms, always thrown together. The combination of that and the fact of being back in London, which we were in December, and having tremendous acclaim as individual actors from critics and from other directors, producers and managements, led to the company shooting off in several directions. This was very disappointing. Obviously we were weakened by that diaspora, and we further aggravated the situation by making a decision to go in three directions. One was that the English company should continue doing, for the meanwhile, small-cast plays to keep the organisation going. Second was that Gavin had been asked to take over the remains of Ken Campbell's Road Show. We felt almost unanimously that he should do that, as obviously he was capable of doing it, and it would add to the growing number of touring groups that we had respect for. This company became Belt and Braces. Gavin was very involved in the idea of the total liberation of the actor. He was constantly scornful about 'the power of the pen' and wanted the actor to be the almost totally autonomous creator of his role and of the whole show. I don't agree with that as a totality but it was something that he wanted to do and he was having quite interesting results. The work that he has done, and that Ken Campbell has done, is valuable and has had an influence on the way we work. The third direction was that David, Liz and I wanted to work in Scotland with a Scottish company. I, for my part, wanted to write a specific piece about the clearances, and at that time the whole monstrosity of the oil exploitation in the North of Scotland, particularly the onshore developments connected with oil. I worked out that the three of us were going to go to Scotland, to find Scottish actors to create a Scottish company, to deal with Scottish problems, to make Scottish plays and so to get more directly involved with Scottish audiences. That was the division in February of 1973.

In England the collective decided they wanted to do a stage version of *Man Friday*, Adrian Mitchell's television play, and Adrian said he would work on it. *Man Friday*, which had a small cast, did a tour which was fairly successful, and continued the work we had been doing. The only problem with that show was that the small cast left the company in England pretty small really. Very gratifyingly a lot of people who had been previously involved, people who had been away for a year, came back and said, 'What's happening? We can't let this stop.' Altogether we found that the demand from the people who had worked in 7:84 for it to continue in England was very great. I then suggested to Gavin that it might be a good idea for his company Belt and Braces, who were then four people, to join forces for a production with 7:84 in England. Mick Campbell suggested doing *The Ragged Trousered Philanthropists* as a subject that is part of working-class culture and which could be a method of getting through to more outside extra-theatrical working-class organisations, which in fact it turned out to be. In fact this is the most difficult problem in this kind of theatre – getting an urban working-class audience to trust you enough to come and see what you're doing. Once it's happened, then they are very loyal and they grow all the time

Barker *Well, you've said what the problem is, how do you tackle it?*

If your work is politically involved, you immediately gain a sympathetic hearing from working-class organisations. In Scotland, for example, we found a very willing ear from the Scottish TUC, from Glasgow Trades Council and Edinburgh Trades Council. On the organisational level it helps people to have confidence in us if they have some sort of political identification with what we are doing or we have political identification with what they are doing. The problem in England is far greater, because in Scotland there is a much greater cultural coherence, for example, among the Glasgow working class and the working class of the Clyde Valley, than there is, say, in the Birmingham area. There is a tradition of variety, comedy and particularly Scottish music; there is even a tradition of Scottish rock which is quite strong around the Clyde. There is a very big tradition of folk singing, folk clubs; the people themselves have a kind of indefinable character. Certain qualities are more or less common to everybody, owing to the incredible battering the Clyde has taken from successive governments during the last fifty years. When you talk about the Clyde Valley working class, you talk about something that is very positive. Of course it also has certain negative characteristics – it's hard to accept totally the image of the 'Scottish working man' as the prime example of forward, progressive, proletarian organisation or thought, but there is an identity to begin with, and this helps. What we do has got to grow from this identity.

In Scotland, in Glasgow, and to some extent Edinburgh, through the Unions, through community projects and tenants' associations and word-of-mouth, there is a very strong level of communication amongst working people. There have been four shows which have been very interesting in this respect in Scotland. There has been *The Great Northern Wellyboot Show*, which was written by Tom Buchan with Billy Connolly and Hamish Imlach and a lot of very good Scottish actors. This was a kind of parable of the UCS [Upper Clyde Shipbuilders] occupation told in a very reviewy style, and when it was done in Edinburgh it was packed every night with working people from Edinburgh and from Glasgow who had come through in train loads to see it because they knew it was about them, and it was funny and it was a good show. Similarly, Bill Bryden's *Willy Rough*, which is about an agitator in Greenock during the 1914–1918 war, attracted an enormous audience at the Glasgow Citizens' Theatre and at the Edinburgh Lyceum, simply because it was intimate with the character of the Clyde. *The Sash* by Hector MacMillan, which is about orange and green factions in Glasgow, drew on the sectarian clash that embodied the immediate interest of the working-class audience. The plays that we have done from the beginning have always had direct contact with the situation in the country at that moment. With the possible exception of *Occupations,* they have all been set in the immediate present.

In *Ballygombeen* and *Musgrave Dances On* we tackled head on the Irish situation at that time. *Ballygombeen* is a very big statement about what's going on in Ireland and has been going on for a long time. In it John and Margaretta tie a very small area of violent repression in the west of Ireland, a small village, in with the overall exploitation of the whole of Ireland, not simply by Englishmen but by the capitalist system as a whole, which operates in the interest of Imperialism. In that play we really got directly involved with an immediate situation, we were actually militants for an immediate concern. In *Musgrave Dances On* we actually confronted the audience and each individual member of the audience with their direct responsibility for what was going on in Derry and specifically with the deaths of the people shot by the paras in Derry on Bloody Sunday.

Barker *How much did you rewrite* Musgrave?

It was amazing how little it needed re-writing once I had done the basic change of roles. I combined the mayor and the vicar into the modern equivalent of both, the National Coal Board Pit Manager, who represented the values that both of those men had. These were paras coming back from Bloody Sunday with the body of a man from that village, who had been shot in Derry before Bloody Sunday. This is one of the reasons the paras went mad on Bloody Sunday, because so many English soldiers were being shot there. It was originally written as an immediate parallel with an incident that took place in Cyprus, the parallel between the Cypriot situation and the Irish situation was very close. In the last act, instead of having the confrontation between two sets of people on stage, we used the hall we were playing in and had Musgrave and his men recruiting from the audience. The house lights were up and the miners and the dignitaries were in the audience and the audience was held by Musgrave and his men at gun point, and the audience itself was confronted rather than having it mediated through another group on the stage. This was horribly powerful because feelings were very high at that time. Gavin, playing Musgrave, found terrible difficulties in playing that man because, as he says, 'I'm talking to real people about something that's real. I'm doing it through Musgrave, through his passion, his madness, but when I see these real people, some of them having the reaction to me as a real person, I find that absolutely maddening and revolting.' He was very near the edge. It was a very effective theatrical situation.

Both plays did really well, but Ballygombeen *got us into several kinds of trouble. One was that in his programme for the Edinburgh shows Gavin had written a highly inflammatory note about a real absentee landlord and claimed some of the events of the play related to him, even giving his phone number to encourage the audience to ring him up and abuse him. We narrowly escaped being sued and having an injunction placed on the tour, but we had to promise not to carry the offending piece in the programme. This we complied with until we played in the theatre nearest to the said absentee landlord, when the theatre management had brought home their programme from Edinburgh and printed the piece in full in their programme, over which we had no control. Then the writs were served, lawyers taped performances, the Ardens were sued for causing slander to be uttered on the stage, and we had to take the show off in the middle of its final week at the Bush Theatre in London.*

One other kind of trouble was a gang of Orange youths who smashed down screens and tried to disrupt a performance.

A third, more serious, was the collection of howls of protest sent to Sir Hugh Willatt, a kindly, liberal lawyer, then Director of the Arts Council. They mostly came from Bury St Edmunds, where audiences turned up for a night at the theatre in black tie with their womenfolk in long frocks. When this cacophony was added to by the Officer Commanding British Forces in Northern Ireland, I was summoned in to the Arts Council:

TUZO MISSILE[24]

9 October 1972

Dear Sir Hugh Willatt

I have just heard that your Council subsidised a play called *The Ballygombeen Bequest* which was recently staged at Bury St Edmunds.

As a lover of music and the Arts I have long admired and been grateful for the work you have done and have been quick to defend you even when privately assailed by doubts as to your wisdom and good sense. But I feel I must now ask you a question on behalf of those under my command as well as on my own account. It is this. When there is so much work of beauty and real merit in need of help is it in any way justifiable to devote public funds to a manifestation of this kind? Naturally I am greatly influenced by the fact that the actions of a large number of ordinary young men, carried out often at great sacrifice and always in conditions of discomfort and danger, were represented as obscene, near-bestial and moronic. These men, as public servants, have got used to criticism, abuse and insult from many quarters. This is part of the business and is cheerfully endured even when based on the grossest determination to misunderstand. They are sustained, however, by constant evidence that the country as a whole is behind them and is ready to support them. This is not simply blind confidence because their shortcomings do not go unnoticed; it is rather a comprehension of the peculiar conditions under which they must operate and a determination to help them so far as this is possible; it wholly transcends political boundaries.

I very much doubt whether the play at Bury would be considered by any reasonable cross-section of the public to be a proper object for their financial support. I myself, of course, must go further and say that such support is in the highest degree wrong.

Sitting where I do I lack reference books. I cannot, therefore, claim to know in detail the Terms of Reference under which you operate. I only know that their results have, in so many cases, been entirely beneficial. I hope you will feel able to write and tell me if I am wildly off the mark; in the meanwhile I am obliged to believe that a very serious mistake has been made.

Yours sincerely   Harry Tuzo

We had only accused the British Army of what we knew to be true and which the European Court of Justice subsequently accepted as true: that there was a policy involving torture through threats, violence, sensory deprivation and the use of 'white noise'. Hugh Willatt was embarrassed to be cast as political censor, and made me promise to let him know if we intended to do anything similar in the future. And just to make sure, he told me our application for an annual grant would not be granted for at least two years, so we'd have to go on from production to production, submitting each script before we could be awarded any money.

The last kind of trouble was that although John Arden had agreed to our taking the show off (it had played for sixteen weeks, and we only cancelled three shows), Margaretta D'Arcy accused us, very publicly, of giving in to the authorities to save our skins.

We survived all these troubles, but as aforesaid everyone was tired with the length of the tour and the misery of the digs on the road and the uneatable food, and various company members were being offered other opportunities.

I have always believed in 'doing my bit' for trades unions and other organisations from which I have benefited. In 1972, after spending many hours in Council meetings over several years, I was Chair of the Film Committee and Deputy Chair of the Writers' Guild of Great Britain. At the 1971 AGM, the Council were instructed to use all means to resist 'anti-Trades Union legislation'. When the infamous

Industrial Relations Bill was introduced by the Heath government – clearly anti-Trades Union legislation – certain members of the Guild Council denied it was anti-Union, refused to agree to any opposition to it, and, when defeated in Council, demanded, and got, a postal vote from the entire membership. When this turned out to be against taking any action, I, along with the International Secretary, Stuart Hood, and the Chair of the Television Committee, Roy Jenkins, all resigned:

LETTER OF RESIGNATION[25]

The decision of the Writers' Guild of Great Britain not to de-register under the Industrial Relations Act is contrary to the official policy of the Trades Union Congress, of which the Guild is a member, and therefore, poses a question of principle for those who find themselves in a minority.

We believe that, as a result of its decision to sacrifice the principle of trades union solidarity by not de-registering, the Guild will find itself isolated from the other trades unions in the entertainment industry and, in particular, from its fellow-members on the Federation of Broadcasting Unions and the Federation of Film Unions, at a time when concerted and unified action is essential. The decision cannot, in the long term, therefore best serve the interest of the individual Guild members.

As trades unionists, who believe that the trades union movement is concerned with more than conditions of employment, and that it is only by presenting a united front to employers and, if necessary, to Government that the livelihoods and standards of the workers of this country can be defended, we find it impossible to continue to serve in office on the Executive Council of a Union which has breached TUC policy. We therefore have no option but to resign from office and from the Executive Council, which we do forthwith.

Meanwhile, Liz, David and I went up to Scotland to start 7:84 Scotland:

THE YEAR OF THE CHEVIOT[26]

Our first gig was on Saturday, March 31st. Bob Tait, then of Scottish International magazine, had got together, in Edinburgh, a conference of 450 people from all over Scotland to discuss what kind of Scotland they wanted. They were politicians, union men, writers, social and community workers, academics, and ordinary people who cared about the future of Scotland. We were to perform our new play for them, before setting off on a six-week tour of the Highlands and Islands. The problem was, as I explained to Bob, by the 16th March we'd only just got the company together, and not a line of the play was written. Could he find somebody else? No. That was what he wanted.

We were scheduled to finish most of the writing by the 31st, so we said, would he accept a reading? Why couldn't we present it as a work in progress, and throw it open to discussion? We could learn a lot, and use intelligent criticism constructively: We had another two weeks to rehearse and finalise the show. Why not let the public in on the process – we could only benefit, and they might even enjoy it? Bob agreed.

On Friday night I stayed up until four writing the last scene. On Saturday we read it, discussed it, rehearsed the songs, changed a few, then went over.

It was the best thing we could have done. The audience at the end rose to its feet and cheered, then poured out advice, corrections, support, suggestions of great practical value, facts, figures, books, sources, and above all enthusiasm. Not because we'd been 'good', or 'clever' – but because what we were struggling to say was what they, and masses of people in Scotland, wanted said. Now.

One hundred shows, over 30,000 people, and 17,000 miles later, we feel even more strongly that the strength of the show is in the expression of what people all over Scotland want to say. Many have come for the entertainment – there are good laughs, good acting, good singing, good fiddling – but nearly all go away heightened in their awareness of what has been, and is being, done to the people of the Highlands.

I'd spent quite a lot of time in the Highlands before anyone mentioned the clearances. And then it was only indirectly. In 1961, someone I'd got to know came round for a drink, and said he'd discovered some old parish registers. This valley used to support 253 families, he said. Now you'll be lucky to find 50.

Then came the stories. From all corners. How the Gaelic language had been suppressed. How the Dukes of Sutherland were hated for what they did to the people when they discovered there was more profit in sheep than in people – how their factors burnt the houses, drove the people to the sea-coast, herded them into boats for Canada, all to make way for the Cheviot sheep, how they forced every tenant to pay one shilling towards the huge statue of the Duke on top of Ben Bhraggie – and at the same time the Sutherlands were building Dunrobin Castle to vie with Versailles in opulence and conspicuous consumption.

Later, John Prebble's book *The Highland Clearances* did an excellent job in bringing this neglected episode of nineteenth-century history to a wider public, as did Ian Grimble's very thorough account in *The Trial of Patrick Sellar*. To me, at that time, it was a source of amazement that so little was known of it outside, even inside, Scotland. To the people there, it was, and is, a burning memory, never to be forgotten, and never forgiven. As late as

1970, the Sutherlands' factor was greeted with 'Baas', and cries of 'Men not Sheep' when he got up rashly to ask a question at a Labour election meeting in Golspie.

For years the Highlands have, to most people, been shrouded in mist. Either the mist of romanticism – the land of solitary splendour, Gaelic twilight, and sturdy, independent, gently-spoken crofters; or the mists of inevitable backwardness – a land that missed the boat, with no resources and a dwindling population, a land inhabited by lazy, shifty, dreamers who cannot be helped, in which nothing can alter. The realities of Highland life, and the Highland people, are very different. The realities are created by the actions of the feudal system leaping red in tooth and claw into an imperialist capitalist system, becoming more repressive, more violent as it does so.

At the first sniff of oil off the east coast of Scotland, things began to jump. First in Aberdeen and the North-East. Then all over. Suddenly villages that did not merit even an advance factory for 100 workers are being taken over by thousands of men in labour camps building oil-rigs, and oil-production platforms. The Highlands and Islands Development Board had failed to do anything about Stornaway's 150 unemployed. Now Fred Olsen's men are talking about Stornaway's need for 5,000 jobs: it happens they want to service and build rigs there. They're even talking about a shipyard. Land prices in some areas have been so inflated by speculators that local farmers can't stay, and in Aberdeen young couples in need of houses are talking about emigrating. International corporations – oil, land, property, building, construction, marine, even catering – are jumping about all over the place looking for millions of dollars. And they don't care what they do to the people to get them.

It was with this perspective in mind that three of us who had been working with 7:84 Theatre Company decided to go to Scotland and take a play about the Highlands 'from the time of the clearances up to the present day', around village halls, dance halls, community centres and schools in the North. We went to Scotland and began to look for people who cared enough for the idea to come and work harder, mentally and physically, than most reckon possible, for not much more than the Equity minimum. We thought of advertising, but the demands looked too ridiculous: 'Needed – people who can act, sing, entertain, and play at least one musical instrument (all superbly well), who are committed socialists, know the Highlands, can drive, and are prepared to join in all the work of the company on a communal basis, and play in a dance band. Apply 7:84 Scotland'. Amazingly enough, we didn't run the ad. But the people came. Three actors I had seen in *The Welly Boot Show* the year before, Alex Norton, Bill Paterson and John Bett. They had worked together a great deal before, and combined an enormous number of skills, acting, singing, guitar, pipes, whisky, commitment, and others. Yet another MacLennan – Dolina, from Lewis in the Outer Hebrides, no relation to the other two. She spoke only Gaelic until she was eight, sang Gaelic songs the way they should be sung, and had years of experience of holding an audience. Chris Martin, who had just walked out of a steady job with a publishing company, and had worked in Chile, South Africa and India, came, in the first instance, to work on publicity. And Allan Ross, fiddler extraordinary, musicman, entertainer, whose great-great grandfather had been cleared from Easter Ross. Ferelith Lean came with us to freeze on countless makeshift box-offices, and dish out the wages. That was the new company.

Obviously I, as a writer, had a very clear idea of exactly how I wanted the show to be. I knew who it was for, and I knew what I wanted to say, and how I wanted to say it. But I also wanted everybody in the company to be intimately involved in the actual process of creating it. I had always fought shy of group-writing before, and still do. This wasn't to be a free-for-all, utopian fantasy: I wouldn't expect to play Allan Ross's fiddle, or to sing in Gaelic, or act. The company didn't expect to write the play. My contribution was my experience as a writer and director, and it was to be used. But there were two things we could do to break down the insane hierarchies of the theatre. Firstly, we could all respect each other's skills and at the same time lay them open for collective discussion and advice. Secondly, we could work as equal human beings, no skill being elevated over another, no personal power or superiority being assumed because of the nature of the individual contribution: no stars, of any kind. And no recourse to the 'I'm an artist' pose to camouflage either power-seeking or avoidance of responsibility to the collective.

So we all sat down, with blank note-pads. I outlined the sixteen main areas or blocks of the play, and how I thought we should approach each one. There was a huge pile of books, cuttings Elizabeth had kept, and other material, on the table. Every one was given one or two areas to be personally responsible for, check what was said, and answer to in public discussion. For example, Bill was given the section on the Highland's military tradition – the numbers killed in the wars, the way recruiting worked, etc. – and he looked through the books, went off to libraries, and military museums to get the facts. When we came to write that section, I knew what I wanted to write, we all discussed it, Bill knew the details, or where he could find them, and either there, with everybody present, or in the evening at home, the section was written.

The form of the play was conducive to this kind of approach. One truly popular form of entertainment in the Highlands, past and present, is the ceilidh. This is usually a gathering at which all, or most, of those present, with or without the aid of the whisky, sing a song, tell a story, play an instrument, have a good blether, and occasionally end up dancing until the next morning. In the past, these gatherings had also had their political side, particularly at the time of the Land Leagues, and stories of Highland history and oppression had been passed on. In the West, they were also one way of keeping intact the Gaelic culture – language, literature, songs and manners. 'Ceilidh parties' also go from place to place to entertain and be entertained, and are very popular. I wanted to keep this form – an assembly of songs, stories, scenes, talk, music and general entertainment – and to tell through it the story of what had happened and is now happening to the people. And to end the evening with a dance, for people to get a chance to talk and have a good time.

As we worked, our knowledge of the subject grew. We invited sympathetic friends with special knowledge in certain areas to come and talk to us. Ray Burnett, for example, who had been beavering away on the history of the Land Leagues. The day he came to talk to us, he had uncovered evidence of soldiers back from the 1914–1918 war occupying land in Sutherland – a phenomenon not mentioned in the history books. After the session, I wrote a song about it. When we performed in Sutherland, the song aroused memories – and old men who had been on those land-raids, and many who just knew about them, came up to us with stories that would make a decent chapter in a decent history of Scotland.

Ray, and our sources, provided us with a problem. We wanted to tell what happened on Skye in the 1880s, particularly in the Braes area, where the resistance to the landlord was particularly effective. The problem was, we had too much material – enough for six scenes, let alone one. After two days, during which the story had been hammered out into a strong narrative, we were desperate. How could we tell so much in a short time? I crept off into a corner of the disused discotheque we were working in, and wrote a ballad. Somebody saw a verse, came up with a tune. We all threw in ideas for the chorus. Some verses got thrown out, others improved. We moved on.

After two weeks huddling round a table, occasionally leaping over to the musical instruments to try something, or moving into the open space to see how a scene might move, we had something to begin to work with. Not the purist's improvised theatre, but a written text that all the company were part of, and deeply involved in, and excited about. Nobody had anything to do that they thought was wrong, everybody knew exactly why every word was there.

And the company had grown in knowledge, concern for the subject, and conviction, through the process. So we went off to Bob Tait's reading.

With the boost of that audience's reaction, and the excitement about the subject we already had, rehearsal became fast and enjoyable. I threw the material at the company, told them they were entertainers now, not Chekhovian actors, and to work on their acts, and bring them in for us all to see. Being good Scottish actors – who had all worked in many different situations, from Ibsen via panto to spieling on strip-shows – that is what they did.

I, and the others, threw in ideas, made sure one part related well to all the other parts, that the political meaning didn't get lost in the gagging or the singing – in fact, that they were *part* of the political meaning – and generally stood back from it all a bit, to provide the necessary objective perspective. After the next two weeks, we began to need an audience again.

All this time, as well as writing and rehearsing, the company was simultaneously trying to turn itself into a dance band, with at least four hours of dance music at the ready. The dance after the show, as I have said, was an essential part of the evening. The task we set ourselves – to provide the music – was formidable. Allan was a brilliant fiddler, with a vast knowledge of Highland fiddle music. Elizabeth, a pianist, had prepared herself by mastering the accordion in six weeks flat. Alex had amazing facility on the guitar, and played rhythm along with the bass line. Bill and Doli sang, Bill played whistles, pipes, piano and I'm not sure what else besides. There the musical talent ended. I fancied myself on the drums, Dave thought he might come to terms with bass guitar. We both got fired by the others after a week, for enthusiastic incompetence. We managed without a bass, and asked Tommy Marshall, an Edinburgh drummer, to join us for the dances, which, to our relief, he did. He also drove, sold programmes at the beginning of the play, and joined in the general work.

Our basic sound was traditional Highland dance music – waltzes, eightsome reels, schottisches, Gay Gordons etc. – and the band providing this was christened the Force Ten Gaels. But we did want to be able to throw in, in some places, a load of rock and more modern sounds, so we created, in honour of Alex Norton, the Nortones, with Allan dropping the fiddle and playing electric bass. Night after night, after a hard day's work, we assembled and rehearsed material, decided on a programme that might work, and slowly began to play with a little confidence and togetherness.

Before rehearsals David and Chris Martin had set off, after long consultations, to the places we were hoping to play. Between us, we had friends or contacts in almost every corner of the North, and they soon made many more friends in the others. The response to what they were proposing was one first of amazement, then of enthusiasm, and then of overwhelming practical kindness. People willingly took on the jobs of sticking up posters, selling tickets, spreading the word, finding accommodation, sometimes even providing it. Dave and Chris booked the halls on the spot, in as sensible an order as they could, balancing free dates, mileage, rival attractions and estimated exhaustion with remarkable dexterity.

The Scottish Arts Council Drama Committee had at first displayed incredulity. They thought Highlanders didn't want to know about the clearances, the politics of oil and such, and anyway wouldn't pay to see a theatre show because they didn't go to the theatre. They threw our estimated budget back in our face, and turned down our request for a small guarantee against loss. We went back armed with the response, and the figures, Chris and Dave had got, and a lengthy explanation of why we thought it would work as we estimated. They had second thoughts, gave us the small guarantee, and have proved more generous ever since. As it happened, our figures were almost exactly right: the Highlanders *did* want to hear their true history told out loud, and they certainly wanted to say something about the politics of oil. An ancient, near-blind, Gaelic poet, the Bard of Melbost, came up to us after a show in the Outer Hebrides, and said: 'I have heard the story of my people told with truth. If I die tonight, I die a happier man.' He, too, had been paying taxes to support the Arts Council. For the first time, he was getting something back.

Our first gig was in Aberdeen. We had one van borrowed from the original 7:84. I spent the last of my fee for writing a movie that never got made on another Transit, with seats. We were on the road, north. The word of mouth from the 'What Kind of Scotland?' reading was good, several Aberdonians had been there, and it had had good notices in the papers. Even so, we were surprised to hear the Arts Centre was full. The show went well, for a first night, and we were staggered to see an Aberdeen audience stand up and cheer at the end. The last section of the show, on the oil rip-off, had meant so much to them, they demanded we come back, which we did, with pleasure, a few months later. Fortunately, as this was one of the few places we played with a theatre-type fixed seating, we couldn't follow with a dance. In the next few days, the band grabbed every minute to rehearse and didn't face the public until the next Saturday night, in Rose-markie hall, on the Black Isle. We were saved there by the imminent arrival of the Sabbath, and had to finish the dance at 11.45, as is the custom on the Highland Saturday, having provided an hour and a half's pretty convincing music: but that was about all we had. The band rehearsed on, and by the following Tuesday really gave one of the best dances we, or Kinlochbervie, had experienced for some time.

Kinlochbervie was the beginning of the real Highland tour. Aberdeen, Stirling, Inverness and Rosemarkie in the first week had been exciting enough. The Chairman of the Highlands and Islands Development Board, which comes in for some rough handling in the play, turned up, with a lot of the staff. He had both legs in plaster, and wore a kilt. I anticipated a rallentando of an exit – it was the same man who, as our Ambassador in Indonesia, had marched around the grounds of the besieged embassy playing the bagpipes to the enragement of the already overheated Djakar-tans – but, whether through inability or masochism, he stayed to the end. It seems to be a deliberate tactic of the ruling class under attack in public, at least in the Highlands, to be seen sportingly taking it on the chin, thereby eliciting admiration from the people they are exploiting for their courage, pluck or open-mindedness.

The Countess of Sutherland did the same trick, many months later, in Golspie, and ensured that the *Aberdeen Press and Journal* carried a report of her sporting gesture. As half of the play is a direct attack on her forebears, and the other half an attack on present-day landowners, which she is, she probably got more than she bargained for, but a few of her tenants were impressed – though not, by any means, all.

Kinlochbervie – it's a few miles down the West Coast from Cape Wrath, a crofting and fishing community, spread out over wild and beautiful hills, with a new harbour, a hotel for the fishing gentry, and a tiny hall on the edge of the water. We arrived about midday, made for the bar, and bumped into a few people Dave, Liz and I knew of old. They were politely surprised that we had actually come, and they and some of the crews from the boats had a bit of an alcoholic get-together with the company. Then we went down to the hall to set up. Already people were waving to us as we drove the vans over, and by the evening the word had brought a full house to see what the hell this was all about. The boats had been kept in by gale warnings, so the crews came too.

In the halls, we used the stages, normally only big enough for a small band, for our 'scenery'. This was a giant pop-up book, like children's pop-up books, only eight feet deep and ten across, made from strengthened cardboard. As you turn each page, a fresh 'set' pops up from in between the pages, in this instance all beautifully constructed and painted by John Byrne, a Glasgow artist. In front of the stage, on the floor of the hall, we put up our own platform, 18 inches high, and the company sits on either side, on the same level as the audience, throughout, when they aren't actually doing their bits. That way, we kept closer to the audience, and had the same intimacy whatever kind of hall we were in. We carried our own lights, set up on stands, and operated by David from his seat amongst the others, in full view of the audience, on a small portable six-way board. All the music is live, some electric, some acoustic. In the middle of the front of our stage, there is a mike, used or not used according to what we're doing.

The show begins as the audience is coming in with Allan playing reels on the fiddle, and the audience, if they feel like, clapping or stamping their feet in time. From that, Bill introduces the show, and gets the audience to sing a song together – with song-sheets held up by the company. From the way that audience in Kinlochbervie, none of whom had ever been in such a thing as a theatre, reacted to the show, we knew that it was impossible to under-estimate a Highland audience. In knowledge, sophistication, politics, history and wit, they were right there, if not way ahead of us. We had never 'written down' to some supposed audience level. It's just as well we hadn't. Direct Marxist analysis of the clearances, long chunks of readings from eye-witness historical accounts, facts and figures about oil companies and the technical-ities of exploration, all were not only grasped but waited for, expected. It's quite a Gaelic-speaking area, and even those few who didn't speak the language joined in with Dolina as she sang. In the modern section, there are several songs to which we added new verses almost every day to refer to local events or keep up with the events as they happen. That night in Kinlochbervie, 250 miles north of Glasgow, in that so-called backward area, the people taught us what theatre has to be about. And that was the lesson we learnt over and over again, in fifty or sixty halls all over the North.

Everybody, from grandmas to toddlers, stayed for the dance. The chairs and benches were pushed to the side, props and costumes cleared, band gear set up, and for the first time the band showed it could do it. They had to. The fiddle was a great hit. For many years, fiddles had been destroyed, as ungodly, immoral and conducive to lustful practices. When it sang out again, light shone in a lot of old eyes, and nobody had to be asked to dance. After an eightsome reel, exhausting to dance, even more wearing to play, Dolina got up to sing some more songs in Gaelic. As always thereafter, even the rowdiest crowd settled down to listen and join in. About midnight, the boats had to go out, gale warnings retracted, but the crews wouldn't go until she sang one for them. So she sang a beautiful old Lewis fisherman's song that defies translation. Dolina's seven brothers and her father and his father were fishermen: she wasn't singing out a fantasy, nor did they think so. Off they went.

About two-thirty we stumbled off, No Alcoholic Beverages having been Consumed On These Premises, of course, to caravans borrowed for the night that nearly took off, gale warning or no gale warning, to B & Bs, or (Elizabeth and myself) to the hotel. We had this honour (it being the beginning of the tour) because we had our children with us – two boys, one five, one six – and they had to stay somewhere where there was someone to baby-sit. All the B & B ladies were at the do, and we knew the lady who managed the hotel. This theory could have lead to some serious class-distinctions, and was quickly eroded, but on that night we were glad the boys had four walls, and not a bucking caravan roped to the rock while we were away. It also gave all of us the way in to the hotel lounge, where someone produced a whisky bottle with a few dregs in it, which was passed around as we sat and tried to work out what we felt about the night, the show, the dance, and the audience's feelings about both. We knew we had a lot of work to do still, but we all felt we now knew not only *how* to work on the show, but also, for the first time as a lived experience, *why*.

The next night was a disaster. Partly because we were tired (the caravanners not having slept at all), grumpy, hung-over, our memory of the night before shattered by the grim realities of striking the gear from a hall that needed an Alka-Seltzer, loading the vans, driving to Lochinver, setting it all up again, finding the digs, finding some food, getting ready again. (Though we did see an eagle being mobbed by two buzzards, and Lochinver is one of the most scenically beautiful places in the world.)

Lochinver suffers from being inundated by what are known as 'white settlers'. The chief of them all, a butcher from Liverpool now known as Lord Vestey, owns over 100,000 acres of Sutherland, including several fine mountains and the whole of Lochinver. He also owns huge tracts of Australia, Argentina, and Brazil, shipping lines, insurance companies, whaling companies, etc., and is into both the docks at Wapping and Midland Cold Storage, the containerisation people, the row over which put three dockers in jail. In the play, he figures as an excellent reason for crofters in the Highlands showing international solidarity and solidarity with dockers in London, amongst others.

Apart from him, Lochinver has many minor breeds of white settler, English and Scottish, retired, or living off investments, or just failed gentry come to find a few forelocks that might still be tugged at them. Unfortunately for us, these people had appropriated us in advance, because we were 'theatre' and they were cultivated. Most of the local people had taken their cue and stayed away. We did have a friend who was working on the huge road improvement scheme into the town, and he brought a lot of his mates, but they sat at the back, and enjoyed two shows – one our lot doing the play, and the other the white settlers at the front trying to stomach it. But the participation was minimal, and the laughter inhibited. Then to crown it all, for the first hour and a half of the dance, there were forty men and only one girl – and she didn't want to get up, not surprisingly. Just as we decided to pack it in, three girls arrived all done up and demanded that we play until two. It was then 12.30. One girl – who can best be described as strapping – then proceeded to display such powers of leadership, eloquence, guile, force, righteous indignation and revolutionary fervour that we almost announced we were going to start again just for her. But the rest had gone home, and we simply hadn't the energy.

During the next few weeks, we moved from village to village down the west coast, as far as Dornie (which was one of the best nights of the tour, in every way), then over to Skye, from Skye to Harris, then Lewis, then back from Stornoway to Ullapool, across to the east coast, up to the Orkneys, and back via Thurso to Sutherland again. Orkney was bizarre. Small audiences in Stromness and Kirkwall, the two main towns. On our third, and last, night, in Orphir a small village inbetween, suddenly hundreds. Apparently nobody in Orkney goes to anything until someone else has gone, and reported on it. A curious sensation at the box-office, waiting for a whole island full of people who are all waiting for each other.

At Orphir we had a good dance, marked by several odd moments. One was near the beginning. A large crowd was sizing us up for a bit too long, showing a reluctance we hadn't expected. However, Allan had met an Orcadian fiddler, who was sitting in with the band. After a while Liz asked him what they were all waiting for. The Evoe Three Step, he said darkly.

After a quick consultation, it turned out you did this particular dance to music we had already played, with little result, for the Gay Gordons. So Bill announced the Evoe Three Step. There was a cheer, the floor filled, and we played the same music all over again. From that moment, the dance took off till early next morning.

At one point, I had to give Tommy a spell on the drums – he'd sprained his wrist. He trusted me on the waltzes, having laboriously knocked all ambition to do more than keep strict time out of my Krupa-based fantasies, so I sat in for a waltz, and concentrated like hell. I was appalled, when, after a few minutes, I looked up to see a crowded dance floor standing stock-still – every one of them. I hastily looked back to my drumming, wondering if I was really so bad they'd just stopped altogether and were about to stampede me off the platform. I furtively glanced again, and there they were, like statues again, only this time they'd changed positions. Not to be thrown completely, I didn't look up again for quite a time, waiting for the bottles, etc. to rain down on me from an angry mob of frustrated Orcadian waltzers. When I did look up, they were still immobile, but in different places again. I determined to brazen it out, to see what happened. After a few more bars of freeze, I almost dropped my drumsticks when, as one man, they suddenly leapt frenziedly around the floor then, again as one, they all stood block-like again to all appearances glazed and baked. It turned out that this was another local craze – the Hesitation Waltz. It vaguely resembles the motions of the St Ola, the ferry to Thurso, though I don't know which was based on which.

We developed a kind of rhythm, to keep us going and to prevent a repetition of the exhaustion of the second night. We travelled, when possible, about eleven in the morning, by road or ferry or both; during the journey, Allan and I drove one van, Dave or Chris the other; everybody else was fairly lively, and, as we were driving through some of the most awe-inspiring country in Europe, we all somehow drew a great deal of strength from just looking out of the window. There were stories of places we were going to or through, songs, jokes, and, for the two boys, school. Apart from lessons from Liz, they were treated to the University of Life, from Bill and Alex, with short courses on jokes, sex-education, wild life, songs, stories, poems, more jokes and Scottish history. They kept diaries with drawings of events and places, and brought their own energy and imagination to the whole proceedings. We either stopped on the way, or found some food and a drink on arrival, met a few people, then set up for the night. Everybody worked on get-ins, which became faster and easier the more we did. Then a quick tech., for lighting and sound levels, then a short company talk about any changes, new verses, new jokes etc. for that night or that place. We rehearsed the changes, checked props and costumes, and if we were lucky found the digs or some fish and chips. The show went up at eight. Some liked to be in at seven, to get organised. Others spent the time in the pub, getting to know the audience, turning up alarmingly near time to start. By eight, Allan was fiddling, the company chatting to the audience or finally sorting out their gear, and when it felt right, we began.

At the end of the show, everybody struck their own costumes and props, I did my roadie bit with the band while the stage was dismantled and the chairs shoved away and the floor swept. In twenty minutes the dance was under way. Allan had an ability to get pissed during those 20 minutes that was unnatural. Everybody needed something to charge up their batteries for the three or four hours ahead. The dances varied, sometimes terrific, sometimes thin, but usually enjoyable. We tried to finish at 1.30, but didn't always succeed. During the dances, those not playing in the band packed and wrapped lights, costumes, props, stage etc. quietly, and at the end, we wrapped the band gear, and everything was ready for loading the next morning. We were generally invited to somebody's place after the dance, and the intrepid went for a wind-down with a few quiet songs, a chat and a cup of tea. Our children slept in the same room as us, and were looking for life and adventure soon after eight the next morning, so Liz and I resigned ourselves to a reputation for anti-social pit-seeking most nights, though not all. By ten, everybody was back at the hall to load, and wearily did so, and after a few groans, we were off again, hairs of dog bristling, with blood-orange eyes. It's a great way to shatter your constitution.

We had Sundays and Mondays off, and usually made for Rogart on the east or Dornie on the west, supposedly to rest and recover, though somehow Allan's fiddle or Doli's singing would draw us into the local, and another, more impromptu, ceilidh would be under way. All found it a physical strain, some found it a social strain as well. Constantly in public, always aware of representing the company, always involved in arguments – historical, political, social, economic. But it was never less than rewarding, because of the nature of the people we were amongst – who gave us more than we could ever give them in every way.

The company held together as people under these circumstances of over-work, of relentlessly being thrown together, no privacy and constant re-working, re-writing, re-rehearsal, astonishingly well. One minor incident, when one got angry with another for being pissed and a bit casual during the show and said so on stage, could have blown up, but a long and painful company meeting sorted that out, and a lot of things looming on the horizon as well. We were very happy, had no time for jealousies, spites and gossip, and were bound together by a common purpose, which was being triumphantly achieved. If any polarisation took place it was the inevitable one, between those with strong political responsibility which was taken as earnestness and commisaring, and those with strong responsibilities to entertaining and pleasing the audience, which were taken as ego-boosting and copping out. But these were not real divisions in any way, though they grew to seem so many months later. The politicos were every bit as entertaining and the entertainers as deeply concerned, in fact. It was only in discussion away from work that these seemed like divisions of any importance. To me, anyway, I have never known a company with as much respect for one another, or as much ability to criticise one another constructively, as this one.

We did our last show of the Highland tour at Bonar Bridge, then set off South on the long drive to Oban. Billy Wolfe, the Chairman of the Scottish Nationalist Party, had seen the show and invited us to perform at an evening's entertainment he was giving to delegates after the party's annual conference. We wrote pointing out that we were not nationalists, and would attack bourgeois nationalism, but he repeated the invitation, hoping our politics would stimulate discussion within his party. We discussed it, and decided to go. There are many socialists in the SNP, who are there for lack of any other party that is not run from London. And it would do no harm for the chauvinists and tartan Tories to get a dose of what we were saying. We were attacked by comrades on the left for going at all, but they didn't know why, or what effect we had, had not read James Connolly or John Maclean, or even, as far as I could tell, Lenin on The Right of Nations to Self Determination, so we left them to their sectarian thunderings and got on with it.

The hall was enormous, the stage a thin slit half a mile from the back, and the acoustics dreadful. We had all of half an hour to sort it out, lighting and all, but we did, and it worked. Reactions differed from various parts of the hall. I shall never forget Liz squaring up to all 500 of them and delivering 'Nationalism is not enough. The enemy of the Scottish people is Scottish capital as much as the foreign exploiter' – with shattering power. Some cheered, some booed, the rest were thinking about it.

At the end, a ten-minute standing ovation, and the company responding with raised fists and a short speech about socialism and nationalism. It was worth doing, and we were right to do it. We loaded again, and drove off through the night to Edinburgh, aching with tiredness, happy.

We did another week of performances in the south – Cumbernauld, Livingstone, Irvine, all small theatres. The word had come down from the Highlands, and we were sold out everywhere. The audiences were different, of course, but their involvement with the situation was strong and positive. What was lacking, and is lacking, is the political organisation that will unite both sets of interests. We knew we were fighting in this void, but hoped that we might step up the demand for it to be filled.

At Cumbernauld a small posse of BBC men came riding out to track down some of our outlaw actors. They ended up taking on the whole show. I thought I saw a way of using the theatre show to create some sort of Alienation Effect in televisual terms, and wrote a screenplay along those lines. After many a hassle, John Mackenzie finally filmed this version of it, with chunks of the company performing the stage show, and other actors doing location stuff.

It became apparent that we couldn't just walk away from Scotland. However, Liz and I and the two boys were sleeping in Dave and his wife Ferelith's flat in Edinburgh, we had a house in London and the English 7:84 were struggling on, and I was supposed to be its Artistic Director. Nevertheless we decided to continue with the Scottish company. I tried to be in four places at once, covered hundreds of thousands of miles, and wrote far too much. Eventually, after sleeping on Bob and Irene Tait's floor, and writing on it to boot, we ended up with a two-roomed flat in Edinburgh.

Our 'office' had been in Dave and Feri's front room, but a friendly film-maker lent us a room in Queen Street, and Feri was installed as our Administrator.

Rather than try to repeat a success, and for other more political reasons, we decided to mount a show for the industrial working class of Scotland:

THE GAME'S A BOGEY[27]

The Cheviot, popular and appreciated as it was, did not touch on the urban misery, the architectural degradation, the raw, alcohol-riddled despair, the petty criminal furtiveness, the bleak violence of living in many parts of industrial Scotland. Nor had we performed *The Cheviot* in the miners' clubs, Trades Council clubs, the union halls of central Scotland. We resolved to do both with the show we mounted after *The Cheviot*, called *The Game's a Bogey*. The title is a Glasgow children's phrase meaning the game's up, or over, or spoilt. In a narrow way it was used with reference to the alternation of Wilson and Heath at that time, the pointless two-party system in which the objects were always the working people; but in a more general way it referred to the state of the lives of many people in our audience. Against these were set the life and words of John Maclean, pioneer Scottish socialist activist and teacher of Marxist economics to many thousands of workers in Scotland in the first twenty years of this century. In some ways that is quite a sophisticated operation, theatrically coping with switches from 1907 to 1973 and then back to 1913 and so forth; historically sophisticated in coping with two periods not in parallel but in ironical distantiation, and politically sophisticated in relating Maclean's words to their historical context, but pointing them, by way of their defeat at that time, through to the consequences of their non-fulfilment today. Anyway, that is something of what we set out to achieve.

I think in many ways it would be better to describe the realisation of the show as an event rather than analysing the text on the page, and the performance that will always stay in my mind was that in the Glenrothes Coal Industry Social and Welfare Organisation. Glenrothes is a New Town in Fife, sitting on an old coalfield. In the middle of the new town, a large glass and concrete building looking like a small light industrial advance factory. Inside, an upstairs bar where members get beer subsidised by the Coal Board, even if they've never been near a pit, and downstairs, at the back, the clubroom, a huge concrete barn with a bar all down one side, tables and chairs for three hundred, a smallish but high stage at one end, and a tiny dressing room behind it. Tickets had been sold at 20p each to members and 50p each to non-members: about 220 had gone in advance. The fame of *The Cheviot* had helped to sell some, others had been press-ganged by our supporters in Glenrothes, others came to see what it was.

We set the show up as well as we could on the stage, and rigged the sound equipment and lighting, and arranged the tables so there was some chance of being seen from the far end, and tried to relay speakers so that we might be heard as well. We put away a Chinese carry-out and a few subsidised pints as the hall began to fill. The bar in the hall, like all busy bars, was making a hell of a noise and a lot of money. The club officials were against our putting any of their lights out at all, but this would have made our lighting plot more than ineffective. A compromise was reached. The noise in the hall was heavy – and boozy. It occurred to all of us that the club would make more money if we *didn't* perform and the audience could concentrate on serious drinking for the evening. But no – we were going to go on: to the end, if we had done our work properly.

The reason I remember Glenrothes so clearly is that it was the very first miners' club we had ever played in, and the very first time we performed *The Game's a Bogey* to an audience in that situation. I was literally terrified: the consequences of failure to please would be direct and painful; the consequences of pleasing but failing to communicate would be indirect but even more painful in the long run. The company were also terrified, but heroic.

On came the band, all acting as well as musical members of the company, in matching red blazers with 7:84 on the pocket. Nobody paid any attention, and as they launched into the instrumental opening, the noise level got higher as people yelled to be heard above the band. On bounced Bill Paterson to do his compere job, off went some of the lights, and up came our lights and follow-spot. As Bill chatted breezily to the audience and introduced, with gags, the members of the band, the general noise level was still high, and the bar very busy and very loud. It was really only when Terry Neason came on, burst into her verses of the opening song, and blatantly vamped them, that something approaching attention was established. The show, ultimately, had a certain amount to say about sexism, but I regret to say that it was in some measure for sexist reasons that we established contact with the members of the Glenrothes CISWO Club. This, plus the fact that she has a good raunchy sort of voice, plus the fact that the whole tempo of the number picked up when she came on, and the band suddenly were able to perform with some attack, all helped to turn a few heads, even those at the bar, towards the stage. The number ends with a big bang, and as a few claps broke out, suddenly police sirens, blue lights flashing, general scramble to get off the stage, and a Goon Show policeman appears running in to the hall – he is about seven feet tall, with an enormously long overcoat, a trilby stuffed on top of his helmet to indicate that he is incognito, a false chin (with a false pluke) to cover the straggling red beard of our fiddler, and a false accent and false height to throw his enemies into confusion. He runs and leaps onto the stage, driving away the hooligans of the band, then informs the audience that he is Lachlan Mac-Donald, in search of Red trouble-makers, particularly one John Maclean, who is stirring up industrial strife among the peace-loving workers of Scotland. He goes off threatening to kill them, smash them, etc. because he hates violence: police sirens sound. Now the audience really are intrigued. His acting of 'Kill them! Smash them!' is strong, and even though contained in a joke, still commands attention. As he goes, the company come back on and tell the startled audience that there really was a Lachlan MacDonald, who really *did* go round trailing John Maclean – and they tell them who this John Maclean was. Bill Paterson, as he adds his bit of information, is putting on the coat and hat of Maclean; he then delivers a reconstruction of a shortish Maclean speech. The audience are now confronted with the history and the politics: they become more interested, rather than less. But we have an unwritten entertainment contract established at the beginning of the show. Lachlan again comes on, and arrests Maclean with a few awful knock-knock jokes, and takes him off, ordering the company to get on with the fun-loving Scottish variety show. Another number ('Let's take a walk down by the Clyde') is the response, a catchy, poppy number, but describing life in the high-rise cardboard cartons that sway from side to side by the silvery Clyde: a nice number, and a few laughs. Then on comes our first modern character, Ina, a young girl of eighteen going out to the dance. She bursts on to do a stand-up comic routine, with terrible jokes about pan-stick and polyfilla, but she gets the audience interested in the character she's playing, just like Buttons in the panto. Then she settles down to dream about Mr Right as she reads her teen-magazine, and Terry and the band perform, for her and the audience, a song about her situation and her dreams, and the fantasy factory: it's a gentle, folk-rock tune that develops with urgency and anger into the section about the lies she is being sold about men and her future. By now, the audience are sitting, taking it in. Theatre has begun to take place.

The point about *The Game's a Bogey* is, really, that it took the trouble to contact and reassure the audiences, to show the signs of class solidarity in a theatrical and personal as well as political way, and to speak the language of the audience but in a new and intriguing way. Anyway, that's what it set out to do. The show goes on to introduce two other main characters, a country-and-western singing Hard Man, who meets up with Ina in a dance and soon has to marry her; and a vicious young pre-punk character called McWilliam singing Slade-type stuff about the game he's got to join. We interact between their advancing stories, at work, at home, at the doctor's in the pub etc., and the relentless and increasingly nasty pursuit of Maclean by Lachlan, and Maclean's speeches about the situation of the Glasgow working class, and other scarcely plot-related incidents or turns involving Sir Mungo McBungle, a local failed industrialist, his wife Lavinia, who advocates portable gas-ovens for trouble-makers and supports Teddy Taylor, and Andy McChuck-emup, a fly wee Glasgow wheeler-dealer, who makes a return appearance after his success in *The Cheviot*. Somewhere in amongst it there is a tragedy, not of one person, but of a whole society. It is the tragedy you feel walking round the streets of Govan, of Clydebank, of the Gorbals – of a hope once burning bright, but now gone out: but not for ever.

Now *because* we had taken *The Game's a Bogey* round and built audiences who knew and enjoyed our work, and who trusted us, we were able in the next shows to develop, to push the style in all kinds of directions, to make increasingly complex statements, to invent new devices within the general framework of a style that we knew would work, even to try out bits we weren't sure of: just to see.

The unifying principles of the company were, amongst others, to keep faith with that audience by going back time after time, by working hard to maintain the highest possible standards of entertainment and imagination, in writing and performance, by developing our personal contacts with the audience, listening to their comments and learning from them, by expanding our political and historical work into areas that were important and showing clearly their relationship with the lives of the audience. We tried to 'keep faith' also by changing, by not simply repeating, either in content or form, the first show simply because it was successful, but to keep thinking, moving ahead of the audience's expectations in all areas. They would follow us now more readily than they would some unknown bunch of middle-class actors. They, in fact, had appropriated us: we belonged to them, and when we did not appear for longer than six months, there were complaints.

BOOM: AN INTRODUCTION[28]

Boom was the third production of the Scottish 7:84 and the second specific-ally designed to tour the Highlands and Islands. In March 1974 we began work on *Boom* while *Game's a Bogey* was still touring.

We toured *Boom* twice during 1974, the first tour in April, May and June, the second in October, November and December. We began to rehearse for the second tour while we were in Dublin playing *The Game's a Bogey*. Sadly, during this period, one of our children became dangerously ill, and my wife, Elizabeth MacLennan, who had been involved very closely in researching and acting in the first tour, had to drop out to look after our son. Vari Sylvester, a member of the English 7:84 company, with roots in Scourie, took over from her.

There has been a certain amount of speculation as to how we arrive at our scripts. Firstly, we do not 'improvise'. Virtually everything, down to the smallest throwaway, is written or discussed before the performance. Secondly, the actors do not write their own material. The shows are conceived and controlled down to the smallest detail by the writer/director, with the fullest consultation, discussion and contribution from the collective company.

Writing and directing a play can never be a totally democratic process. They are skills which need aptitude, long experience, self-discipline and a certain mental disposition in one individual. They demand leaps in the dark, liberated instincts, arrogance of the imagination and autocracy of the intuition.

What I was trying to do in 7:84 Scotland was to move forward from that concept of the writer, without jettisoning the whole writing process. To demystify the role, without castrating the talent.

This is an extremely difficult and dangerous operation. Even though a certain amount of our income was from a state organisation, the Arts Council; even though we were working for largely working-class audiences; even though we had no entrepreneur or impresario or capital-owning investors to satisfy; even though we had previous experience of successful collective work and collective organisation – we were (and are) still working within a capitalist economy, with bourgeois cultural and ideological values dominant in society as a whole and exerting their pressures on each one of us individually.

How were we going to move forward? Basically, by trying to see our job *not* as expressing the writer's individual state of mind, psychological obsession, etc., but rather as finding the way to present to certain specific people certain specific facts about their lives, or facts that affect their lives, using an equally specific form. In other words, our job was to act as mediators between people and a chunk of their present history. Further to that, it was our job to present alternative ways of doing things to this audience and, because we were mostly socialists, to show socialist alternatives.

The 'specific people' were the people of the Highlands and Islands. The facts we wished to present were about two main areas: ownership of land, and control of oil development. The 'specific form' was that of a Highland village hall concert. We knew the audiences well: some of us from living in the Highlands, some from our previous tours of *The Cheviot*. This play had raised the land and oil questions in an historical context. They were, and are, the two most important social, economic, political and cultural questions for the Highlands, and it was necessary to spend more time on them and see them as urgent contemporary problems affecting the lives of everybody. The form was familiar to us from *The Cheviot*. It was not the same form as a ceilidh, but not very different. And we knew it would give us a certain amount of freedom.

All three elements were the result of decisions taken by the collective. On the whole they were suggested, or initiated, by me; then discussed, elaborated on and decided on by the collective.

The small group going on the tour sat down together in the disused disco we used for rehearsal in Edinburgh. I had not written a word. We knew the main areas the show was concerned with, and I had a very loose structural idea; to use the characters Angie and Janet as the running story to link and relate the other elements to a recognisable Highland reality. Liz had amassed huge piles of relevant newspaper cuttings through diligent work every day for the previous six months. She and I had, via contacts, begun to find the facts about how many children left their homes the minute they left school, and David MacLennan had got hold of some of these exiled young people and interviewed them to discover their feelings now they were living in Glasgow or Edinburgh.

As in our previous shows, we spent the first few days talking generally, then itemising areas, then breaking these areas down into blocks, with detailed ideas as to how we should present what we wanted to present theatrically and musically, and who was to be involved in each sketch or song. Not only were my ideas up for scrutiny, discussion, amendment, but the whole company was throwing in their ideas which were taken up, knocked down, analysed by everyone else and fed into the growing pool of unrealised material that was to be the basis of the show itself.

An example of the way this worked: Alex Norton desperately wanted to do a running character of an eccentric lecturer who came on every ten minutes with lantern-slides and tried to get his lecture going, but met with a fresh disaster every time. This was a purely theatrical instinct and obviously the sort of thing he would do well. But what was he lecturing on? I had my doubts about the viability of more than two or three appearances anyway. But Alex was insistent there was something in the idea. He didn't know what, but he had a strong feeling for this character. When we were discussing the way the HIDB [Highlands and Islands Development Board] failed to make any serious impact on the economic structure of the Highlands, failed to invest money in, for example, buying up Kildonanstrath and using it as a model for collective agricultural development in the Highlands, Liz remembered an eccentric retired engineer with a nutty scheme for a self-loading toothbrush factory whom she and I had met some years before. She pointed out some of the more bizarre and trivial ways the HIDB were spending their money, and the strange characters we knew who were getting money from them, and we realised that here was Alex's man. The next morning we discussed the idea with the company, and we had a hilarious session devising schemes the man might be getting money for from the HIDB. We agreed that we had some possibilities, theatrically and politically, and certainly tied in with the main theme of the play. One of the ideas I had was that he should devise ways of using up natural resources that were going to waste, like bracken, sheep-shit and sloughed off snake skins. Alex got a gleam in his eye and suggested a glove-puppet snake in a basket. We then devised the memorable snake-skin and I reckoned he should have a string vest on underneath. That night I went home and wrote a monologue for this character, whom I christened McQuirk. It was partly based on the laughs we'd had that morning, in feeling it was aiming at the character Alex was after, but in the actual writing of the dialogue all sorts of new and bizarre ideas flowed in, from snake and chips to, in the second monologue, a whole fantasy about whelk-breath-powered monsters. In rehearsing it, Alex came up with some fresh touches, and we were able to incorporate several new gags as we worked out the business.

On the more directly political material, this again had to be written, but only after discussion. Angie's big speech at the end when I first wrote it was half the length it is now. I was quite pleased with it, but Dave MacLennan thought it didn't say nearly enough and was in danger of being negative, or wishy-washy. I argued hotly against him, then, having proved to my satisfaction that he was wrong, went home, and rewrote it to incorporate everything he'd said was missing. He was, of course, absolutely right.

The research continued through rehearsals. One night Dave and Liz drove up to Blairgowrie to talk to an 87-year-old ex-forester who, we were told, had some interesting stuff on land ownership. This was John McEwan, who had done an immense amount of painstaking work all on his own to try to find out from the flimsy evidence available what no government since 1871 had dared to find out – who owned the Highlands? He was delighted to give us a free hand with his findings, on condition that we put them to some use. We did. Dave and Liz came back with maps, charts and figures that exposed the appalling power a tiny handful of landlords have over the land and resources of the North of Scotland. On the first tour, everywhere we went we read out the figures for the county areas, and then detailed figures for the areas we were in.

My job, as writer to this show, was complex. In the first place I was a contributor to a general discussion, which became hourly more detailed and involved the elements of history, research, reportage, investigative journalism, Gaelic song, fiddle music, new songs, instrumentation, acting flair and intuition, props, costume, scenery, personal abilities and limitations, satire, poetry, economics, social structures, institutions (public and private), politics (practical and theatrical, Scottish, Cuban, Tanzanian and Chinese) and the entertainment values appreciated by a Highland audience in 1974.

In the second place, having been involved deeply in this complicated discussion, I had to digest it and regurgitate it as something with a shape, a form, an overall meaning and a coherent, recognisable tone of voice that would work for the audience, that company, in the time available.

In the third place, I had to add, or breathe into the material floating around, another dimension – that of the individual humanity, the uniqueness, of the main characters. This is where no group creation can work because an individual character like Angie or Janet is created from endless half-conscious details: a turn of phrase, a way of looking at things, a rhythm of speaking and, above all, surprise – for every human being is surprising but the instinct for the right kind of surprise and the right moment can rarely be felt by a committee. It takes an individual to create imaginatively another individual, in the first instance. The actor, of course, then takes over the job from the writer.

Having written the piece, I then had to become the director, laden with practical problems of all kinds, trying to keep the feel of the whole thing coherent and physically interesting, as well as helping actors and all concerned to realise their jobs to the best of their ability.

I think I can say, quite honestly and fairly, that as far as the first ten performances or so were concerned, I failed. Some of the material didn't work, the whole thing was under-rehearsed, the order of the first half of the show was wrong. It lacked rhythm, flow, variety, pace, surprise. The audiences were generous. They saw the good things and bore with the bad. There can be no excuses, but rehearsal-time had been far too short, constantly interrupted by most of the company going off to perform *The Game's a Bogey* in the evenings. We were much too small in numbers, the work-load, was enormous on every single one of us, and we became increasingly tired and slow.

In Lochcarron, Allan Ross, Dave Anderson, Liz and I were sharing digs. We sat up very late after the show and get-out, quietly taking it apart and piecing it together again. We all found some more energy and got up earlier, got into the halls faster, and rewrote and re-rehearsed. An opening night every night for three weeks.

I don't know how we survived. Tempers frayed, and broke, one or two allowed their morale to sag, to lose objectivity, passions flared up, quarts of whisky went down, some fists rose, some hearts sank. But the show was making more sense, had more life, more punch, and was being greatly enjoyed all over the West and the Hebrides.

By the time we got back from the West, the show really was moving well. On the last night I went into the foyer to discover one distinguished BBC cultural producer, plastered out of his skull, stumbling round complaining that the politics of the show were too Maoist. I thought of the crowds in Barra and Lochmaddy, and the school kids in Dingwall, and decided that the show had done a good job.

Perhaps my proudest moment arising from all this work, and much more besides, was when, several years later, I was able to persuade Raymond Williams to change his mind about the possibilities of making theatre for the working class: they were perfectly happy to pay attention and come out to theatre, provided it paid attention to and came out to them. Oddly, it would appear that such activities had never before been conceivable.

In addition to servicing the demands of two companies performing the length and breadth of Britain, not to mention Belgium and Holland, I was also 'doing my bit' for writers by working on the Arts Council's new writing committee – the Arts Council of Great Britain in London, that is: I have never been asked on to any Arts Council committee in Scotland. At that time the ACGB's policy was enlightened, and was creating the great flowering of theatre-writing that marked the 1970s. I fought many battles even then:

SOME THOUGHTS
ON HOW WE SPEND OUR MONEY ON NEW DRAMA[29]

As the change in New Drama Officers has coincided with a desire of the Committee to have a hard look at the present system of distributing the available funds, the Committee has decided to devote much of its next meeting to a discussion of its work. Unfortunately, it seems unlikely that I could get away from rehearsals in Dublin for this meeting, so I have noted down a few points which may be useful in that discussion.

Grants for Individual Plays

If the basic aim of the Committee is to encourage the writing and production of good new plays in this country, then the system of guaranteeing a minimum income to the writer from a production of a new play, coupled with a subsidy to the theatre involved for taking the risk of putting it on, is in principle one good way of achieving this aim.

However, two questions present themselves.

(i) We have recently (I don't know how) withdrawn the production part of the grant from most theatres. The theoretical justification for this was that their grant covered the putting on of new plays anyway. In practice, it means we have taken away the financial inducement to put on new plays, and indirectly reduced the subsidy to theatres who do. If theatre managements do not want to put on new work they will have a thousand justifications for it. They will still get the money. If they do put on new work, they won't get any extra help from us. We have, in fact, reduced the chances of new plays being put on. This seems to me totally wrong.

In other words, the money which the New Drama Committee should be using to encourage specific and valuable projects is being handed out as part of a lump sum with very little guarantee of its proper use. I would propose that the New Drama Committee should control this money in the coming year '75/76 ensuring that it goes where it will do most to promote new drama.

In any event, the production grant should be reinstated as soon as possible.

(ii) The second question is whether £250 is a high enough guarantee to the author for a full-length play. My own experience is that work in film and TV is necessary to subsidise writing for the theatre, and I am sure that this is true of almost all writers who do not aim at West End success, and who continue writing for the theatre over a number of years. This will in many cases result in new plays not being written at all, as TV and film careers are very demanding and can become all-embracing.

If we genuinely wish to raise the standards of writing in the theatre, and to maintain a flow of new and exciting work, we must examine the implications of this £250 figure not in isolation but in terms of the lives of the writers who are likely to produce the work.

Commissioning Fees

The operation of this scheme has been questioned by the Committee with good reason. The theory is that a theatre may offer a straight fee, which is not an advance, but an extra lump-sum to a writer when commissioning a play. In this way highly-paid writers (recent examples being Dennis Potter and Trevor Griffiths) can be given more money to write for a rep, or small theatre. It has been questioned because it is a form of arbitrary discrimination. Many theatres don't know about it, or at least never apply for it. Those who do apply exercise a sort of inverse means test on the writer, not bothering to apply for the poor, but forced to bother for the rich.

Clearly, clarification of the scheme and publicity would help to solve some of the mess. But it is hard to justify some of the assumptions behind it, except in terms of the money offered to these writers by competing TV and other interests. Again we come back to the implications of the funding in terms of the lives of the writers concerned.

Bursaries

Here the Committee finds itself directly involved in writers' lives. It has often been assumed that these bursaries are exclusively for new, young writers, with talent and proof of their ability, to allow them to 'set themselves up', to have some breathing-space from other jobs and work as full-time writers for a year without starving. This is one excellent use of the bursary and should be continued. But again we come back to the question of the writer who devotes their life, or the best part of their writing life, to the creation of new works for the theatre. Clearly there will come a time when many such writers will need a year free of financial anxieties and distractions to develop an idea, a series of plays, a new phase in their creative lives. We are, at the moment, able to help more 'established' writers in this position (viz. John Antrobus), but we should make sure that it is known to such writers that we can do this (it is not known to most) and the bursary should not be a once-in-a-lifetime award.

General

1. Writers' income from other sources is becoming more insecure. Films are not being made, the number of single plays on TV is being reduced, and television is becoming less and less open to new, experimental or challenging writing of any kind.

2. The Arts Council's regional policy has successfully stimulated theatrical life outside the metropolis, and new audiences have sprung to life throughout the country who can, and do, respond to good new work.

3. There are a lot of good new writers, and good developing writers, at work in the country. It is quite conceivable that, given the right help, this country could produce a really vigorous, non-centralised theatre in the next ten years, different from that of the Royal Court era, but possibly more exciting.

Therefore we must ask ourselves, as a matter of urgency, whether we are in fact giving the right help. We should look at the answer in three main areas.

1. The Theatres

It is no good having plays if the theatres are not there to do them in. The Arts Council has helped create the theatres and to keep them alive. But, as indicated above, the withdrawal of the production subsidy specifically for help with new plays was a serious error, a discouragement. It should be reinstated and increased. The small proportion of the overall subsidy for each theatre which is supposedly there to help with new plays should be taken away and put into the New Drama production guarantee fund and used for help with definite projects. The present idea of 'reviewing' a theatre's new play record and adjusting their following year's subsidy according to what they have done seems most unsatisfactory.

The role of the Dramaturge in theatres has been under discussion. It is vital not to confuse this role with that of the Attached Writer. The Dramaturge in theory seeks out new plays (as well as old ones), commissions, encourages, protects writers, reads scripts, umpires director-writer punch-ups, and maintains literary law and order. I confess I have never been fond of Dramaturges, wherever I have encountered them. In practice, they are powerless tools of the director, become part of the bureaucratic fabric, and are content to be over-ruled by everybody. In any event, the New Drama Committee's funds should not be considered for this purpose. If the director needs a Dramaturge as part of their machinery, then the theatre's general subsidy should take this into account. New Drama money for theatres should go to directly encourage the production of new plays.

2. *Individual New Plays*

To date, apart from the Bursary scheme, the Committee has seen new writing as a series of individual plays popping up for consideration. As I shall indicate later, this is something we ought to examine. But new plays do pop up from all kinds of amazing directions, and if good or interesting or unusual enough must, of course, be helped on their way. If the theatres know they will get help they will be more willing to do them. The guarantee to the writer, however, of £250, seems grotesquely out of proportion. The 'going rate' for a 75-minute TV play is between £1,000 and £1,500. A full-length play for the theatre makes at least five or six times the demands on a writer's time and talent than a TV play. Obviously the New Drama funds will not stretch to £10,000 per new play, but the disparity is apparent. I would suggest that any new play worth putting on should be worth £500 to the writer, and that £500 should be our minimum guarantee. This is, however, still looking at new plays as disconnected phenomena.

I would suggest that we go beyond this.

3. *Encouraging Writers for the Theatre*

It seems that the dimension of thinking which is missing from our discussions at the moment is that concerning the livelihood of individual writers for the theatre. Clearly, this is a very difficult area. It will be objected that to become too deeply involved with supporting writers could lead to a State-authorised list of permitted authors, that playwrights should be like ships that pass in the night, silent, blinking out their signal, vanishing, that the Arts Council should not be held even notionally responsible for a writer's livelihood, that we should be concerned with encouraging new drama when it appears, not writers. All of these are evasions of responsibility.

What I propose we should be considering is a structure that will enable a good writer to be confident that they can survive as a writer for the theatre alone, without debasing their standards.

At the moment this is possible only for a very few who have become, usually rightly, stars in the metropolitan firmament. The potential vigour of the next decade in the theatre depends on building on the Arts Council regional policy's achievements in theatre-building, raising of production standards and creation of audiences, by enabling writers working and living all over the country to devote all their creative energy to filling those theatres with exciting new work.

Proposals

1. I have deliberately not discussed the fourth scheme the Committee handles – attachments to theatres. This is because such a scheme usually involves a lot of non-writing work – reading scripts, writing programme-notes, organising local writers' groups, etc. This seems to be a vague attempt to institutionalise the writer by giving them other people's jobs. The scheme could, however, be made into one simple way of keeping a writer alive and working within a practical theatre context, and often works well this way.

At the moment, the theatre has to match, on a pound-for-pound basis, the Committee's grant. Many theatres cannot, or will not, do this. I would propose that theatres should be encouraged to offer yearly attachments, re-newable, to writers, the cost up to £2,000 per year to be borne by the New Drama Committee. The writer's only obligation would be to live or work in the area of the theatre, and to write plays for it. In this case, no individual play guarantee would apply for the writer, but the theatre should receive the production grant.

The appointments would obviously have to be approved by the New Drama Committee.

In this way, writers who would benefit from this method of work could do so, and some could spend a period of their lives moving from theatre to theatre, as directors, designers, etc., currently do, secure that they were going to be paid, and could get on with writing.

2. The attachment scheme would not suit some writers. It presupposes a willingness to commit your work to one specific outlet, which may inhibit quite a few. It presupposes a relationship with an Artistic Director, which some may not have. In these cases I propose that the Bursary scheme could be made available without commitment to a theatre, selection being made directly by the Committee (with the help of the readers), on the under-standing that if selected, the writer will devote their energies to theatre work for the period. We already pay writers' guarantees direct to the writer, there would seem to be no sensible reason why we should not pay bursaries

direct. The bursaries should be renewable for a limited number of years and subject to the criteria of work done for the theatre and proposed projects, and should not be reserved for new writers exclusively. They should be worth up to £2,000 per annum and subject to six-monthly review.

3. The number of attachments and bursaries available at any one time will be limited. Writers who are not receiving them will still be writing plays. If we consider £2,000 enough for a writer who has a bursary to work for a year, at the present guarantee of £250 per play, the non-bursaried theatre writer will have to write eight plays per year to live, or find some other source of income. Little wonder that our readers complain so bitterly of the standard of plays submitted or that so many shoddy plays are circulating. I would propose that we raise the standards expected for a play to receive subsidy, and raise the author's guaranteed royalties to £500. In this way a writer could reasonably spend three months exclusively on a play – which is not long, God knows – and could hope for second and third performances. The commissioning fee should be abolished and a £250 advance made available in certain cases.

This structure is aimed at supporting in a slightly more realistic way those theatre writers who genuinely have the talent and the desire to write new and independently-minded work for the theatre outside the West End. They may only have the talent, or the desire to do so for a limited number of years. They may move into the National/Aldwych/Royal Court orbit, and opt for international stardom or go to Hollywood, write soap operas, or turn to sugar-boiling, who knows? The important thing is that a talented writer should be able to live by working for the theatre, and at the moment most can't.

I think I should declare, or at least clarify, my interest.

I am one of the few who have survived by working almost exclusively in the theatre for the last four or five years. I would not personally benefit greatly from any of the proposals I have made, but I did waste at least four years, if not more, of my life struggling to keep alive in TV when I should have been writing full time for the theatre. I don't know if what I might have written would have dazzled posterity or not, but I deeply regret not having written it. I don't think other writers should have those regrets when it could be within our power to prevent it.

So much for my bias. Quite apart from that, I believe the theatrical health of our country depends now on its writers. Our job as a Committee is to allow them to write the new plays which will be so important in entertaining, expressing, instructing, elevating, galvanising communities throughout the country in the future, and will keep the theatre alive through the next decade.

Sorry I can't be at the meeting.

1975 was the Year I Did Too Much. 7:84 England produced a tour of Fish in the
Sea, *directed by Pam Brighton, for which I did many re-writes and several new
songs; after that we at last got annual funding from the Arts Council in London,
so I was able to audition and set up a regular company, and write and direct* Lay
Off *and* Yobbo Nowt *for them, and direct Shane Connaughton's* Relegated; *in
Scotland I wrote and directed* Little Red Hen; *and on a visit to Amsterdam
I wrote a short play,* Oranges and Lemons, *for John Bett and Jenny Stoller, who
toured it round Holland. Liz was touring with* Little Red Hen, *so I had the boys
to look after a lot of the time. It was an exciting year.*

LITTLE RED HEN[30]

Little Red Hen was the sixth major production, which toured mostly in the
industrial areas of Scotland from September to December 1975, also being
performed subsequently in Ireland, and at the Shaw Theatre in London in
June 1976.

Wherever we go in the industrial areas of Scotland – and Clydeside in
particular – we meet up with an older generation of working-class militants
who constantly astonish us. Active, articulate, passionate and well-informed,
they draw their strength and conviction from the days of the 'Red Clyde' –
days when the naked greed and ruthlessness of the capitalist system were
plain to see; days when John Maclean, Jimmy Maxton, John Wheatley, Willie
Gallacher and many other great activists and speakers expressed the
demand of the Scottish working class for the overthrow of capitalism and
the creation of a socialist Scotland.

During the 1914-1918 War, Glasgow was the centre of opposition to the
senseless slaughter in the trenches, the exploitation of the workers in their
factories to keep the slaughter going, and the rent-profiteers who owned
their homes. After the war, in 1919, Glasgow workers led the strike for a 40-
hour working week to absorb the unemployed. There were 30,000 unemployed in Glasgow, and thousands more coming back from the trenches
every week. On Bloody Friday, trouble flared up at a mass meeting in
George Square. That night, the soldiers arrived and set up machine-guns on
top of buildings in the city centre, and a howitzer in the City Chambers. The
leaders were arrested. There was no violent revolution. But the anger, and
the activism, continued. By 1922, the movement was so strong that ten out
of the twelve Glasgow MPs returned at the election were socialists.

That generation saw Scotland on the move – in a big way. Today, we are
told, Scotland is on the move again. The UCS (Upper Clyde Shipbuilders)
work-in, the activism of the Scottish miners, the promised economic miracle
of the oil industry, the up-surge of nationalism – all point to an atmosphere
at least of energy and debate.

In *Little Red Hen*, we try to take a look at that earlier time of high hopes, and at the present moment of aspiration, through the eyes of one of that older generation. What went wrong with the first period – which ended in the misery of the 1930s – may be of interest to people today who are working, as she [the 'Red Hen' of the title] did, for a better future for the people of Scotland.

At the beginning of March 1975 I tried to document what 7:84 England had achieved and what was still to be done:

THE PRESENT SITUATION OF 7:84[31]

7:84 exists to communicate with as wide an audience as possible, with particular emphasis on audiences of the working class and the potential allies of the working class – students and progressive elements in the professional, petit-bourgeois, and technocratic sectors.

Our main objectives have been, are, and will be:

(a) To de-mystify, i.e. to reveal the class nature of our society, and the full extent of the oppression of all kinds *in* this country and *by* this country, to the people capable of changing it. And to stimulate them to change it, by showing that it can, and must, change.

(b) To celebrate the alternatives to capitalist values: to show that entertainment, gags, language, music, theatrical vitality, depth of thought and strength of expression belong to the people and *not* to the bourgeoisie, and have more to do with revolution than with monopoly capitalism.

(c) To give the working class confidence in its own culture, to celebrate its progressive characteristics and attack its backwardness from a position of trust.

(d) To entertain and enliven what is loosely known as 'the movement'. And in the process, to try to move the looser elements in it towards sharper-thinking, positive (Marxist) attitudes and away from reformism, populism, anarchism and dropping out.

(e) To fight individual battles against the oppression of individual capitalists and to show their relationship to the internal struggle against the capitalist state and the international struggle against monopoly capitalism.

(f) To assert, against the deadening creations of the present power-structure, not dogma, infallibility, potted archaic theory or a party machine, but the immense potential of humanity, of individual people.

(g) To attack, within the theatre, the glossy, the sham, the slick, the pseudo, the lying, the corrupt and corrupting corpse of commercial and official bourgeois theatre, and to make it look as dead and deadening as it really is.

(h) To be good at it: to learn from our audiences.

What Has 7:84 Achieved?

During the four years since it began it has:

(a) Communicated to many thousands of people in many different situations, effectively and in some cases overwhelmingly powerfully, a socialist view of humanity and of our present condition. Not all of these audiences have been middle-class theatre-goers. Most have been strongly moved by what they saw. A lot of politically conscious people have come out of our shows entertained, enlivened, happier – strengthened. A lot of politically unaware people have come out feeling very differently about what politics means in terms of people's lives. A lot of complacent theatre-goers have come out, or walked out, shaken, angry, even violent – but not so complacent.

(b) Built up a circuit, and a reputation for high standards of theatrical, and mental, excitement.

(c) Arrived at a position where a considerable audience has been built up for our political position. Up to now this position has been non-sectarian, non-dogmatic, and non-compromising Marxist dialectical materialism. In Scotland, we are working towards approval of separation and a Scottish workers' republic, while attacking nationalism and guarding against dividing the working class of Britain. It recognises the vital role of theory and analysis of history, but insists those are constantly changing with the changes in the national and international situation, and should be seen in the perspective of an informed, open and honest assessment of what is real today, if not tomorrow.

(d) Moved into a position of strength, in terms of experience, organisation, reputation, contacts and finance.

What Is Still To Be Done?

(a) To reach a mass popular audience on a regular basis.

(b) To develop a large enough group of people working together permanently, committed to its work: writers, actors, stage management, directors.

(c) To develop serious political work within the group.

(d) To maintain a working atmosphere of trust, openness and freedom in which people can flourish as individuals and grow as artists.

Organisational Problems

During its first year 7:84 was run by a fairly benevolent dictatorship. This was a conscious decision, and necessary to build the company's strength to a position where it could become collectively controlled.

After one year, the devolution of power was attempted. It failed because many of the people who said they wanted power were away at the Royal Court or Nottingham when there was a break. Several attempts at company or collective control have floundered or ended in disaster for two main reasons:

The company has never had an annual grant, so has had to move from tour to tour with little continuity of work.

Attitudes varying from opportunism, via gross irresponsibility, to anarchist childishness, in some members of the collective.

However, since the end of the first year, collective decision-making of a kind has been practised, and a small hard core of politically aware people has kept up continuity and a sense of purpose within the changing fortunes of the various companies.

The Present

The present tour of *Fish in the Sea* was got together by the determination of the hard core of the collective to keep the work of the English company going. Sandy Craig as administrator, Pam Brighton as Director and the present group of actors and musicians have all put in a great deal of energy, talent, political commitment, good will and hard work, often under difficult circumstances to get the company going full-blast.

Pam Brighton was doing a great job directing Fish in the Sea, *with design by Bill Dudley.*

7:84 ENGLAND RESURGENT — MID-1970S[32]

Fish in the Sea was really the resurgence of 7:84. There were some very good people: musicians Mike O'Neill, Mark Brown and Chas Ambler, actor-performers like Hilton McRae and Colm Meaney, who were very important in that period. Sandy Craig had come back which was great because he knew the company, knew me and was a very good administrator with a lot of ideas. We were able to interview people in the round, as it were. So the whole basis was not 'You're right for the part' or 'I've worked with you before and I know we get on' – it was on a much more open basis of a lot of people knowing people who were coming in. We were able to be firm about political commitment and involvement and about what the company was for, what it was doing and what kind of gigs we were going to play.

LAY OFF

Chrissie Cotterill came in with *Lay Off*. I saw her doing a gig in the East End for old age pensioners and thought she was someone who had direct contact with the audience, big, simple direct communication, a wonderful immediacy, a very unpretentious stage presence. Mike Barton came and he was very, very good and Hilton McRae, a wonderful singer and a very flexible, talented actor with great physical dexterity.

Knowing that we'd got a year to work we were able to do a lot of things; like we would have an hour's discussion every morning before rehearsals began. At the beginning it was based on Mao's essay on collectives, applying it to our situation and the national political situation. We also had regular voice and physical training. We had regular company meetings where everything was discussed and decisions were taken collectively about that show and the future policy of the company.

We started off with an idea that was to do with multi-nationals, I wanted to do something about multi-nationals . . . but through discussion it became apparent we had to talk about nationals – how big firms grow up. We really built up a whole picture of business and industry within one country until we got to the interval, where we had a big corporation about to go multi-national. After the interval we went into the operations of multi-nationals, mostly American and a whole section on Chile. At the end we had a section about how organised labour was beginning to fight back, how contacts between plants in different countries had been made . . . in the end it was about organising against multi-nationals.

There were endless songs . . . marked by a tremendously confident performance. They were all high-octane performers. It was a terrific feeling of energy and imagination, all within the shape of this extraordinary saga. It was a very exciting thing to work on, and the response of the audience was great. We did over a hundred performances of it. We played in occupied factories, because there were still factories being occupied in those days, back rooms of pubs, in theatres . . . everywhere.

Then we started to work on . . . two ideas. One was to do the nationalised industries, specifically steel. Or alternatively I had a specific yen to do something along the lines of Gorki's and Brecht's *The Mother*. Not an adaptation, but to start totally from scratch, with the idea of a working-class mother learning about political involvement. The company fancied doing the second, so I began work on that. There had been complaints that in *Lay Off* the women hadn't had enough to do, so, again it was appropriate to do *The Mother*.

Mortimer   *Is that an argument that had come up before?*

The arguments came out of a performance at the Unity when some London women's libbers had objected to the number of men in it. I thought they were wrong. They were understandably over-reacting to centuries of oppression everywhere, even among their friends and allies . . . but that was another good reason for *Yobbo Nowt*.

YOBBO NOWT[33]

Brecht's adaptation of Gorki's novel *The Mother* tells the story of a working-class woman's growth to political consciousness and militancy in Russia at the beginning of this century. We had all met on our travels many women who were going through a similar process. The story, of course, turned out to be almost completely different from Gorki's. But these were the sources, literary and real, from which came the story of Marie.

In form it is not exactly a musical comedy – though it is definitely musical, and a comedy. With Mark Brown, who composed the music, I set out to explore several ways of relating music to speech and story-telling: the sung narrative, straightforward character and situation-songs, plus scenes in which the characters cut from speech to song, and scenes completely set to music.

On looking at the show again, one feature of comparison with both Gorki's novel and Brecht's play is striking. In telling this story today, we could not show Marie's learning experiences as including the vital strength of a coherent mass Marxist movement. We know from our own experience, and that of the many people like Marie whom we meet throughout Britain, that such a movement is our greatest need. It is to this movement of the future, and to all those in the company, and who have helped the company, that I dedicate this play.

This was a truly enjoyable period in 7:84 England's work:[34]

What was good was that we were touring both *Lay Off* and *Yobbo Nowt* and we had two very different styles that everybody was on top off. This was the peak of 7:84 activities in England.

In January 1976 we started work on a play by Shane Connaughton [*Relegated*], which he hadn't written and kept bringing bits of to rehearsal. It was difficult. I was shattered by the previous year and the company was very tired. The additional problems were the play, which wasn't very good, and that it was set in Stoke-on-Trent and for the first time I got really angry with the company because I'd asked them to learn the accent. The women worked on it, but the men were just plain idle. They sounded awful and that gets you down, listening to the wrong accent all day.

We opened at Bracknell Arts Centre and it was all right. Harriet Walter was wonderful. I suppose we could have got away with it under different circumstances, but none of us were happy. It was proposed that we take the play off and substitute *Lay Off* or *Yobbo* for it. Shane wasn't there. I was going up to Scotland to see *Honour Your Partners* and a delegation from the company were going to see Shane and explain what happened. Shane came to the conclusion that I'd removed it because I wanted my plays to go on and not his . . . this paranoia about 7:84 giving writers a bad time was bandied around. It's totally untrue. I was shattered by the whole experience. I'd put an enormous amount of effort into directing it. Far from rejoicing, it made me feel sick. It led to the disintegration of that company because we were committed to 28 weeks and we just toured, toured and toured until the following June.

Then I wrote a play called *The Rat Trap*, which was a short thing with a lot of music. It was really an attempt to get some life back into the company. It was deliberately over the top and a lot of fun to do. But it was still this feeling of having to lift everybody up, and I began to get pissed off with it all, frankly. I just said, 'Right, I'm not actually going to direct this lot. I'm going and I won't be back,' because I couldn't bear it any longer. That's the way I remember that year, as a kind of decline: people getting more tired, pale, sick-looking, lethargic and lazy. I think they were still genuinely committed to what they were doing, but they couldn't get the enthusiasm or the energy together.

Subsequently the English 7:84 fell alarmingly frequently into various traps to do with political correctness, one such being what was called ultra-democracy. At various times 'the power of the pen' was challenged, and a project like Ragged Trousered Philanthropists *split into many sections, each one given to a different actor or technician or musician to go off and write; Gavin Richards, whose policy this was, also challenged the role of the director, only accepting that role, as he put it, 'to stop anyone at all trying to be the director'. At one point the jobs of the administrator and the PR gig-getting person were put on the line, so the company could take it in turns to administer the company's business affairs and its relationships with venues. The administrator however was not allowed to act, or play the piano – because they couldn't. Some skills were respect-worthy, others clearly not. We never had this syndrome with the Scottish Company, who mostly felt very fulfilled being allowed to do what they were good at.*

Here's a fairly typical document of that period:

INTRODUCTION TO 7:84
FOR DIRECTOR APPLICANTS[35]

The Company

I. ALL DECISIONS relating to production and touring are taken by the Company in democratic debate, or delegated to individuals or groups who are answerable to the Company. All members of the Company receive the same wage, and have an equal right to participate in decisions.

2. The Company's basic artistic policy is to provide good socialist theatre, incorporating music, with a specifically Marxist but non-sectarian analysis, in the interests of the working class, primarily in England and Wales at the present time.

3. We hold as equally important the development of socialist collective methods of working and we therefore oppose any tendencies towards bourgeois hierarchical, authoritarian or manipulative working. The work process should take place in a spirit of open and constructive criticism and self-criticism. Any major differences must be referred to a full Company meeting. At least one half-day per fortnight, within working hours, shall be set aside for such a meeting.

4. The Company places great value on the contribution of individual skills, provided always that these are subservient to the collective work and to the overall political and artistic aims of the Company.

5. Decisions relating to the long-term policy and finance of the Company are taken by the Collective of eleven Directors of the Limited Company, five of whom are members of the present Company, and six past members. The Collective has no control over the internal working of the Company on individual productions or tours.

The Director

From the above it will be clear that we regard the role of Director as that of one who has a skill to contribute, not an authority to wield. The functions and responsibilities of the Director are:

(i) to provide an 'objective eye' in putting the play into performance.

(ii) to organise rehearsals and co-ordinate the various individual contributions to the production: i.e. design, staging, music, lighting, acting and writing.

(iii) to contribute to the on-going work of the Company by taking collective responsibility with other members for policy decisions; in particular by ensuring that the current production reflects the artistic and political objectives of the Company.

The Director shall be employed for the rehearsal period, from 3 January 1977 until the second week of performance; and in addition, part-time at mutual convenience for discussions with author and Company before rehearsals start. The Director, together with others employed for the production period only, shall be consulted and shall have the right to participate in any decisions affecting that production, after they have left the Company.

The Interview

This will be held in the form of a Company meeting with chairperson etc. Please do not be intimidated by a large number present; we are not an examining board. The process is intended to provide the optimum opportunity for mutual exploration of common views and differences, given our limitations of time and the desire to see as many applicants as possible. Among the things we would like to know from you are:

(i) your personal background;

(ii) your politics;

(iii) your professional experience;

(iv) your views on past 7:84 productions, on our overall political and artistic policy, and on the role of the Director in collective working.

In conclusion, we would emphasize that we are not looking for the person who will conform most exactly to our existing views and policies, but the one who can contribute most creatively to developing them.

This English tendency reached its apotheosis in the next production, Our Land, Our Lives, *after I had left them to it:*

94

OUR LAND, OUR LIVES[36]

The company decided to ask Steve Gooch to write a play. The play appeared and it seemed to me to be terrible. The jokes weren't funny and the dialogue didn't sound like dialogue. And there was this dreadful democracy within the structure of the play, that everybody had a large, long monologue; all the parts were almost to within a syllable, the same size. I think it could almost stand as a classic example of the reason that May 1968 failed in Britain, as it epitomized all the mistakes: crushing of individualism, of difference between people. Frightened democracy, in the sense that one felt all the parts were equal out of a sense of fear rather than out of a sense of celebrating everybody's equality. At the same time the whole thing was incredibly arrogant, because it assumed that people were going to come and pay money for this. That's the real thing about the 1970s, the automatic assumption of the right to be maintained at the public expense. That, to me, is the underlying reason why Margaret Thatcher is there now. Even a lot of working-class people have foolishly been misled into thinking that this is the way to solve the problem of people assuming that the public should support them because they are intrinsically worthy of support.

I didn't come down for any rehearsals. I was just another member of the collective, and we said we would not interfere unless something drastic happened. I came down for the first dress rehearsal and was distinctly underwhelmed by the whole experience. The tour went on and I kept getting phone calls saying, 'We must have a collective meeting'. Eventually Liz and I decided that it might be an idea to go and see the English company. We drove with our two boys being sick in the back of the car, to Stranraer, over to Larne, then across Northern Ireland to Coleraine, where it was opening a brand new theatre at the university. It was packed and this show came on and it was diabolical.

We decided to have a collective meeting and proposed that the show be taken off, there and then. It was a strange time and didn't do the company any good at all.

It was at this meeting that one actor, new to the company, was asked what good it would do a working-class audience to see a bad show. He proudly replied: 'They have the right to see us fail.' As it was, several venues had already told us not to bother coming again. The show was taken off to avoid further damage.

While all this was going on, the Scottish company felt confident enough to be openly critical of one of the worst failings of many in our audience: booze. I did a lot of research, as did the company, on what exactly the culture of getting drunk was, and how we individually related to alcohol, then I wrote, and we tightened up, and then toured, Out of Our Heads:

OUT OF OUR HEADS[37]

How on earth can you write a play about booze? So much has been talked about it, so many mythologies have grown up around it, so many books, poems, stories have been written about its influence, so many hell-fire sermons preached, so many hymns against it sung – what can you add to it all? Surprisingly very little medical research has been concluded on its actual effects on the mind and body – and a great deal of what is accepted as 'common sense' is pure rubbish. Surprisingly very little sociological research has been done on exactly why people drink, and almost none at all on why different societies, drinking the same liquor, get 'drunk' in different ways, recognise different forms of 'drunken' behaviour. And, not surprisingly, very few political thinkers have made connections between the root problem of living in a competitive, manipulated industrial society, and the particular uses to which we put alcohol.

Medically, drink simply stops the oxygen circulating in the brain and the nervous system. To this extent it does interfere with our consciousness, and drugs our bodies. What seems to happen is that we take advantage of this feeling of lack of control over ourselves, to justify certain kinds of behaviour. But this behaviour is not actually 'caused' by alcohol – the presence of alcohol gives us an excuse to indulge in it. If alcohol 'caused' people to do things, then we would presumably react in much the same way, the world over, to an excess of it. Clearly we don't. Some societies go berserk, some sit in loving circles, some allow sexual freedom, others have no sexual reaction at all, some sing sentimental songs, others chop each others heads off – when 'under the influence'.

Every society, in fact, teaches its young how to 'be drunk' – it has built a code of behaviour that is permissible to its members who get drunk, and this code is very clearly defined. In Scotland, for example, wife-beating is fairly tolerable when a man gets drunk, but not among certain groups of Mexican Indians. Again, in Scotland, violence flares up easily in a group of drinkers – but not at all on Ifaluk, one of the Caroline Islands, where 'a slightly bleary look about the eyes, and a tendency to be jovial or sentimentally friendly' are the only effects of a hard night's battering the booze.

One conventional wisdom about drink is that it releases the animal instincts, somehow dis-inhibits the mind from the normal moral code, and anything goes. But it is obvious that this only happens within strict limits. There are a few individuals who may use drink to justify extremes of violence, or animality, but on the whole, most drunken Scots know very clearly that although they can sing, or dance in the street and be excused, they mustn't throw bricks through windows or strangle cats. So they are not 'uncontrollable' or even completely liberated. They are conforming to a code, defined by society, and passed on, with modifications, from one generation to the next.

It must follow that the code of drunken behaviour allowed to the Scottish working man, as opposed to the native of Ifaluk, is strongly connected with the life style of the Scottish working man as opposed to that of the Pacific Islanders. Violence in one, joviality in the other, why? This is the extremely complicated question that we try to look at in this play.

The single most striking feature of the life of working people in Scotland today is alienation. The basic alienation comes from the fact that in their work, they are selling their labour to other people to use to make profit. Few have a deep personal desire to make the products they produce, or find their work satisfying, or gratifying to any of the creativity that is within every human being. A great part of their lives is sold, for cash. And the purpose of their work is generally not for the good of the community, but to create a surplus: profit.

When they have free time, enjoyment is now usually measured in terms of commodities – films, colour television, clothes, package holidays, cars, restaurants, nicer furniture, electrical gadgets, and booze. The desire to feel part of a community, part of humanity, is now more difficult to fulfil – inhuman 'filing-cabinet' architecture, supermarkets replacing the corner shop, the devices of mass-consumption split up people more and more.

As a class, the working class is socially alienated – their traditional values, they are told, are inferior to the dominant values of society: they lack the social graces, the charm and politeness and assurance of the upper classes they see on the telly every night. So they are either alienated from society or mimic their masters (another form of alienation – from themselves).

Women are alienated, starting at an early age, from what they might want to feel, by the pressure to conform to a male image of what a girl should feel. Likewise boys have to conform to a manly image, or suffer for failing. The relationship between a man and a woman has to struggle through this network of images, and is distorted by it. All these different kinds of alienation create multiple splits in the personality. So what makes you feel whole, complete and in charge of your destiny? Booze, according to the code. Maybe that is what is underneath so much working-class drinking: the need for an excuse to feel complete.

But there is more, much more, that we have decided to use drink for in Scotland. To give us a chance to be emotional for example – not a very sober thing to do. To give us courage to bewail our human condition: the sober thing is to button up your fears.

The play tells the story of a working man and his wife caught in all this; their friend Davey, who sees that if you drink because things are wrong, you won't change them, because you'll be drunk; and their works manager and his wife, who are caught in the same trap. The play only scrapes the surface of the problem, but we hope it will at least raise it in a different way.

In Scotland our working methods and thinking about popular theatre were developing in tandem. One of the oddest consequences of the tour was that I was asked to write a piece for a guide to the best pubs in Edinburgh and Glasgow. I did my best. [The following piece was written by John in response to the theatre critics' wearisome notion that 'good theatre' is only about nuance, and theatre is 'bad' when it contains 'blacker than black' villains. – Elizabeth MacLennan]

SOME USES OF STEREOTYPE[38]

The conventional reaction to 'stereotypes' on stage is one of shock-horror-blunder. To see a character portrayed on a stage with no effort to present a picture of that character's subjectivity and, what seems to be more important, without automatic and uncritical emotional sympathy, is considered somehow immoral. A character must be 'rounded', we must see both the good in them and the bad in them, we must see them as fallible but lovable human beings, or else we are 'distorting' them, making them into stereotypes, therefore into non-human beings, in order to purvey propaganda; *but,* the argument runs, since we have already 'distorted' the objects of our attack or approval into non-humans, our argument is invalid, because it applies only to the stereotypes we have invented, therefore does not apply to Reality.

There are times when to use what are called 'stereotypes' on stage is the only way to tell the truth about a social situation or a historical movement.

Perhaps it would be as well, before going further, to say what I do *not* mean by 'stereotype'. I don't mean lazy naturalism that aims at a 'rounded' character and fails through lack of observation or invention. Nor even the creation of cliché characters, the callow grasping at the obvious that marks a lot of agitprop theatre – the boss with the silk hat, the worker in honest dungarees etc. Nor do I mean the symbols of theatrical rhetoric found in poetical plays, usually called 'the woman', 'the poet', 'the young man' etc. Nor do I mean their cousins found in Expressionist and sub-Expressionist political dramas, known as 'the worker', 'the unemployed', 'the man of the people'. Above all, I do not mean the noble tractor-driver of socialist realism, the impossible hero of Stakhanovite drama whose productivity is matched only by his devotion to Stalin.

One of the main problems of grappling with contemporary reality whether in terms of theatre, social history, or political analysis, is the truly massive amount of confusion and mystification thrown up around the social processes and the individual within those processes. One central manifestation of this is the determined attempt to erode the concept of 'class'. If a coal-miner can earn more per week than a dowager Duchess on a 'fixed' income – in itself a highly dubious proposition – then surely the idea that the Duchess is a member of the ruling class is a laughable anachronism?

In the presence of such deliberate and depoliticising mystifications, clearly one of the main problems in presenting images of contemporary society is going to be to reveal the true nature of the social forces in that society.

Let me explain this a little further. Let's take a complex naturalistic creation from one of Tennessee Williams's early plays – *Baby Doll*. Here was a highly individual, fully rounded, good-and-bad, psychologically individuated and explored in depth 'real person' on stage. But a world-wide audience appropriated her as a symbol – as a manifestation of what was in fact a new configuration of social and cultural forces in post-war Western society. What is interesting here is that the term 'Baby Doll' became used for a time as a way of referring to a certain age- and class-specific sexuality. It had become a useful word in the language, a way of referring to an unnamed phenomenon; it had ceased to refer to a piece of naturalistic character-building.

In a similar, perhaps less marked way, almost all 'characters' created on the stage are in fact emblems. Whether the author and actors like it or not, they become generalisations in the perception of the audience.

Furthermore, it is often forgotten that these 'characters' are not analysable or static case-histories: they move, they act out their reality in the play – they become a necessary part of a structure, they become defined as opposed to other characters, falling in love with X, trying to murder Y, trying to persuade Z. The audience perceives them as functions within a narrative, as fitting in with a whole set of other forces in the force-field that is the play. They are necessarily conceived by their author as in part determined by the other characters, the needs of the rest of the play. The demands of form, of a narrative, of an emotional gestalt, or of a coherent statement, mean that every character is forced into a shape to suit them; is, in some way, stereotyped.

Anyone who has seen or helped an actor in a naturalistic play to 'create' a character will know that, as Stanislavski suggested and Lee Strasberg made emphatic, he or she will strive to find the character's 'super-objective' in the play, and break down their role into subsidiary 'objectives' for each scene, perhaps for each line. Around and about this system of objectives, the actor will add what they imagine are appropriate graphic details, provided from their imagination or memory or both.

Most writers of the 'post-Chekhovian' theatre, will in fact create their characters in bold outline, with more or less significant detail added later for verisimilitude. I would like to suggest that the notion that the audience is conned by these processes into regarding an actor on a stage playing a character as anything approaching a 'real' person is ridiculous. They apprehend the subjectivity of a real person, true – the subjectivity of the actor. They also apprehend the function of the character in the drama, and they see what *kind* of person the writer/director/actor is trying to make us see. They check the observation of the writer/director/actor with their own observation of that kind of person in real life, and derive a certain amount of pleasure if it is accurate, and complain as they walk home if it is inaccurate.

What I am suggesting, then, is that even in the most dedicatedly 'naturalistic' theatre, there are two categories of perception of a character. One is the process of recognition of a type of person. This is the essential part of the creation of the character, and relates to the 'super-objective'/ the function in the gestalt/the socially useful image. It is on this level that the ideological intervention of notions of 'roundedness', good-side-bad-side, human ambivalence etc. are *really* made.

The second category of perception of a 'naturalistic' character is that of checking up on the accumulated details that writer, director and actor have smothered the archetypal core of the character with, like some rich sauce or gravy. Now it is usually rather generously assumed that these details are 'organic', and I can hear the cry that a whole idea for some characters grew from a tiny but significant detail observed in life or invented in rehearsal. And of course it is quite possible, but what this is really saying is that the idea of the stereotype came in a blinding flash from a detail from the working out of the stereotype.

The famed liberal demand for an author to present the case for both sides of a character, for 'rounded' characters, has its validity in another sphere from that of verisimilitude and detail: but verisimilitude is the banner that it waves to reassure its supporters and confound its enemies. It shifts its ground – not ever wishing to be identifiable as ideological – onto the subsidiary territory of 'recognisably real human beings'. What this *does* do, is provide a form of writing and perceiving contemporary reality which allows the deliberate mystifications and confusions of the opinion-forming devices of the capitalist state to operate unchallenged.

This is where a more direct, honest and open use of stereotype can serve to open up a dialogue with the audience about the nature of their perception, and can allow the writer/director/actor to bring into motion real social forces, in a direct, honest and open way.

It was about this time that my friend Clive Goodwin upped and died, leaving us all seriously bereft:

CLIVE GOODWIN[39]

Clive Goodwin died on 16 November 1977 on a visit to Los Angeles. He had a brain haemorrhage outside a hotel where he had been talking to one of his clients, Trevor Griffiths. He staggered back into the hotel for help, but the hotel simply called the police, who handcuffed him, threw him into a police wagon, and after a cursory examination decided he was drunk, and locked him into a cell for the night. When they opened his cell in the morning, he was dead. It has been established that although the haemorrhage he suffered was large, had he received prompt medical attention, he had a chance of living. In America, whoever calls for medical attention for another person is responsible for paying the bill. Clive was killed by capitalism, as surely as Steve Biko. Or many thousands daily in the cities of America.

To write about Clive Goodwin so soon after his death is a difficult, and, in several unexpected ways, a painful experience. It is painful because I now realise how little I knew of him, even though I have known him well for over twenty years; and because, the more I think of him, and what he actually did and was in the course of doing, and could have done, the more I realise how much we have all lost.

He was born in Willesden, a stone's throw from Grunwick's. His father was a waiter in a posh restaurant in London. He went to the local Grammar School, and did reasonably well. During his National Service, he was recognised as a useful sort of bloke, and given a commission. This entree into the Officers' Mess was to lead to an awareness of class, a shock of recognition that never left him. As happened with many intelligent working-class children creamed off in this way, and in others, he quickly learned the rules of the game. As happened with rather fewer, he retained the ability to use this experience for the benefit of his own class, rather than see it used against them.

Clive went into the theatre as an actor. He trained at the Central School, and was apparently quite good at it. But this was in the mid-50s, the time of the reactivation of English theatre, and it was here that he first showed his value to the left. With some friends he started a magazine called *Encore* which grew to be a vital ingredient in the development of the English theatre at that time, which was not only a forum for current ideas, but which also introduced to the English scene the thinking of theatre-workers abroad, past and present. Its presence raised the level of discussion and knowledge of all of us who were then working towards a new kind of theatre, and gave us a sense of confidence and of not being alone. The value of Clive Goodwin was that he didn't just think it would be a good idea. He did it.

In the theatre proper, Clive got involved with Stephen Joseph's Theatre-in-the-Round company, in London and in Scarborough. A true child of his time, he even played Jimmy Porter, as well as getting *Encore* to publish Pinter's *The Caretaker*, and a special issue devoted to the work of John Arden.

At the time, Granada Television was still waving a slightly tarnished left-wing banner. It was natural that Clive should move in for a time to help them to find and encourage good socialist writers and directors. His long friendship with Ken Tynan then led him into working with Tynan on an Arts programme called *Tempo*, featuring regular spots from the *Beyond the Fringe* team, and films on the many different roles of art in society. All the time he was learning the executive skills of the professional servants of the dominant ideology within their most important medium. All the time he was introducing exponents of a counter-ideology, like R.D. Laing, Joan Littlewood, Adrian Mitchell and many others, to audiences brought up on the mandarin culture of the early 1960s.

The friends he had at this time were mostly poets, painters, film-makers, writers, actors, directors and a great many of the rich and trendy of the time. From them he got a sense of intellectual stimulation as well as the vicarious excitement of being up with the times. He marched to Aldermaston, campaigned for the legalisation of cannabis, even worked as a disc-jockey for a time. He ran a film-clip request programme that ran bits of Busby Berkeley routines for the first time on British TV, as well as other even less likely requests. Underneath it all, there was an awareness of the importance of this experience to the unspecified future. In his extraordinary zeal to do, and to learn, he often got involved in ventures which appeared merely flippant, or 'trendy lefty', or even just 'trendy'. But his instinct was always sure – 'we', that is the left, needed to be in amongst this lot, somewhere. We must be intimate with the specifics of the present.

In the middle 1960s three things happened which set him on the course that was to make use of all this, and to lead to his unique contribution to socialism in Britain. He married Pauline Boty, painter, actress and socialist; he started his literary agency; and, a little later, he started *The Black Dwarf* paper. Pauline's unbounded health, optimism and imagination concentrated his mind on the positives, on the creative. They moved in to a huge, cheap flat on Cromwell Road, and Clive decided to start an agency for writers. When Pauline was pregnant with their first child, it was discovered that she had cancer. She survived to give birth to a daughter, but soon after died. Her testament, which Clive read to a memorial gathering, was a message of undying hope, of solidarity with the oppressed, and of certainty about the future that gave all of us more than courage. Determination.

Through his agency, Clive helped many young writers to see their work in performance. Through his extraordinary combination of skills, experience, contacts in the media, allied with his clear perception of the need for socialism to do battle with the ruling ideology on its own ground, he became more than an agent. He became a polarising presence, a living expression of one element of the contradictions within the media. His personal contribution to the development of the work of Tony Garnett, Trevor Griffiths, Jim Allen, Jack Gold, Barry Hines, Ken Loach, Simon Gray, Dennis Potter and many others cannot be estimated. What became quite clear was that, because of Clive, the left-wing creative forces were not going to be stifled, or isolated. Not just from each other, but from the movement, and from action. A visit to his flat became synonymous with some form of action. Meetings, discussions, general chats, always ended up with something happening, somebody doing something. It's not hard to see why, for several years, a plain-clothes motor-car was unsubtly parked outside his door, with shifts changing regularly. He was often tempted to offer the occupants a cup of tea, but he didn't want to compromise them.

In amongst all this, at the beginning of May 1968, he started *The Black Dwarf*. To launch it, he got together the many skills he possessed, with those of friends like the poet Christopher Logue, writers David Mercer and Roger Smith, journalists and politicians like Tariq Ali, Robin Blackburn, Sheila Rowbotham and other members of the *New Left Review* Board, and the resources, financial, literary and agitational, of many others. He worked all day at the business of the agency, and most of many nights on the paper, and still managed to appear cool and laconic. The paper became a rallying-point for the non-aligned and the members of the smaller left groups, and it united people in action – in demonstrations, campaigns, in imaginative coups, in reporting the suppressed events of the time, and exploring the jungles beneath British society. It was, like everything else Clive did, of its time. But, precisely because of his close connection with events, he was never unaware of change. In reviewing the film *Woodstock* for *The Black Dwarf*, in 1970, he wrote:

> Of course events (unlike good films) can get overshadowed by other events. Earlier in the same week that I saw *Woodstock*, four students were murdered by the National Guard on the campus of the University of Kent, Ohio. The familiar liberal optimism of American youth, that the film catches so well, suddenly seemed hollow and sad. It was no longer a celebration of life, but a wake.
>
> Maybe there can never be another Woodstock. It ought to mark the end of the movement that has outrun its issues. Drugs, long hair and freaky music have become irrelevant. The questions now emerging are about the survival of capitalism, and those questions need thought as well as feeling.

Shortly after he wrote this, *The Black Dwarf* folded in order to merge with other groups to launch a new weekly socialist magazine, which ultimately became the ill-fated *7 Days*. There are many reasons still unanalysed, even unknown, for the disaster that this ambitious project turned into – indeed, it would make an interesting research project. But throughout, Clive fought for a paper that was readable, popular, efficient and effective. After its collapse he concentrated fully on his work in television, film and theatre.

In this, he became increasingly aware of the complexities of these media, and expert at handling them on behalf of the writers whose work he believed in. He also became increasingly aware of the need to combat the growing monolithic control systems of British television, and in a brilliant paper on Censorship delivered at the 1977 Edinburgh Television Festival, published in *Socialist Challenge*, No. 12, he combined energetic research with his own experience to make a concrete class analysis of the operation of the medium that will remain of great value in the years to come. Characteristically, he combined it with a demand for action: for the release from the BBC's forbidden shelves of certain material. He gained a partial victory. Action was taken.

Clive as a person is not an easy subject to write on with any great authority, even for those who knew him well. He could appear flippant, yet deeply serious, arbitrary, yet combatively consistent, flashy, yet modest, fashionable and faddish, but somehow not bothered by anything but the deepest issues, cynical, but naively optimistic, a fantasist, but profoundly realistic. His main qualities, however, were concerned with his political practice. He was an ideas-man of the left, a practical entrepreneur of the left, and a comrade dedicated to making the victory of his own class (which he considered inevitable) a worthwhile victory. He was a man of action.

In Western European capitalist society, the left can all too frequently dive back into the womb of dogma, its own history, its private language, its own internecine disputes, its own pietisms. Outside there is a world where people's minds are acted upon daily by the most cunning devices of advanced capitalist ideology. The economic movements, the social shifts may come and go, but they are seen through the eyes of the BBC News Editor, the *Sun* subeditor, the pages of the teenage magazine. Records can be sold in millions, films can be packaged and sold to millions of people before they are even made. Beer ads can penetrate the national consciousness, the views of a fascist clique can occupy the minds of the media-men and through them, the nation. But the left can still be disagreeing over trivia, and the great urgency of the need for a socialist society can be reduced by Robin Day to the squabbling of a few cranky nut-cases. In this situation there are two levels of attack for the left. One is the long-term, patient work of education and clarification of the relationship between events, properly the work in theory and organisation of the mass Marxist party that we haven't got. The other is to launch an immediate counter-offensive using the devices popularised by the ruling ideology, to question those very devices, that ideology. This is not easy, and contains many traps and pitfalls for those trying to practise it. But Clive Goodwin saw the need for this, and was quite sure of his own class position, and so could hack a trail through this jungle without fear. It was in this area that he was at his most creative, his most joyful. It gave him great satisfaction to dream up a striking headline, a good poster, a good name (like 7:84, which was his), or to place a good piece of socialist television in the right spot. To call him an ideas man for this is to demean the strength and seriousness of his purpose, but it was in this realm of counter-propaganda that he excelled.

He was also a practical entrepreneur of the left, in that he made things happen. In struggles at the point of industrial production, the left has a great history of effective struggle. The struggle at the point of ideological production is one that the left is all too often prepared to lose. Because to win requires skills and qualities which are all too similar to those of the enemy. Clive had these skills, and was secure enough in his personal convictions not to be afraid to disguise them in order to win a struggle, particularly one for the writers he believed in.

But he was also an entrepreneur in another sense. How often has the left in Britain fumbled and lost ground simply because no person or party had time or energy to call a meeting, to find a room, to phone a few people? This failing made Clive very impatient. He moved on events and issues in the directest possible way. And he did it with deceptive ease. In this area he will be greatly missed by many, in Britain and abroad.

A few weeks before he died, I went with Clive, Liz, and Howard Barker to Grunwick's picket-line to add what we could to that particular battle. It took place within a few yards of the place he was born, a fact he was proud of. It was entirely characteristic of Clive that he then insisted on taking us to look at a building he was angling to get a cheap lease on to turn into an Arts Centre for the area. He had never deserted the working people he grew up with, and was planning to go back with some of the things he had learnt and been excited by. It would have been an interesting place had he lived to see it through. It was also entirely characteristic that he went straight from the picket-line to a smart Italian restaurant to eat tagliatelle with a television producer who was interested in some work by one of his writers. The incongruity was the incongruity of our time. Neither struggle was diminished by the tagliatelle.

Anthony Barnett has written of Clive being the child of the victory of his own class. This was indeed his special quality.

For Clive, the presence of capitalism was absurd, and unbelievable. That the world should be like this was for him far more unlikely than the possibility of socialism, which he regarded as our proper human reality . . . So he stepped out into this world as if he was a member of that future one. As if, by some twist of fate he had been catapulted backwards into the wrong time, and now he had to earn a living in a society that could not possibly be his society.

That is true. He was very much of his time, minute to minute, year to year. But he carried the future with him, and the way towards it became more real for those who knew him.

7:84 was often accused of excluding writers other than myself. In England during the 1970s and 1980s we put on and toured plays by Trevor Griffiths, John Arden and Margaretta D'Arcy, Adrian Mitchell, David Edgar, Jim Sheridan, Steve Gooch and Shane Connaughton amongst others. Here's an account of what we did in England between 1976 and 1979:

WRECKERS & TREMBLING GIANT[40]

I'd been asking David Edgar to write for the company for years and eventually he came in and worked with the remainder of that company in communal discussion and produced *Wreckers*. I went into one discussion and everyone had got their subject they wished to have in the play and there was David trying to do this incredible synthesis about the docks, the rag trade, feminism, the Labour Party and Stalinism. Which is really what Steve Gooch had been led into . . . basically just a really nice guy conscious of democracy and over-conscious of trying to please everybody.

I was interested in doing a comic-strip play about capitalism and that was *Trembling Giant*. The whole idea of it was that capitalism was this dwarf which turned into a giant, became more powerful, prospered in the 18th and 19th centuries and then was shaken by wars, the workers rising up and the Red Giant of the East. Now this Giant was moribund and being propped up by the very workers whose blood he was drinking. Jim Sheridan who had come to see us when we were doing *Musgrave* and *Ballygombeen* came and directed that. But there's something about allegorical plays and working-class audiences that doesn't quite fit . . . they thought it was a bit tittish. If you want to say something about capitalism, say something, don't dress it up in all this paraphernalia. So I don't think *Trembling Giant* completely worked.

JOE OF ENGLAND

The next show was *Joe of England* from a basic notion of *Diary of a Young Man*. The show itself, I felt ultimately, was disappointing. We had a terrible time in rehearsal. The place was a room above a pub in King's Cross, and we couldn't get access in the morning because the guy who ran it wouldn't get up to open the door. Then we kept discovering we were locked in the room during the afternoons. At three o'clock he'd close the bar and lock us in because he had a huge Alsatian he let roam. So we ended up pissing out the window! It was a nightmare! We wasted weeks trying to create an atmosphere out of this lunacy! Eventually we got the whole thing vaguely organised, got the band in and the minute they started to play the police came round, summoned by the person next door. The police were banging on the door, which was locked and we were locked in the rehearsal room upstairs. It made concentration on the show absolutely impossible. We moved back to a church hall in Marylebone, but by this time it was a little late. It was scrappy in the end. I think on the whole it felt flimsy.

It was the year when Callaghanism and the heavy tread of the police federation running the government became apparent. *Joe of England* was a response to the nihilistic feeling one got at that time that politics was becoming pointless on a parliamentary level. They were beginning to sort out inflation but everyone was very fly; all socialist principles had been abandoned and the ability of Callaghan and his cabinet to absorb opposition and the militancy of the working class, cast people with any principles into a certain gloom and cynicism about the way people in the country were going. So to have this boy coming to the heart of the nation he is so proud of, to see it in need of a transplant, was what the play was about.

VANDALEUR'S FOLLY

We'd been talking to the Ardens about doing *Ballygombeen Bequest* again, which was now called *Little Grey Home in the West*. The case was sort of resolved, although it was never very clear to me how it had been resolved, except they had used the company's non-involvement in the case to their advantage. Somehow they had come to a settlement on this basis. When this happened we said 'come and talk to us', and we met about us doing *Little Grey Home in the West*. They said, why don't you do our new play about the co-operative at Ralahine on the condition that we direct it? We had a meeting of the policy group, and I put forward the proposition that the Ardens might make a mess of it, they might make a triumph of it. Either way they deserved the right to do it. We had tremendous respect for them. We placed the company entirely in their hands for the period of that production. The limitations on their actions were those that were inevitable: that we played a certain number of dates to a certain kind of audience, the amount of money and the amount of organisational input we could offer. We said they had no need to take anyone from 7:84 and that the decision was entirely theirs as to how to proceed, who to take on, where to rehearse, etc.

John wrote a draft of the play while Margaretta was in New York, and we were very excited about it. Margaretta came back and she went off with John to re-write what he had done. It was very long, but it was very exciting. It was called a melodrama and was written in this kind of rollicking doggerel that went along at a cracking pace. During the writing process the company was being put together. All were interviewed by 7:84, John and Margaretta. We were there because we were part of the contract with the actor, to explain what the company did, what the life was, etc. The company was put together and the production went into rehearsal.

When I saw it all the natural spontaneous contribution of the actors was being taken out and replaced by a kind of staccato, fast, rather flat delivery – nobody seemed to be able to pause to develop a moment or a character. As the awareness came that it was still very long, lots of cuts happened and I think a lot of the cuts came at the wrong places and some of the most effective moments were cut in almost a masochistic way. It had the effect of hitting the audience repeatedly, like a boxer hitting a punch bag. The audiences got rapidly tired, though intrigued, then more tired and slightly bored, then more tired and a bit angry. By the end, most audiences were left indifferent, a great pity because I thought the play was good and the company were very talented.

The problems that arose were many, but the basic problem was that the show was not getting the kind of response it deserved from the critics or from student or working-class audiences. It was hitting people very hard and without a great deal of seduction. In a way that was pretty well how Margaretta could have been feeling about the English audience. She was pretty angry with English people, by the way things were going in Ireland and the absence of any passionate response from the English audience, the English working class, the English left. I think she saw it as part of a campaign to startle English audiences into a realization that there was a history to the Irish troubles and that they ought to care a bit more about them.

The other problem that arose with that tour was the question of the display, which initially was going to be a display of photographs and material related to Ralahine, co-operatives in general and Robert Owenite co-operatives in particular. What in fact turned out to be the display was a whole lot of Provisional IRA posters. They may not have been called Provisional IRA posters but that is what they were. They were up for the first performance, but apparently they were pretty soon damaged . . . indeed thrown away by audiences. One of Margaretta's main complaints was the company refused to put up their posters, which is absolutely not true. The other thing that went wrong was a very contentious crossing from Liverpool to Dublin. I was not actually on the boat, so I'm not able to bear testimony either way, but it did sound odd.

It was the first time off the company had for something like three and a half weeks. They got on the boat and as far as I can see went to the bar. Margaretta thought this was absolutely outrageous. It was in some way the

English indicating their reaction to Ireland by getting drunk, belittling somehow the seriousness of approaching Ireland. The result of all this, plus some incidents on the quayside when we were supposed to be met and they didn't turn up, made Margaretta extremely annoyed. From that point on Margaretta was disgusted by 7:84 and decided that we were the enemy. 7:84 was fascist or neo-fascist, certainly an anti-Irish organisation. The very sad thing is that *The Ballygombeen Bequest* had been a brilliant success, particularly the production of it. Seven years later they found signs of incipient neo-fascism in it, which they didn't show any signs of pointing out at the time. It was a great rewriting of history.

In Scotland, David Anderson wrote a musical show, which basically was all-singing, occasionally dancing, very little talking. When I came into rehearsal and the entire company was now a band, all playing rock music, I realised we were no longer a straight theatre company: we'd always had songs and a lot of music, but this was a new, interesting and different kind of theatre. The band formed themselves into Wildcat Stage Productions, with the help, in their inaugural year, of half of 7:84's grant. I went to Cambridge for a break, and delivered the lectures that became the book, A Good Night Out.

I should cite at length a kind of summing-up lecture I gave in Cambridge, an attempt to work out what we'd all been doing or trying to do for the previous ten years. It was published in Theatre Quarterly *as a response to David Edgar, but it was never written as such. Indeed David arrived and spoke after I had delivered my piece, and I was quite taken aback by what he was saying. I thought it wrong, and said so (without, I'm glad to say, losing David's friendship).*

THE THEORY AND PRACTICE OF POLITICAL THEATRE[41]

Several important features of the relationship between the economic structure of society and its literary self-expression arise from a consideration of Raymond Williams's work. One is that the directness or determining nature of this relationship is thrown into question. Literature, which I take here to include theatre, can often appear to have an autonomous development of its own, connected only tangentially with the modes of production, ownership of the means of production, and the state of play in the class war. This development can be affected by internal factors of uneven development, by other elements in the social and cultural life of the society – even by individual talent, or the absence of it.

Secondly, in any period there are likely to be three main elements of literary production – the residual, which draws its sources from a previous period but is still effectively alive in the present; the dominant, which exercises hegemony over the period culturally; and the emergent element, by which, and I quote, 'new meanings and values, new practices, new relationships and kinds of relationships are constantly being created. But it is exceptionally difficult to distinguish between those which are really elements of some new phase of the dominant culture, and those which are substantially alternative or oppositional to it – emergent in the strict sense, rather than the merely novel' (Raymond Williams, *Marxism and Literature*, p. 128).

It is important that when we examine the political role of theatre in a society, that both the theatre, the society, and their relationship should be seen in all their complexity.

Three Sectors of British Theatre

There are three different sectors of theatre, each with its own mini-ideology, each with its own relationship with the changing economic base of our society, and each with its own structure: one, the commercial, or West End theatre; two, the orthodox subsidised theatres: the subsidised establishment: The National and Royal Shakespeare companies, the main reps, etc.; and thirdly, the fringe, or touring theatre.

Each of these sectors corresponds very loosely to Williams's categories. The commercial or West End theatre can be seen as in many senses residual, but active. In structure it resembles a nineteenth-century small capitalist enterprise, with investors, with a management, employees on the lowest possible wages, and a product which it hopes to market for a profit. It is a high-risk investment in theory, but can offer compensatorily high dividends.

The central contradiction in this category is the old one between the social or group-effort means of production and the private ownership of those means. This is alleviated to some extent by allowing star actors, writers, directors, designers, sometimes lighting designers, to take a small percentage of the gross income thus making them junior partners in the enterprise, and by the exercise of the traditional theatre ideologies – 'the show must go on' plus the obvious appeal to the vanity of the individual actor or writer of becoming famous through involvement in a successful show, this 'fame' is also an economic incentive, as it often leads to film and television engagements which pay a lot of money.

The ideology contained within the product of this system is usually residual in the extreme. Indeed, nostalgia is one of its main preoccupations, as a glance through the West End listings of any newspaper will show. That again derives from its audience, since the West End audience is to a great extent the bourgeoisie and professional classes of London. But not entirely. A large and important sector which is working-class – the coach parties from Northampton for the big musicals and the comedies with TV stars, edging into a world of unreality for the evening. These last two sectors of the audience are drawn in by a massive publicity machine, which promotes shows like motor cars. The end result of the whole process can be a truly fabulous profit. Residual it may be, but active it certainly is.

The West End was once the dominant sector of theatre, but this has changed. The dominant sector of theatre now, financially as well as ideologically, is the subsidised establishment; the National Theatre – the British Leyland of showbusiness – the RSC, the major reps like Nottingham and Sheffield which echo in style, structure, product and ideology their big brothers on the South Bank, at Stratford and the Aldwych [where the RSC had its London base]; and following trimly in their footsteps the lesser reps, the art theatres, the studios and the more pretentious of the amateur companies.

The 'correspondence' between the changed economic structure of British capitalism, now using a servile state machine to prop itself up, and the economic structure of these theatres, propped up by millions of pounds of public money, is immediately apparent.

As power-structures, these theatres reflect the nationalised industries: they are capitalist structures. But without the need to make profits. What they need to make is the individual reputation of the new masters – and to balance their books, give or take a few million pounds. Sometimes they have a spurious air of democracy, even worker-representation on their boards, and, to enhance their reputation, sometimes they even tackle bold subjects, like the Russian Revolution, safe in the hands of Robert Bolt [whose play about the subject, *State of Revolution,* was staged at the National Theatre in 1977].

But they are dominant in the sense that their product is recognised generally as what we must all aspire to appreciate. Or create. Or imitate. Ninety-five per cent of British actors, directors, and so on would like to work in these institutions. And when we think of the highest levels of theatre art in this country they are what come to mind – even though they may lapse from time to time below their own exalted standards.

In what are now known in this context as the 'regions' the audiences can have a certain amount of social variety, but those which are generally aimed at, which lurk at the back of the director's mind, are from the cultured, higher-educated professional or managerial sector – the AB readership, on whose behalf the reviewers assess the suitability of the production.

The Nature of the Fringe

All this so far has been very schematic and left a great deal unsaid. The first and most important omission is the recognition that within both the West End and the subsidised establishment there are contradictions. There are elements of class struggle – economic, social and, vitally, ideological. Both sectors are of necessity open to new blood, new ideas; both contain people of good-will, anxious to encourage change. Even socialist change. Although their overall effect, if they succeed, is all too often to turn the genuinely oppositional into the merely novel, they are by no means monolithic.

All this preamble is by way of setting out the necessary context for examining the third element, roughly corresponding to the *emergent* element, in our theatre: the 'political' theatre, usually found on the fringe, touring, or in the smaller subsidised companies. There is little point in talking about the fringe as a whole – its components are too various, their *raisons d'être* varying from principled Marxist interventionism, via simply providing employment, to unpaid exhibitionism.

But some features of the fringe are significant. Firstly, it is organised in groups or companies, created by an act of will or initiative. When that original impetus dies or fails to grow the group usually dies, unlike the larger institutions. Secondly, most groups active on the fringe draw subsidy from the state, via the Arts Council, or from local government via Regional Arts Associations, or a combination of both. Most are dependent on this for survival. Thirdly, most groups are small enough to see themselves as organised on a co-operative or democratic basis. Fourthly, most fringe groups aim at audiences outside those which regularly attend the West End or the National Theatre, and, fifthly, most fringe groups demand an application of their member's talents and a degree of involvement different from that of the other sectors of the theatre.

All of these features have positive and negative potentialities. At the negative extreme they could create an egomaniac subsidy-sucking pseudo-democratic group of freaks, performing rubbish for an elite of similar freaks. On the other hand, these features do offer the possibility of a highly principled, creative, Marxist cultural intervention, giving back to the public something valuable for a small amount of public money. Organised in a genuine democracy, demanding new skills and imaginative efforts to create a new kind of culture of the highest standards, for and of the working class, so enriching the Labour Movement and helping it to make its ultimate victory a worthwhile victory.

It is because of this potential that the fringe theatre must be taken seriously by Marxist theatre workers, critics, and audiences, it is because of this potential that I would like to categorise it as the emergent element of theatre in Britain today and examine its theory and its practice.

Defining the Theatrical Contribution

I would like to look more closely at the three main areas of activity of political theatre in a capitalist society as I've described them. The first was the challenge to the hegemony of bourgeois ideology within the theatre institutions themselves. Trevor Griffiths has tried to do this with two plays at the national theatre; David Edgar with *Destiny* at the Aldwych; John Arden and Margaretta D'Arcy with *The Island of the Mighty*, also at the

Aldwych; Edward Bond, Howard Brenton, David Hare, with plays at the National, the Aldwych and the major reps. The plays of Brecht have been used for the same purpose, and some of Sean O'Casey's.

It is no doubt useful to the general movement of socialist ideas to have them aired prominently, to enter the national (or at least the metropolitan) consciousness, on a certain level of seriousness, and occasionally to draw into those theatres certain politically conscious members of the Labour Movement. But, good as these works may be, the process is not contributing to the creation of a new, genuinely oppositional theatre. They become 'product' and the process remains the same; they are in constant danger of being appropriated in production by the very ideology they set out to oppose.

Poor Bertolt Brecht has suffered greatly in this way. But he is dead. The Ardens raised hell at the Aldwych five years ago for precisely this reason. In Trevor Griffiths's *The Party*, at the National, the character of an old Marxist revolutionary from Glasgow was taken over by Lord Olivier, and became a vehicle for a star to communicate with his admirers.

The process, the building, the wages structure, the Publicity machine, the free interval drinks budget, all these can turn opposition into novelty. But it could be short-sighted to deny the value of trying. This challenge to the dominance of bourgeois ideology on its own ground is important; it creates allies for the movement and is a weapon to use, and we are not in a position to throw any weapon away.

Outside the Institutions

At certain periods in the past, some of the bolder companies, like the Liverpool Everyman, the Victoria in Stoke, the Playhouse in Nottingham, the Northcott in Exeter, the Belgrade in Coventry, even the Royal Court in London have embarked on policies of presenting socialist plays. Some of these companies have tried to make their theatres attractive to working-class audiences, some have even created a style of presentation that is anti-bourgeois – of building a relationship between the theatre, the performers, and the local working class that makes the theatre more the property of its audience. Here I think Peter Cheeseman's work and Alan Dossor's work in Stoke and Liverpool should be mentioned.

But few of these theatres have escaped from the power structures of capitalism. All, to qualify for subsidy from the Arts Council and the local authority, have to have a board of directors, generally local worthies and councillors. They appoint an administrator and an Artistic Director, both of whom, while having a certain amount of autonomy need board approval for their plans, and answer to the board for their success or failure. Within this framework, the Artistic Director can consult members of the company on the future programme, can have company meetings to sort out problems in a communal spirit and so on, but few actually do this.

It is to the other two areas that I would like to turn. They are the areas that I am most familiar with and have thought a great deal about, both concern making theatre for working-class audiences, first and foremost; and both present immense questions of theory and massive problems of practice.

The first area is that of the direct interventionist theatre-piece – polemical, openly political, and whose avowed aim is to gain support for a particular party or position inside the working class, and among its potential allies. The support demanded can be for a strike, a struggle, fund-raising, or a piece of legislation; or against a piece of legislation; or concerned with a more general issue, like grasping the salient features of a particular firm, or the way ACAS [Advisory Conciliation and Arbitration Service] works, or the way racism works, or sexism, or the press; or it can be support for an even more general attitude to, and understanding of, the operation of (say) multinational corporations, the role of the British army in the north of Ireland, or indeed the way the Labour government operates.

The problems which arise with this kind of theatre are, of course, immense. I am not particularly bothered with the aesthetic categories of the thing. I spend too long arguing with actors who bring abstract, received notions of what is right and wrong, and proper and improper, correct and incorrect in the theatre to spend any more time on worrying about the correct categorisation of style, convention, and the consistency thereof: it works if the audience get it with the same sense of wonder and rightness and relevance that you as a group got it with – if the instinctive reaction is not jarred by any incongruous worries, if the subterranean connections are made and the scene itself is gripping, for good reasons. That's the end of aesthetics. These problems solve themselves.

The real problems with this kind of theatre lie in three main areas. One has to do with the actual organisation of the company, the second with the nature of the people who work with it, and the third with political organisation on a national level – which leads on to a host of others.

Organising the Company

It is the nature of any fringe theatre group that its membership changes constantly, and hence the contradiction that the new membership of that company may wish to redefine its objectives and aims. There will be conflict and a certain amount of ineffectuality about the company if these two forces – the original impetus and the redefinition – are not worked out on a proper political level.

So why not have the same company all the time? This is a practical problem. People have to survive and many people find that they can't take it. To make an intervention you need consistency of purpose and identity and a growing relationship with the audience, but to stay alive as individuals you need variety, breaks, time to read, time to wash your socks, time to see other people's work, and so on. To make a democracy within that sort of shifting situation, you run a very good chance of diluting your interventionist possibilities.

The Needs of the Performers

The second problem area involves individual company members. The basic attitude of socialist performers, as far as I'm concerned, should be that they are on the same level as the audience, they are there to do things for the audience because it's their job and because they have the skills. They can play the fiddle or sing or show other characters clearly. They can time a gag. They can make an exit. But at the end of that they can be the same again.

It's like watching a plumber work. He comes in, has a cup of tea, has a fag. And then when it comes to the actual plumbing, he is on, it is his turn, he does it, and everybody has to watch it because he knows what he is doing. At the end of it, he puts the tools back in the bag, has a cup of tea, has another fag, and goes, i.e. returns to exactly the same level as the people whose pipes he is mending. Or whatever.

To take a more specific example, I think of the fiddler in the Scottish 7:84 company, whom I have watched often in pubs, who would sort of lean over the bar and talk to everybody, so that they soon know he's a fiddler, and he knows he's a fiddler, and he knows they're going to say 'give us a tune', and they know that they're going to say 'give us a tune', so eventually he will be persuaded to pick up his fiddle and play, and he will play for an hour and a half, pure magic. Then he will put the fiddle away again and not vanish behind a curtain, or go to his dressing room, or wait for the chauffeur-driven car to appear at the door, but have another pint; he's generally pissed by then anyway.

Coping with 'People Problems'

The average actor's mentality is a product of late romanticism, a hangover from the 1890s; a product of a concept of art as ultimate sensibility. There's a huge amount of bullshit taught and spoken in drama schools and in the reps on this mystique of the actor, the mystique of the artistic sensibility, and similarly a great deal of bullshit, mystique and late romanticism about the roles of the director and writer. There seems to be an unwritten rule that to be truly creative in the theatre you must be a pain in the arse, otherwise nobody knows that you're being truly creative.

First then, there's the problem of people subscribing to the mystiques and the bullshit. Secondly, there are a lot of people with no interest in entertainment skills, or in developing further other skills. Thirdly, lower middle-class actors don't think the working class will appreciate their art. Fourthly, a lot of actors from the working class have used acting as a way out of the working class and into the ranks of the middle class, and they don't fancy risking falling back again. They'd rather run an antique shop in Barnes – quite a few do. Fifthly, there's the problem of individuals who have no politics, are not interested in politics, but who have the necessary skills. (This problem in some ways is preferable to that of the individuals who have strong populist or anarchist politics, but who think they are Marxists.) Sixthly, there is the problem of the socialist theatre worker who joins the company and becomes engrossed in political theory, and particularly in the organisation of the company, and gets turned in on the company, seeing it as a socialist utopia and forgetting about the actual intervention and the audience, even! Seventh, many find it difficult to make criticism and self-criticism on a high political level, to see the politics of acting – for example, the way a half thought-out performance can have a political meaning. Eighthly, is the desire among a lot of actors to create a sensitive performance and preserve it, come what may. And if it fails the audience is to blame. There are a lot of people who become actors because they want to be liked, and this presents a great deal of difficulty, either when you are in the position of having to criticise or be criticised by your fellow-workers, or when you are in a position of having to perform a character with a certain amount of detachment, or a character who is not likeable.

Pros and Cons of Party Affiliation

Should a theatre group belong to a party? There are many reasons why they should. First, to be part of something which provides a political channel of action, assuming that people are agitated by what you say. There's a possibility with a political party of follow-up to make the involvement of the audience more permanent, and not just getting everybody going and then leaving them to it, it raises the possibility of the audience becoming active, becoming the actors, not passively receiving. There is a further benefit in belonging to a party: within the group itself there will be more coherence or identity of purpose. But there is a practical problem, which is the present situation of the left in this country. The heritage of labourism means that the mass party of the working class is Labour. The heritage of Stalin and Stalinism is that the Communist Party is feared and is characterised as totalitarian, dictatorial, by many people in the working class and in society as a whole.

Now if a company openly identified with the position of the other groups – the Communist Party of Great Britain [CPGB], the Workers' Revolutionary Party [WRP] or the Socialist Workers' Party [SWP], there would immediately be a tendency for the audience to become a faction and for the others to stay away. The WRP at one point put on shows and some of them were very good indeed. I saw one in St. Helen's, for example, which was about the English revolution in 1649, which was very well done, but was attended by only a very small handful, of whom I would imagine 90% were WRP members, most of whom had seen it before because they had been attending all the other performances.

The question of affiliation to a political party or organisation raises the issue of what theatre 'can and should do', the single-issue agitprop piece very rarely actually persuades anybody intellectually. Rather it is a show of support – part of a publicity machine. Evidence of energy in that cause which impresses the ditherers and the 'don't knows' in the audience. It can relate a single issue to wider questions, thus informing the audience, but it rarely changes their prejudices.

In some single-issue pieces there is an organisation, a strike committee, a local group, a tenants' association, or such, towards which to direct the audience's further action. The political follow-up is then structured anyway; but in the wider-issue agitational pieces (particularly the ideological agitational pieces) about the repression of women, about the role of the police, or the army, or the multinationals, or labourism, or racism or fascism, the problems do indeed become more complex. If the ultimate aim of the group is the strengthening of the organisations of the working class surely there should be some organic link with one of those organisations, and one which has clear political aims?

The answer to this question is 'yes', but no political fringe group that I know of is organically linked with a party at this moment. As far as I know, Red Ladder, Belt and Braces, the two 7:84 Companies, Pirate Jenny, The Women's Theatre Group, Monstrous Regiment, North-West Spanner, Common Stock, Recreation Ground, and so on are all politically independent. Yet all are attempting to raise consciousness and to agitate on issues which demand political follow-up and coherence, which they can't provide. Does this then make them politically ineffective? The answer is in my opinion 'no', but it makes it more difficult for them to be politically effective.

What we have is a Labour Movement, which is increasingly moving apart from its national bureaucracy. On shop stewards' committees, trades councils, in certain union branches, on action groups, on solidarity groups, in the universities, in tenants' associations, on community projects, in women's groups, and of course within the Marxist parties and groups, and even within the Labour Party there exists, on the ground, a massive and not entirely incoherent number of militants who are closely involved with the everyday struggles of the working class.

They combine across party and sectarian lines on certain issues, broad and narrow; and many have a strong practical sense of the way towards socialism. Their support within the working class is volatile, which is not surprising since the moment they show any sign of winning a struggle they become the most reviled group of individuals in society, turned by the screeches of the media and the major parties into the lepers of the Welfare

State. They interconnect in action. On a theoretical level there are huge disparities between them, and frequent political clashes, but they exist as the real core of the left Labour Movement, and it is the failure of left-wing politics in Britain that they do not have a unified party to assist them.

Given this situation, it is indeed better and more effective for a socialist theatre group to relate to this cross section of people than to one or other of the factions who are bidding to control them. These are the people who bother to organize the shows, to get an audience in, to carry the can if the evening is a flop. They are also our major critics and our major sources of feedback, they recognise the value of raising the awareness of their work-mates and neighbours, not only on single economic issues, but also on broader issues which involve political and class-consciousness.

A good series of events in an area can help to raise the level of militancy and can in the process give confidence and a sense of depth to the move-ment. A good show can and should also cheer these people up and help them to feel in touch with a larger, if loosely defined, socialist movement, this is one practical reason why I don't think that theatre groups do or should join with a party.

Single and Complex Issues

I would like to develop one other aspect concerning the wider-issue pieces which form the bulk of the output of the political companies. The broader the issue raised, the more complex the argument becomes, and the more complex the statement of the play consequently needs to be. Major ques-tions of form present themselves; it's not enough simply to organise an argu-ment schematically in theatrical terms, you are no longer simply dressing a piece of agitation with theatrical devices, you are trying to stretch the possibilities of theatre itself. In short, what in purely agitational terms began as a broad single issue has led to the need for a new kind of theatre.

In this situation, received notions of what theatre is begin to creep in, and to inflect the thinking of the writers and the company, and the director, towards the values of 'real theatre'. It is important to identify these received notions as the source of much confusion: 'real theatre' in this sense is the term for the dominant mode of theatre – in our case, that of the subsidised establishment. The ideological values of that theatre are ultimately based on the ideology of a class structure and a management structure and an audience which are all opposed to the values of socialist structures, socialist theatre, and the working class: the demands of working-class audiences for a new kind of theatre cannot be satisfied by populist or oeuvrierist inflections of an old, bourgeois kind of theatre.

Clearly, to fulfil the role of agitation on an ideological level within the working class requires a certain amount of attention to working-class forms of entertainment. I believe that in spite of the immense difficulties in specifying them, there are important and significant differences between the cultural values and traditions of the working class and those of the middle class and there are equally important differences between their respective theatre values and traditions.

In Scotland, I used one of the old silkie legends, about the seal-wife who leaves her coat behind, and whose husband hides it to stop her going back to the sea, to put together a Highland show about what was going on around the shores of, and in, the Minch. We had one of our best tours with The Catch *(or* Red Herrings in the Minch*), and the audiences were bigger than even those for* The Cheviot. *Indeed it was a feature of our tours that the audiences continued to grow right to the bitter end. This may explain why we get a little tired of the attitude which goes: after* The Cheviot, *mere repetition. The later shows were never published, which may explain their comparative lack of attention.*

THE CATCH[42]

From the Hebrides to the Scilly Isles, the story is much the same. Decisions are made, which affect the lives of whole communities, in the name of some higher authority, which in turn will invoke the 'national interest' or our international commitments, or simply 'government policy', to over-rule any local opposition. This tendency to authoritarianism from the centre (i.e. London) has been greatly increased since May 1979. Grinning Mr Heseltine [Secretary of State for the Environment 1979–1983] now dictates to local authorities exactly what their policies must be, regardless of their pledges to their electors . . . The police take orders from nobody, elected or appointed, . . . The lofty 'consultation processes' of the Scottish Office are increasingly just another method of forcing the decisions of the ruling faction of the Tory party down the gullet of the Scottish people, who did not vote for the Tories in the first place . . . The Ministry of Defence seems to operate by making its commitment to NATO first, and then bullying the rest of us into accepting their consequences whether we like them or not . . . and the whimsical dictates of the incompetents who run the EEC are allowed to outweigh the urgent needs of the very people whom they are supposed to be serving . . . And the vast array of secret police activities, phone-tapping, Special Branch infiltration, agents provocateurs, and of secret government controls of the media, and of all the democratic processes is all controlled from the centre to make sure that the other central decisions go through without any serious opposition.

In this climate, what began, when we first discussed doing a 'fishing play' back in 1975, as a historical piece, has now become a wander through a chamber of grotesque horrors. As we looked around the shores of the

Minch, we saw increasing evidence of the insulting way this part of the world is treated by the rulers of the military-industrial complex.

Stornoway airport, for example, is the centre of an incredible operation of cynicism and duplicity. The Ministry of Defence, acting as agents of NATO, first of all pretended that all they wanted was to extend the runway for the new generation of planes at a cost of £6 million. By 1981, this had grown to an enormous up-grading programme, costing £40 million. Whereas NATO use of the airport was strenuously denied in 1976, it is now being sold as of the utmost strategic importance.

The conflicts between local desires and central government needs is an ancient one. There are many ways of resolving them, from medieval clan warfare to Fascistic dictatorship. What is clearly needed is a process of resolving these conflicts openly, with the full range of information being available to all; an honest, unbiased, unprejudiced hearing of all points of view; and a final decision taken with the community involved fully represented on the decision-making body. Until such time as this happens, there is little wonder that riots go on in the streets, and in people's minds, the length of the land. For we are told that we must believe in our democratic society, be proud of it, be part of it. And almost every action taken by central government since 1979 has been designed to exclude us from this very democracy. And when we cease to believe in it, then the door is wide open.

My Cambridge lectures produced a book – A Good Night Out *– which has remained in print for the last twenty years, but which was met at the time with some fairly aggressive reviewing. I was invited by* The Guardian *to respond. I did:*

LIVING DANGEROUSLY[43]

To write any book today based on the existence of class is a dangerous undertaking. To write a book of theory about the theatre, and then to continue to make theatre, is hazardous in the extreme. To do both – and to question the right of white, well-fed, sensitive but sophisticated literary critics to sole ownership of the definition of theatre or, indeed, Art – is tantamount to suicide while the balance of the mind is disturbed. It is certainly guaranteed to invoke the urbane howls of Irving Wardle in *The Times*, and the *Guardian*'s intrepid reporter (otherwise known as theatre critic of Scotland's own *Sunday Standard*), Ms Joyce McMillan.

To go further and to accept an invitation to reply is clearly crazed, kamikaze behaviour. Nevertheless to remain silent is to appear to accept, as a people's artist should, the just criticisms of those Zhdanovs of the bourgeoisie. Therefore one must reply and be damned.

To take the most trivial first. Ms McMillan omits from her less than frank piece some essential background information. At a meeting a few weeks before she wrote it, at which I was guest speaker and she was chairperson, she was savaged by a large audience for the ineptitude and class bias of her own reviews. Furthermore, her own views on my book and the work of 7:84 were thoroughly exposed as uninformed and inaccurate.

Shortly afterwards Ms McMillan announced she was going to write an article for the *Guardian* comparing 7:84 with the Actors' Touring Company's production of *Don Quixote*. Now ATC (London) were touring the Highlands inspired by the success of, and with a great deal of initial help and practical encouragement from, 7:84. Their presence in Fort William could well be seen as a political consequence of our work. Still, I predicted that ATC would be used by Ms McMillan as a stick to beat us with - and that was what she did.

Ms McMillan came for two days to Wester Ross to see 7:84's production of *The Catch*. In Ullapool and Achiltibuie, integrity poised, she scanned the faces of the audience for the 'shining, wistful look in their eyes', which *Don Quixote* had aroused, and lo, she was disappointed. She found only that they sang 'obediently', when asked. Stakhanov would be proud of them. The main plank of her argument is that *The Catch* is artistically weak, which is somehow due to my theories. And she elicited the unlikely statement from her Ullapool landlady that 'Wester Ross still has a Tory MP. They [7:84] need to try something new, something different.' Car bombs, perhaps?

Ms McMillan's opinion poll (showing 100% of those asked sadly shaking their heads) could easily be discredited. There are many letters in 7:84's office, Harold Hobson's review in the *TLS*, a thousand unsolicited handshakes, and not a few shining eyes – perhaps not so 'wistful' – as well as John Fowler's account of the Stornoway performance in the *Glasgow Herald*, to prove her perceptions wrong, her methods discredited, and her conclusions valueless.

If *The Catch* is less exquisitely wrought than *Don Quixote* it is due to my failure to write a masterpiece, not to the theories in my book. We, too, relentlessly pursue 'skill in performance, sensitivity to the audience's response, complete honesty and integrity in making aesthetic decisions'. For me, these are neither in theory nor in practice secondary to the political and class orientation of my work. Many people find them in what we do: I am sorry that Ms McMillan, for whatever reasons, does not. She should have come to Stornoway: we were all sea-sick. Wonderful copy.

The Times, also noted for the complete honesty and integrity of its aesthetic decisions, printed a curious piece by Irving Wardle, in which my critical attitude to the social aspects of the work of the Royal Court in the early Sixties was used to line me up with those philistines in the Arts Council of England who are making threatening noises at the Royal Court (and 7:84 England).

In a disgraceful travesty of my own position, he accuses me of ingratitude to George Devine (whom I knew, loved, worked and argued with), of wanting to close the Royal Court (complete and despicable rubbish), and of not recognising that the English Stage Company fought for the subsidy system of which 7:84 is a beneficiary.

What the bilious Mr Wardle does not know is that a few years back, while on an Arts Council Re-Assessment Committee, not alone, but against heavy odds, I fought tooth and nail to keep the Royal Court open. In trying to define the work of the Court in class terms, I may have upset Mr Wardle for some reason, but I was not trying to close it down. He, on the other hand, was giving more than a nudge and a wink to the Drama Panel in the direction of dispensing with these 'stultifying' studio theatres and fringe venues outside London. It must be nice to be a white, well-fed, sensitive but sophisticated literary critic living in the metropolis.

While Mr Wardle failed to engage at all with any of the central ideas of my book and grossly misrepresented those ideas he did latch on to, Michael Billington, in these columns, did at least show some seriousness of purpose in tackling what I was struggling to say.

Alarmed by his attack on what he took to be my belief that my way was the only way of making theatre, I hurried to the book, to discover that this could perhaps be inferred from my over-polemical assertions. I hasten to assure him and your readers that such a Proletcult absolutism, nay, 'partisan polarity', is a million miles from my belief, practice or nature. In fact, I quote Sanchez Vazquez, who 'warns against the dangers of decreeing that there is only one way of, say, making theatre'. I then add: 'We must be certain that there are many.' That seems pretty straightforward.

More alarming, perhaps, is that Michael Billington took from my book the idea that I make a fetish of working-class culture, and am prepared to jettison the Western European literary and theatrical heritage because it is 'too posh for the working class'. Even Joyce McMillan recognises that this is not my desire. I should be a hypocrite and a fool if it were.

But I do suggest that writing, like the other skills of the theatre, 'has to be performed not only with a command of the traditional methods, but also with a critical and creative attitude to those methods when put to serving new purposes'. Just like T.S. Eliot, I am involved in re-ordering that inheritance in my own private pantheon, giving Langland more importance than perhaps he deserves, elevating Skelton and Wyatt over Surrey and Spenser, Ben Jonson over Webster, Bunyan over Dryden, Gay over Sheridan, finding the more intellectual aspects of the Romantics more exciting than their lusher, more sensual pieces.

None of this may show in my work, but it is an essential condition of working within a rich tradition that one re-defines it constantly. In throwing out the murky bathwater of Stoppard and Pinter, I do not intend to jettison the baby of European culture: I need it, and use it, daily.

Billington's most interesting thrust, which I see no reason to parry, is that many working-class people enjoy productions like the National's *Passion*. So they do, and why not? They also enjoy good productions of Chekhov, Molière, Shakespeare and Sophocles. It would be good if they got more of them, done with the same vigour, imagination and skill as Bill Bryden brought to *The Passion*, and done somewhere that they are likely to be able to see them.

Meanwhile, *The Catch* continues to tour the west and east coasts of Scotland; 7:84 England's *One Big Blow* leaves the Dublin Festival for the Welsh valleys, then goes to Sweden and, if it's of any interest, my next show is a version of Aristophanes' *Ecclesiazusae*, with music by Mikroutsikos: I hope this doesn't disappoint those people who are busy building an image of me as an uncouth, philistine Rasputin – (there is only one quality of Rasputin's that I aspire to: a certain resilience against assassination attempts).

One of the most vehemently argued-over passages in A Good Night Out *was my description of the demands of a working-class audience as opposed to a middle-class audience:*

A GOOD NIGHT OUT [44]

The first difference is in the area of *directness*. A working-class audience likes to know exactly what you are trying to do or say to it. A middle-class audience prefers obliqueness and innuendo. It likes to feel the superiority of exercising its perceptions which have been so expensively acquired, thus opening up areas of ambiguity and avoiding any stark choice of attitude. In *Lay Off*, for example, a show with the English 7:84, we spoke straight to audiences about what we thought of the multinationals. In a factory occupation where we played the show at Swinton, just outside Manchester, there was no problem whatsoever. It was appreciated that we said what we thought. Equally in Murray Hall in East Kilbride there was no problem. But after a performance in London in Unity Theatre, a socialist publisher came up to me and said, 'I don't like to be told what to think, I preferred *Fish in the Sea*.' Now the national press who saw the show felt patronised, but not the working class of Manchester because they knew we were saying what we thought and they were prepared to weigh it up. Some critics even said they thought we were patronising the working class; but in fact, they were, because the working-class audiences have minds of their own and they like to hear what your mind is.

Second, *comedy*. Working-class audiences like laughs; middle-class audiences in the theatre tend to think laughter makes the play less serious. On comedy working-class audiences are rather more sophisticated. Many working-class people spend a lot of their lives making jokes about themselves and their bosses and their world as it changes. So the jokes that a working-class audience likes have to be good ones, not old ones; they require a higher level of comic skill. Comedy has to be sharper, more perceptive, and more deeply related to their lives. The Royal Court audience, for example, doesn't laugh very much, and most comedy in the West End is mechanical or weak; in a club, it is vital to have good jokes and sharp comedy. The nature of much working-class comedy is sexist, racist, even anti-working class. We all know the jokes about big tits and pakis and paddies and the dockers and the strikers – there are millions of jokes current in these areas. Therefore, without being pompous about it, comedy has to be critically assessed. The bourgeois comedy, largely of manners, or of intellect, tends to assume there is a correct way of doing things and that that is the way of the average broad-minded commuter or well-fed white, etc. Working-class comedy is more anarchic and more fantastical, the difference between the wit and wisdom of the Duke of Edinburgh and Ken Dodd.

Third, *music*. Working-class audiences like music in shows, live and lively, popular, tuneful and well-played. They like beat sometimes, more than the sound of banks of violins, and they like melody above all. There's a long submerged folk tradition which is still there. It emerged recently as a two million sale for a song called 'Mull of Kintyre'; but standards of performance are demanded in music and many individuals in working-class audiences are highly critical and have high standards about the music in shows. But the music is enjoyable for itself, for emotional release, and for the neatness of expression of a good lyric, or a good tune. Middle-class theatregoers see the presence of music generally as a threat to seriousness again, unless of course it is opera, when it's different. Big musicals, lush sounds and cute tunes are OK in their place, but to convey the emotional heart of a genuine situation in a pop song is alien to most National Theatre goers. Music is there for a bit of a romp to make it a jolly evening.

Fourth, *emotion*. In my experience a working-class audience is more open to emotion on the stage than a middle-class audience who get embarrassed by it. The critics label emotion on stage mawkish, sentimental, etc. Of course, the working-class audiences can also love sentimentality; in fact, I quite enjoy a dose of it myself, at the right moment, as does everybody, but emotion is more likely to be apologised for in Bromley than in the Rhondda Valley.

Fifth, *variety*. Most of the traditional forms of working-class entertainment that have grown up seem to possess this element. They seem to be able to switch from a singer to a comedian, to a juggler, to a band, to a chorus number, to a conjurer, to a sing-along, to bingo, to wrestling, to strip-tease, and then back again to a singer, and a comedian and a grand 'Altogether' finale, with great ease. If we look at music-hall, variety theatre, club entertainment, the *ceilidh* in Scotland, the *noson llawen* in Wales, panto, and through to the Morecambe and Wise show on television, you can see what I'm talking about.

The middle-class theatre seems to have lost this tradition of variety round about 1630, when it lost the working class, and it has never rediscovered it. The now-dominant strain in British middle-class theatre can be traced back to Ibsen by way of Shaw and Rattigan, and so on. The tradition is one of two or three long acts of concentrated spoken drama, usually with no more than five or six main characters. The actors communicate the plot by total immersion in the character they are playing, and move around on a set or sets made to look as much like the real thing as possible. The variety within this kind of theatre is more a question of variation of pace and intensity while doing essentially the same thing throughout. I make no value judgements on these formal elements, merely note that the bourgeois is no less bizarre in its essence than the popular, and one might be forgiven for seeing more creative possibilities in the latter. However, the received opinion is that the former is more serious, and is more capable of high art.

Six, *effect*. Working-class audiences demand more moment-by-moment effect from their entertainers. If an act is not good enough they let it be known, and if it's boring they chat amongst themselves until it gets less boring, or they leave, or they throw things. They like clear, worked-for results: laughs, respectful silence, rapt attention to a song, tears, thunderous applause. Middle-class audiences have been trained to sit still in the theatre for long periods, without talking, and bear with a slow build-up to great dramatic moments, or slow build-ups to nothing at all, as the case may be. Through TV, radio and records, working-class audiences have come to expect a high standard of success in achieving effects. They know it comes from skill and hard work, and they expect hard work and skill.

Seven, *immediacy*. This is more open to argument, even more so than what I have stated so far. But my experience of working-class entertainment is that it is in subject matter much closer to the audience's lives and experiences than, say, plays at the Royal Shakespeare Company are to their middle-class audiences. Of course there is a vast corpus of escapist art provided for the working class; but the meat of a good comic is the audience's life and experience, from Will Fyffe to Billy Connolly, or from Tommy Handley to Ken Dodd. Certainly in clubs, pantos and variety shows this is the material that goes down best. A middle-class audience can be more speculative, metaphysical, often preferring the subject to be at arm's length from their daily experience. It prefers paradigms or elaborate images to immediacy, an interesting parallel from *Timon of Athens* to, for example, a comedy directly about the decline of the private sector.

Eight, *localism*. Of course, through television, working-class audiences have come to expect stuff about Cockneys, or Geordies, or Liver birds, and have become polyglot in a way not very likely some years ago. But the best response among working-class audiences comes from characters and events with a local feel. Middle-class audiences have a great claim to cosmopolitanism, the bourgeoisie does have a certain internationality, interchangeability. I can't imagine Liverpool Playhouse crowds reacting very differently from, say, Leeds Playhouse, or Royal Lyceum, Edinburgh, audiences to the latest Alan Ayckbourn comedy. They all receive it, anyway. Just as they all get imitations of the National Theatre and the Royal Shakespeare's 'Aldwych's greatest hits'. Yet this bourgeois internationality must be distinguished from internationalism, which is an ideological attribute that ebbs and flows in the working class alarmingly, but which can be there.

Nine, *localism*, not only of material, but also a *sense of identity* with the performer, as mentioned before. Even if coming from outside the locality, there is a sense not of knowing his or her soul, but a sense that he or she cares enough about being in that place with that audience and actually knows something about them. Hence the huge success of Billy Connolly in Glasgow, of Max Boyce in South Wales. Working-men's clubs in the north of England depend on this sense of locality, of identity, of cultural identity with the audience. There are few middle-class audiences who know or care where John Gielgud, for example, came from. They don't mind if he is a bit disdainful when he's in Bradford, because he's a great man, an artist, and he exists on another planet.

There are many other broad general differences but these are enough to indicate that if a socialist theatre company is interested in contacting working-class audiences with some entertainment, they can't simply walk in with a critical production of Schiller, or even a play written and performed in a style designed to appeal to the bourgeoisie of Bromley, or even the intelligentsia of NW1. A masterpiece might survive, of course. I'm not saying that the working class are incapable of appreciating great art in the bourgeois tradition. They may well be, but if a theatre company wants to speak to the working class, it would do well to learn something of its language, and not assume that the language of bourgeois theatre of the twentieth century is all that is worthy of being expressed.

There is a danger that in schematically drawing up a list of some features of working-class entertainment I am indulging in what is called 'tailism', i.e. trailing along behind the tastes of the working class, debased as they are by capitalism; and merely translating an otherwise bourgeois message into this inferior language. It is a real danger and I have seen people with the best intentions falling into it. But this is not the present case for two important reasons. One is, as I have already said, that these features of working-class entertainment must be handled critically. To enumerate once more: directness can lead to simplification; comedy can be racist, sexist, even anti-working class; music can become mindlessness; emotion can become manipulative and can obscure judgement; variety can lead to disintegration of meaning and pettiness; effect for effect's sake can lead to trivialisation; immediacy and localism can close the mind to the rest of the world, lead to chauvinism, and 'Here's tae-us-wha's-like-us'-ism; and a sense of identity with the performer can lead to nauseating, ingratiating performances with neither dignity nor perspective.

The second reason is this. Given a critical attitude to these features of working-class entertainment, they contain within them the seeds of a revitalised, new kind of theatre, capable of expressing the richness and complexity of working-class life today, and not only working-class life. In terms of theatre they are some of the first sounds in a new language of theatre that can never be fully articulate until socialism is created in this country. But before then we can work to extend those first sounds into something like speech by making more and more demands of them, by attempting bolder projects with them, and above all, by learning from our audiences whether we are doing it right or not.

Lest this be thought to see theatre as therapy, however, I gave a talk to a largely local-authority gathering:

MAKING ART POPULAR — OR MAKING POPULAR ART?[45]

One of the preconceptions about art is that it is 'universal', that a work of art is appreciable by anybody who is educated to it. First of all I would like to say that in my experience art is very far from universal. It just occasionally can be translated from one language to another but this is not its most important characteristic. Art is a high level of living communication between living people and clearly for that communication to take place the people have to speak the same language as the art, or have been trained to speak the language of the work of art. When I say language I don't just mean words, I mean the whole apparatus of approaching a work of art. Art very rarely rises above this language barrier and even more rarely rises above the language barrier created by class. The 'class signifiers' of most art experience are clear and specific – the most apparently transcendent opera, for example, is saying 'this is not for you' to many millions of people. The concern, about being able to get anything at all from opera, is written into the contract with the audience. Where is opera advertised? Which newspaper readership takes in large amounts of opera for example? How much does it cost to get in? Once you are in what on earth is this story supposed to be about? Once you've got over that problem there are many people who cannot listen to the sound of opera singers for three hours. These are maybe apparently philistine reactions but they are nevertheless true and honest reactions of a great many people to opera.

Secondly, art is not a fixed or permanent commodity, a set number of texts or paintings or statues from Aeschylus to T.S.Eliot, or from Greek busts to Henry Moore. Not only is it a constantly growing and developing organism, but it also rearranges its own past constantly, throwing out 'great' works every decade and replacing them with forgotten, even despised pieces that have been relegated to the dustbin. Change is what art is about. Nor does art fall, as is often thought, freshly minted and complete from the skull of the innocent 'carrier'. Every artist is created by his or her age – *their* gift is unique of course, their talent their own, but their language comes from their lives, their times and their history. They are people with a world of people about them. On the other hand, I think it is equally important not to be confused by the idea of art as some kind of social psychotherapy. One of the most vital tasks of the educator today is of course to liberate the creative imagination of every child – I think even Tories would agree. But alas – once liberated, it is doomed to be firmly imprisoned again by the time the child reaches 16, or goes to work. It is one of the most vital tasks for all who are concerned with the future well-being, the future psychic health, of our society, to combat this foreclosure of the imagination. So, let us make a clear and necessary distinction: liberating the individual imagination; making the materials for 'creative play' available to all, irrespective of class or of age; the spreading of the joy of self-discovery and self-expression through artistic means to the whole of society instead of just a few, is one task of immense importance and one which every socialist administration, local or national, should place at least on the same priority level as street-lighting or relief roads.

This should not be confused with another task, the nourishment of the arts. A body of work does exist in all the artistic disciplines which varies in its accessibility to the entire population, but which has a degree of skill, a weight of thought, truthfulness, an aptness of expression which few participants in the general 'creative play' area, and indeed very few of those who are spending their entire lives at play, are going to achieve. For this reason, this body of work, and let's be exact, the standards that this body of work implies, are also of immense value – sometimes of a long-lasting value, but this is not the most important criterion. This stuff is called art.

Now let me say straight away that the upper reaches of our class-ridden society, and I'm afraid that I believe it is class-ridden, have declared ownership of this commodity. They have put it on a high shelf so only those with the appropriate, expensive step-ladder can get at it. This has given it a bad name, and caused people like myself to appear to be attacking it from time to time. To accuse us of attacking art, however, is a ruse, a deceitful tactic employed by those who wish to keep it for themselves alone, on the high shelf. Neither I, nor I'm sure, others would say art has no value if it's not immediately enjoyable by every voter: what I think I would say is that class control of the step-ladder must be removed, that more people should be getting more joy from more art.

There is one model or thought-pattern, which has dominated this sort of discussion for far too long, and it goes like this:

HERE, up here, we have Art – Universal, a fixed commodity. HERE, down here, we have the Ignorant Worker.

To move THIS to THIS requires the Ignorant Worker to go to night-classes, Workers' Education Association courses, Further Education, Open University, or buy a set of Teach-Yourself-Tom-Stoppard volumes. In this way, the Ignorant Worker, slowly, painfully, with mounting joy, approaches the heights of what's called the 'Appreciation of Culture'. Alternatively, the Ignorant Worker sticks to bingo and the boozer, and waits in the hope that the next generation will acquire the education and become inward with the great.

This is the great *Education-to-Art* theory, and exercises the minds and indeed informs the decisions of many worthy and distinguished arts administrators. It does, of course, contain more than a grain of sense; but in my experience to date, it has achieved very little in the way of joy, in the expansion of the consciousness, or deep artistic experience. It is inert in three main areas.

Firstly, it assumes a denial of any value at all in the cultural experience which is already part of the way of life of the Ignorant Worker. Put in the centrist terms of Arnold Wesker, it becomes the patronisation of the farm-labourers in his play *Roots*, who are seen as worthless, basically, culturally worthless. Put in the pseudo-leftist terms of David Edgar, it becomes the argument that capitalism has so corrupted the culture of the working class that it is entirely a negative force which has to be combated. In the terms of the last, Labourite, Secretary General of the Arts Council of Great Britain, it becomes the expression, as is often the case, by a man who has 'risen above' his own class, of his own distaste for his own early experiences. Whichever of these, it relies upon a false and deceitful image of working-class life and culture.

Secondly, it relies upon an *inert* concept of this art to which we must all aspire. I've already asserted the volatile and constantly rearranged, constantly challenged and changing nature of the Pantheon of great art. This theory, in its pathetic small-mindedness, assumes that to appreciate theatre the Ignorant Worker must learn the language of Shakespeare – or to appreciate music, the Ignorant Worker must learn to swoon to Richard Rodney

Bennett. They have such an arrogance in forcing their own narrow gallery of excellence onto the world, and such a life-defying puritanism in their insistence that art *must* be an experience filtered through a cultural education, that it is little wonder the Ignorant Worker shrugs their idea of art aside and goes for some more direct and comprehensible experience even if it is less than high culture.

Thirdly, this theory is inert in its idea of the relationship between the subject and object, high and low. Somehow, it is always the worker who must *learn,* who must – *improve*. It is part of the nature of this model of thinking, that the worker's experience of life, views, philosophy, imagination, is not capable of contributing to art – seen as a collection of the world's greatest hits – whereas art can illuminate his or her dark existence like the beacon on a Salvation Army's lighthouse.

There is the alternative model to this which I probably find even worse and that's called the *Left Populist* model in which Shakespeare is brought to the Ignorant Worker dressed up as Boy George, *Hamlet* is a rock concert and the interpreter of art feels obliged to reduce all subtlety and discretion to crudity and dig-in-the-ribs in the interest of persuading the local authority it is taking culture to the masses.

What I would advocate is a three-pronged attack on the inertia of those three main concepts.

First of all, the idea of art itself.

For far too long this has been an alienated experience, a filtered experience, even a simulated experience. Let us re-scrutinise the canons of art for works that will speak more directly to people today, that will grapple with experiences that mean something to us, that will engage the imagination of the unemployed, the industrial worker, and the youth looking for an Opportunity Programme, as well as the comfortably-off professional classes. This means finding the right works, presenting them in a way that places the meat of the work – be it theatre, opera, music, painting or dance – as a challenge to the experience of life of the audience – that invites discovery and comparison with today rather than passivity and a mild archaeological interest.

To grow, to develop and bite harder, each artistic discipline does need an area of experimentation. It needs the right to have *some* bold but incomprehensible adventures, *some* breaking new ground to keep rolling back the frontiers of our understanding of our own human nature: so don't let's be philistine about this – remember Ibsen was considered some sort of soccer hooligan in his time. There must be experiment, and a civilised community will value and encourage experiment because it leads to re-evaluation and change.

Secondly, we must re-assess the traditional high artist's dismissal of working-class culture.

The most exciting feature of the positive initiative taken in the last decade by some socialist local authorities is that the working class is asserting its demand to be taken seriously by cultural organisations. It was the GLC [Greater London Council] and definitely not the Arts Council of Great Britain, who made the cultural community of London aware that they had to go for contact with *all* the people if they wanted the support of all the people. Likewise, bold policies in Liverpool and in Sheffield are changing the nature of cultural pre-conceptions in these cities. In Glasgow, the District Council's support – enthusiastic and articulate – for ventures like 7:84's *Clydebuilt Season* and now *Mayfest* – have meant that working-class people and their history enter directly into the cultural life of the city.

This leads really to the third area where a dynamic, dialectical approach must replace inert cultural preconceptions – that is in the relationship between the popular audience and the future of artistic creation. *If* we can demolish the notion of art as expensive – with support and subsidy – as only for the rich, and the middle classes – by positive discrimination in redistributing the cultural wealth – as inaccessible and incomprehensible, as a dimly perceived second- or third-hand experience, to do with fanciful folk in funny costumes in other lands – by the efforts and inspiration of our creators of cultural production. *If* we can demolish the notion of the working class as *outside* culture, as the masses with vapid tastes and corrupted minds – by getting to know, explore and trust working-class people for a change. *If* we can encourage the growth of a new generation – and the regeneration of an older one – by a determined policy of refusing to allow industrial society, late capitalist soul-destruction and/or unemployment to kill off all imaginative life in the adult working class of our society. And *if* a society can be created in which it is not necessary for a person with great artistic talent to embrace the bourgeoisie in order to be recognised – *Then* the working class could enter fully into our national culture, and our national culture will be the richer for it. Let us never forget it was James Bridie who rejected Joe Corrie's plays, who rejected Ena Lamont Stewart's plays, and who himself produced *Mr Bolfry*. The cultural experts of the great middle classes continue to make eternal idiots of themselves and by simple class bias to elevate the second-rate into first place and remain blind to the true art when it comes along.

We must try to make possible a new, wider definition of art which includes the experience, the lives and the perspective of life of the working class, in which society is no longer embarrassed by creative play, in which society no longer fears the power of the imagination, in which making art popular and making popular art are drawn closer together.

1979 TO 1988: HIGHS AND LOWS

I shall never forget Christopher Hill's look of bafflement when I revealed – in March 1979, in Cambridge, the night before the referendum on Scottish devolution – that I was entitled to vote in it. I had to deliver a lecture at two the next afternoon, but Christopher clearly felt I should have somehow made my mark. Unfortunately, like many others in Scotland, I did not believe either that we could win 40% of the entire population, including those who didn't vote, or that it would have any meaning if we did. After my rather strenuous 'break' in Cambridge, I came back to Scotland, and found a similar monumental apathy. I decided to do something about it:

JOE'S DRUM [46]

Joe's Drum was written in April and May 1979 as a direct response to two major events: in March, a majority voted for a Scottish Assembly, but due to 'arrangements' made in Westminster, they did not a get a Scottish Assembly. In May, at the General Election, a tiny *minority* in Scotland voted for the Conservatives, and, due to events south of the Border, they *did* get a Tory government. At the same election, the vote for an ever-more-right-leaning Scottish national party was dramatically reduced, and the SNP seemed destined to a massive decline.

These events came at a time of confusion and apathy in Scottish politics, and of yawning tedium in Scottish cultural life. The younger generation of students seemed just not interested in politics, and the young marrieds of all classes seemed content to scrape together their own pile of consumer goods and cosiness, to the exclusion of any involvement in public life. Within the working-class organisations, many of the unions had recently elected right-wing leaders, and the TUC in London seemed content to follow a line that must have satisfied the CIA. The political groups of the far left got less support in the election than the National Front, and the Labour Party under Callaghan was distinguishable from the Conservatives only by being marginally less rhetorical in its pursuit of a smoother-running capitalist economy. And the inflation that had changed all our lives seemed to be caused by factors way beyond our control.

The overall effect of these events and feelings was to give the individual person, at work and at home, the impression that she or he was powerless to affect any decisions or even to be involved in any decisions. There was a dangerous bored fatalism in the air, an uncharacteristic passivity that amounted almost to acceptance of defeat.

In these circumstances, *Joe's Drum* was both an expression of anger and frustration, and a tocsin to alert the audiences to the full monstrosity of what was going on. In performance, it clearly aroused many echoes, and seemed to say what a lot of Scots wanted to hear in 1979. It is to be hoped that the drum will go on beating into the 1980s, to waken us from our curious hibernation.

After that initial burst of anger, I suppose we began a more considered response in the plays that we did. The next show was Swings and Roundabouts, *where I decided what was needed was a way of showing the audiences the reasons for socialism – close, intimate, detailed, daily-life reasons – analysing the values of capitalism in daily life and what they do to us.*

SWINGS AND ROUNDABOUTS[47]

There are some moments in all our lives when we become acutely aware of ourselves – wedding days, twenty-first birthdays, days when a friend or a parent dies, or just days when everything goes wrong – times when we become conscious of ourselves as defined – as what we are: as no longer a mass of possibilities, but a reality: a human fact. It is at one of these moments that Andy and Ginny, Freddie and Rosemary find themselves thrown together in our play. In spite of their similarities as 'people', there are social forces that enter their most private thoughts – the forces that have helped to define them: as women and men, as working or ruling class.

In this play, we have tried just to present this group of people in a story, to indicate the social forces at work in their lives, and the effects and consequences of those forces on their consciousness, and to invite you, as audience, to draw your own conclusions.

I suppose that play was pitching the way that 7:84 was going to develop because the next one we did was Blood Red Roses. *This was another rather domestic, detailed, in some senses naturalistic treatment of a woman militant in Scottish industrial society. In 1975, in England,* Lay Off *had ended with the story of a woman militant in Scotland who organised a triumphant multinational strike against a multinational corporation. After this, her story, in real life, developed: she was made a victim, and fired from every subsequent job. The multinational just closed down the plant she worked in, and 1,200 people were left unemployed. Writing* Blood Red Roses *was a way of coming to terms with this development, and with all that had happened during the 1970s: the enormous growth of militancy which seemed to spread through most of the industrial working class – certainly those who took part in unions through 1975 and 1976 – then this awful erosion of militancy, this apology for using the word 'politics', this terrible tendency to back away from anything that sounded red or even pink. The show was a way to try to come to terms with the fact that these changes were going on: to assert, as Bessie does through-out the play, that the fight will go on, that this is a temporary setback. We've got to look for the ways to keep on struggling through into the future but we've also got to think of ways to connect with people other than those we used in the 1970s.*

BLOOD RED ROSES[48]

Fashion is a double-edged sword. On the one hand the rippling flow of clothing-styles, ideas, excitements and prejudices gives colour and richness to life. More, it can give the feeling of humanity trying out an endless variety of postures in its restless search for progress towards a better life – a feeling of positive explorations . . . trouser-suits, Cohn-Bendit, structuralism, the Anti-Nazi League.

On the other hand, fashion can perform a valuable role for the capitalist state. For it can effectively safeguard the status quo by seeing every form of opposition to the status quo as a flash in the pan – the seven-days-wonder of the burning bra, the trendiness of Leftyism, the passing of the Winter of our Discontent – now made glorious summer by this hero of Bovis: and even Sir Keith Joseph [Secretary of State for Industry 1979–1980], and monetarism, and Milton Friedman [American economist who invented and popularised monetarism], they too will pass on as fashions come and go.

But beneath the glittering surface of punk, ska and Abba, the status quo goes marching on, to coin a phrase. The struggles of the working class to protect the advances made in their standards of life go on. But they have suffered, are suffering serious setbacks. And militancy in those struggles, particularly industrial militancy, is now distinctly out of fashion.

In this situation, it seemed important – if a little unfashionable – to take a longer look at one of these militants, and at the whole question of what 'fighting' means in the age of the multiple war-head. And to try to see where exactly the battlefields are, and who is on whose side . . . At the same time, the play tells a story, an adventure story in its way . . . about some people – real in many particulars, not based on the life of any one individual, but on the experiences of many.

I began work on what became the Clydebuilt Season. *I asked Linda MacKenney, a young ex-student I'd been aware of in Cambridge, now living in Edinburgh, to see if she could research the hidden stream of working-class drama written and performed in Scotland in the first half of the twentieth century. She produced a detailed catalogue of over fifty plays, some not so distinguished, others very interesting indeed. With help from Glasgow District and Strathclyde Region, we put on a season at the Mitchell Theatre, Glasgow, and toured each production.*

Nobody had heard of these plays; they weren't exactly old favourites. They were old vanished masterpieces, some of them. The reason we did that season was twofold. Firstly, it was to try to fight against the bourgeois writing or re-writing of history and, particularly, theatre history. The history of Scottish theatre says that the dominant playwrights of the 1940s and 1950s were people like James Bridie. Now I just don't agree. We did these shows first of all to bring out the work of Joe Corrie, secondly to bring out the work of Unity, which made a massive contribution to the theatrical wealth of Scotland and thirdly to bring out particular work like Ena Lamont Stewart's Men Should Weep. *These pieces have been ignored; they've been cut out of theatrical history – it seemed to me that this was completely wrong, that this is the way the working class loses its history, its self-awareness; it loses, if you like, a cultural richness. The reason we wanted to do the* Clydebuilt Season *was to explore new, different styles from our own 'house style', as it were – to try to broaden the possibilities, to use new people, to get involved with new designers, new actors in particular.*

THE CLYDEBUILT SEASON[49]

Much of what is called the Working-Class Struggle is, in the long run, a struggle against the oppression or exploitation of the whole of humanity. While it may appear, quite frequently, that class struggle sets one group of human beings bitterly, indeed destructively, against another group of human beings, its ultimate purpose is to unite all people on a different basis: one of co-operation and unity in the common cause of defeating war, disease, hunger, lack of decent housing, ignorance and natural disasters wherever in the world they may be.

But this struggle is conducted in many different ways, some good, others evil. In the capitalist countries, the crimes of the left are never forgotten. Stalin's purges and murders and betrayals; the Kremlin's (and Castro's) treatment of dissidents; the brutalities of the Chinese Cultural Revolution; Hungary 1956, Czechoslovakia 1968, Afghanistan, Poland – where next? – all these events are given maximum publicity by our media. They are used to discredit socialism, and to support a ruling class in Britain and America which has created the misery of unemployment on a massive scale in order to maximise profits.

While the crimes of the left are trumpeted by the media, the victories and achievements of Socialism are rapidly written out of history altogether. Worse still, they are forgotten by the succeeding generations working for the same cause.

In a very small way, this season of plays is an attempt to remind our audiences both of the ultimate humanity of the working-class struggle, and of the long, rich and neglected tradition of the way it has been fought.

In Scotland, the Labour Movement has always had a strong cultural side: it has generated its own poetry, novels, songs, films and, of course, plays. But how many of these works are in print, let alone read? The works of Joe Corrie, and the Unity plays, are 'not remembered'. That means that they ARE remembered, but by the 'wrong' people. It is partly in order to bring to mind the cultural breadth and maturity of the Scottish Labour Movement, that we present this Season.

The earliest play, Joe Corrie's *In Time of Strife*, was written in 1927 in the wake of the General Strike, out of the sorrow and confusion of a massive defeat. The latest, *Gold in his Boots*, was written in 1947, when a Labour Government was struggling to implement socialism, and – while certainly not one of the best plays to emerge from popular theatre – it is a fine example of the kind of show presented by the Unity Theatre in its heyday – a time of comparative victory.

From the naturalism of Joe Corrie to the musical-poetical narrative ballad of Ewan MacColl, *Johnny Noble,* the season presents proof also that popular theatre has a wide range of styles and form, to take it way beyond social realism. Perhaps the most exciting play in the season is Ena Lamont Stewart's *Men Should Weep*, where many of today's concerns with the position of women in society are shown to have been debated in the working-class movement for many years.

In the course of the season we hope also to show how theatre makes the connections between local divisive class-struggle, and the common cause of the movement towards a better life for all humanity – not just a few. If they achieve that, they will have done their job.

There was a huge response to this season, and to my great satisfaction we helped to reinstate several of these playwrights in the history of Scottish theatre, particularly Ena Lamont Stewart and Joe Corrie. However, no texts of their plays were available. I proposed 7:84 should extend its publishing activities. We produced two plays, Men Should Weep *and* The Gorbals Story, *and an ambitious collection of Joe Corrie's plays, poetry and verse. In addition Linda MacKenney has produced a history of* Scottish Popular Theatre 1900–1950, *and she started the Scottish Theatre Archive in Glasgow University Library where scripts of most of the 50-odd plays she unearthed can be read. After the first performance of Giles Havergal's wonderful production of* Men Should Weep, *a journalist asked Ena how she felt: she said, 'I feel exhumed.'*

Encouraged by the success of this branching out, we then struck out in another direction:

GENERAL GATHERING[50]
POLICY DOCUMENT

1. GENERAL GATHERING will have as its main function to present the great classics of World Popular Theatre, from Aristophanes via Shakespeare to Dario Fo, in such ways as to make them alive for a Scottish popular audience today.

2. By World Popular Theatre is meant that current of great theatre written to be enjoyed by the mass of the people rather than a small, educated class or coterie: Molière rather than Corneille, Ben Jonson's comedies rather than his masques, Ballad Opera rather than Congreve, Arden rather than Pinter, but including Euripides as well as Aristophanes, Chekhov as well as Gorki, and Shakespeare's tragedies as well as his comedies.

There is no hard and fast line to be drawn, but the intention should be clear, and the final choice of play will depend on suitability for the audience and a strong desire to do it, rather than on the niceties of history. The other main criteria for plays will be:

high literary value;

potential for theatrical magic;

accessibility to the audience – by way of relevance, comedy, music, or some other connection with contemporary life and taste.

Suitable plays that leap to mind are: Aristophanes, particularly *Birds, Lysistrata, Ecclesiazusae*; Aeschylus – *Agamemnon;* Sophocles – *Theban Trilogy;* Euripides – *Alcestis, The Oresteia*; the English Miracle plays, and some of the Tudor Interludes; *The Thrie Estaitis; Everyman;* Shakespeare – *Macbeth, Lear, Othello*; Ben Jonson – *The Alchemist, Volpone*; the 18th Century Scottish ballad operas; Gorki – *The Lower Depths;* Chekhov – *The Cherry Orchard, Uncle Vanya*; Ibsen – *Peer Gynt;* Synge – *The Well of the Saints, The Playboy of the Western World*; O'Casey – almost everything; Hauptmann – *The Weavers;* Büchner – *Woyzeck;* American Popular theatre – Odets, Rice et al.; Joe Corrie; The Glasgow Unity plays – see our Clydebuilt Season; Holland – the *Fat People* play from Werk Theater; Mnouchkine – *1789, 1792, L'Age d'or* – (with possibility of Ariane Mnouchkine directing); Arden – *Serjeant Musgrave's Dance*; Brecht – *Mother Courage, Mahagonny* (chamber version); Dario Fo – a selection of scenes from several plays.

The point of the output of the company will be to use Scottish actors and language and popular theatrical conventions to make these plays really work for Scottish popular audiences.

3. By Scottish popular audiences, we mean primarily the non-theatre-goers, the working people of Scotland, the young people in school or on the dole, the people who make up the bulk of 7:84's audience on the road, but in the case of GENERAL GATHERING, wider. GENERAL GATHERING would go about finding this audience by making their productions tour to the heart of communities throughout Scotland, as well as to fill larger theatres in the cities. We would hope to create special relationships with certain areas, notably the Western Isles, Highland, Grampian, Lothian, Tayside and Strathclyde regions – while obviously not excluding others.

With the experience and contacts of 7:84 behind us, we feel that we are uniquely well placed to create an audience for these plays, and a service to this audience. We would expect it to be wider than 7:84's audience in that we want GENERAL GATHERING to play in schools, and to attract those who might not respond to 7:84's political position.

GENERAL GATHERING will have a separate function and discipline from 7:84. It is not intended that the shows will have the same direct, interventionist political content as the usual 7:84 shows – which obviously does not mean that Aristophanes can be non-political! The main political purpose of GENERAL GATHERING will be to recapture the history of popular theatre and re-present it to the people of Scotland. This is very different from – though related to – the work of 7:84, and obviously relates strongly to the *Clydebuilt Season*.

On a theatrical level, we feel that 7:84 knows how to reach popular audiences, and can use this knowledge to bring the classics of popular theatre back to the audiences they were written for. We would use directors who have worked with or learnt from the theatre of 7:84, and performers who will know how to reach the audience. The return benefit to 7:84 will be twofold; firstly it will give a greater diversity of experience to 7:84 company members, in every way, and secondly it will allow 7:84/GENERAL GATHERING to hold together a company for a whole planned season of work, rather than from tour to tour.

Organisationally, GENERAL GATHERING and 7:84 would apportion the amount of time spent by the staff on each. There would be no question of this being a hidden subsidy to 7:84. The advantages of integrating the work of the companies will very obviously be of financial assistance to both – setting up another, separate organisation to do the work of GENERAL GATHERING would be far more expensive; sharing the overheads will make 7:84 more cost-effective.

Conclusion

The urge to create GENERAL GATHERING comes from various sources: from the experience of a good company working together on the Clydebuilt Season; from 7:84's need to provide more for their audiences – more variety, more demanding plays, more stimulation, more knowledge of the power of theatre; from a deeply-felt conviction that the future of the theatre lies in re-building a mass popular audience rather than in pursuing the vanishing theatre-goer; and from the combination of a great body of theatre-work of the past, a strong group of theatre-workers wanting to stay together and grow together, and an audience in Scotland which will respond to this new initiative. All three exist – to combine them, we need GENERAL GATHERING.

Unfortunately the first show, Women in Power, *was a disaster.*

WOMEN IN POWER[51]

I had started with the *Thesmophoriadzusae* by Aristophanes, the story of the women of Athens dressing up as men, getting into the parliament before the men, and voting that as the men had made such a mess of things, the country should be run by the women. To this I added or interpolated a short, outrageous version of *Ippes, The Knights,* in which the men respond by showing what happened when one particular woman came to power . . . They are driven off by the women, who have a big party, leaving some of the men quite happy to join in, others still stuck in sexist abuse: it was full of songs, terrible old jokes, and startlingly modern notions about the liberation of women. Of course Aristophanes was an old sexist mickey-taker, but as a writer he couldn't help himself – and where he went out of order, I had simply cut whole scenes, and/or replaced them with songs. On the whole, though, I was very close to the original. Let me give you what I noted a few weeks after the event:

What were we trying to do with these daft old pieces? Why revive them at all? The answer for me lies in the real subject-matter of Aristophanes. This is not so much in the 'political' area – though it connects, intimately – more in the really dangerous area of the unspoken – some would say unspeakable – areas of the collective psyche.

The fifth century BC in Athens produced a civilisation which – even though it had problems – has never been equalled in history. It produced works of art, plays, poetry, history, philosophy, that stand today as pinnacles of their genre. The real subject-matter, for me, of these plays was what Aristophanes was telling us about the state of the Athenian psyche that produced all this, and the huge gap which this reveals between our own consciousness and theirs.

All this, of course, in the context of comedy. And very old comedy at that. When the papers complained that the jokes were old, I was tempted to remind them that they were in fact 2,300 years old, and still doing quite well.

But it was the nature of the comedy that was going to reveal the profounder connections between the ancient Greek fertility and our contemporary Scottish aridity – if we had ever got to it.

From the beginning there was a huge built-in resistance within the company to this level of the play. In the production, I was asking the actors to explore this level. The connections between uninhibited play with cocks, shit, body-sweat, lust, erections, women's lusts and fantasies, body-hair, and all the bodily functions – and the beautiful poetry that haunts the play, the magnificent boldness of the political and sexual-political ideas of the play, and the atmosphere of fruitful creativity in which the play was first made.

We never took this explanation beyond the first stages. Inhibition, fear, personal worries about being seen in public involved in this sort of thing, particularly among the majority of the women, even anger and shame, nipped the whole proceedings in the bud.

Because the major concentration of the play is on the women's psyches, and the main rehearsal problems lay in opening them up, the men grew restless and resentful of this unexpected lack of prioritisation. There was a demand for more attention to be paid to the men – and the women wanted to get on with blocking the piece, and to stop wasting time with this exploration, which they thought – perhaps all too correctly – would lead nowhere.

This created in me a sense of deep-down failure even before we had properly begun. We never actually reached the level on which the production should have operated. I doubt if we ever could have.

All this was accompanied by a rather negative attitude in rehearsal. Bold strokes, experimentation, non-naturalistic inventiveness were openly laughed at, and mutual trust was destroyed. When the men did come into rehearsal with the women trying things out, the lack of support was embarrassing, the level of sexual politics a disgrace to a progressive company.

So the real subject-matter of the piece led to my trying to find things in the production which I failed, as a director, to release in the company. In my own defence I can only say that I doubt if anyone could have achieved this kind of release under the circumstances. The cast was suffering deeply from the very distance from the underside of the psyche that the rest of western Christian capitalist (or, at the moment, socialist) societies seem to be experiencing, and the same distance from the sources of Aristophanic comedy. Therein lay the source of most of my problems.

The net result of all this was that the production was imposed rather than discovered. I was unwilling to accept what seemed to be the direction in which the cast wanted to take the real meaning of the plays – and consequently was in some tension throughout. It would undoubtedly have been easier to have simply accepted the suggestions thrown up by the majority of the cast, but this would have led to my remaining as director only in a cynical and resentful way. So I tried my best to produce something that would be nearer to the cast's sensibilities, but not too far from my own sense of style.

The result was a major disaster. We were due to open to the world's press, during the 1983 Edinburgh Festival, in the Assembly Rooms Music Hall on a Monday at 7.30. Due to ridiculous scheduling by the Assembly Rooms, we had grossly inadequate time to get in and light. When we did, they had made such a spaghetti of the lighting cables in the roof, with far too many companies coming in, that we sat up all Sunday night trying to find which plug came from which lights. The company were called out at seven on the Monday morning, and in mounting tension and fury suffered a technical cock-up of the worst kind. By 6 pm we still hadn't finished the lighting cues, the sound was a disaster, and the company screwed up like snapping fiddle-strings. At 7.30 we opened to an audience who knew everything was wrong. Everything. The reviews gloated over our shame, the Festival audiences stayed away in their millions, and the cast were mutinous. They held a meeting in Glasgow to which I was not invited, and came to a full company meeting armed with resolutions.

The main problem was ostensibly that the 7:84 Board saw that if we continued to tour the show we would probably lose over £16,000. If we took it off immediately and paid everyone their full fees it would lose only three thousand pounds: so they decided we must take it off. If not, we could not proceed with the autumn show, and would end up in great money problems which would give the SAC a reason to close us. It was a deeply unhappy time, and one that I don't care to repeat. At the full company meeting, various members of the cast said they had told me so in rehearsal, that the men had better lines than the women, that Aristophanes 'had not written a socialist or a feminist play', that the part Liz MacLennan played was more positive only because she was my wife, and that this was a problem too, creating exclusivity, and that basically it was all my fault. The company's main anger was that the show was coming off. They wanted it to continue, and felt 7:84 was being paternalistic in ignoring their wishes, even though they would not be affected by the cancellation of the next show, and would of course be paid in full for the whole tour. At that meeting I vowed I would never again direct actors in the theatre in Scotland, being unable to cope with their attitudes, and feeling unable to communicate with the majority of the company or elicit an imaginative response. On the whole, I stuck to this vow until I left 7:84, and it has had very serious consequences for the company.

The debacle in Scotland was fast and furious. After the enormous critical triumph of the Clydebuilt Season *only two months before, suddenly we had failed – albeit with one show out of 20 – but it was sufficient for our political enemies to put the boot in, in a big way. General Gathering would receive no more money from the Arts Council – the whole concept was torpedoed gleefully. 7:84 Scotland itself was to be treated with a suspicion bordering on contempt from the new Arts Council Drama Committee.*

MEANWHILE, BACK IN ENGLAND

7:84 (England) was on the up. In 1980 we produced a revival of Barrie Keeffe's play about police harassment of young blacks, called SUS, *and one of our biggest hits, John Burrows's* One Big Blow, *the six-man play with music by Rick Lloyd about a miners' brass band; the company for that play then became The Flying Pickets and went to Number One in the charts.*

In 1981 I wrote a play for Alfred Molina and a new and excellent company.

NIGHTCLASS[52]

'The Queen is above politics.'

'The state, if such a thing exists, is a distant, lofty, impartial apparatus seen only at royal weddings. It too is above politics.'

'We live in a democratic society – our country is governed by the people for the people.'

'We live in a free society, where anyone can express their beliefs and not suffer for it.'

Many people believe these statements to be true. But the English Constitution is a slippery eel: unwritten, concealed in its vital operations, inflexible in appearance, in fact it is constantly and subtly accommodating to a variety of pressures.

Our Constitution is nothing less than the way power is distributed and controlled in our society. Historically, it was the people with the power who made the rules. In the past, however, popular agitation resulted in large changes to those rules – like reform of parliament, votes for men with no property, votes for women, the jury system, the right not to be put in prison without specific charges being brought, public, indeed, local, control of the police, free speech, the freedom of the press – these, and many other such, are there to safeguard the liberty of the ordinary individual against the power of the powerful.

Today we have a Government which in the name of conservatism is destroying all that is best in our constitutional tradition – and in the name of freeing individual enterprise, it is destroying individual liberty. In the name of removing State Control, it is building a terrifyingly strong, centralised, integrated system of State Control.

At such a time, it seems reasonable to air some arguments on the subject of the Constitution, and the State. In our play tonight we see these arguments amongst a small group of individuals who have come together for a night-class on the subject.

In England we opted for a circuit of 40 or so venues which we could visit on a regular basis and with whose audiences we could develop a relationship.

POLICY STATEMENT 1981/82[53]

Over the last few years we have felt our impact on audiences has been dissipated somewhat by the irregular nature of our visits. This has been partly due to reliance on Arts Association 'weeks' and partly due to an over-ambitious desire to visit every corner of England. What we are now planning is a regular eight-week schedule of one night stands in eight areas of the country, which we will visit regularly twice a year. We will also open each of the two new shows every year in one place for the best part of a week and at the end of eight weeks on the road would hope to present the show in London for a short period.

This would mean we would have much more regular contact with our audiences. It will also mean that we can plan our schedules well in advance. In the event of one venue having problems with publicity, or its performance space, we will then be in a position to help in order to maintain continuity rather than abandon it, as tends to happen at the moment.

This means that for the next three years we will be presenting two new productions and filling, roughly 20–24 weeks touring commitment. Over and above this, we still intend to take out shows to Holland, Belgium, Ireland, as we have done in the past, and hopefully, to visit Germany and other countries that have shown interest in our work.

In the next three years we toured shows by Claire Luckham, Peter Cox, Jim Sheridan, Miles Malleson and Harry Brooks, Chris Bond, Farukh Dhondy and others, including a show animated and directed by Paul Thompson of the Canadian Theatre Passe-Murailles.

We spun off a group who performed for picketing miners and their families, and got cut by Thatcher's new top man at the Arts Council, Sir William Rees-Mogg, now Lord Mogg of Spite-under-Spleen.

I contributed three shows and the Malleson adaptation before the axe fell. In Rejoice! *I wrote and directed a version of* Pygmalion, *in which a High Tory, Jack Browning, bets he can turn an unemployed black youth into a perfect entrepreneur, and succeeds all too well. Sandy Craig asked me about him:*

REJOICE![54]

Craig *In* Rejoice! *I was surprised how I found Jack Browning as a Tory. He seemed to be stupid and misguided, but not someone you should hate, and dislike, and fight against.*

Well, Tories as such are very plausible. When you say that Jack Browning is presented as likeable, of course the whole of the second half is an analysis of how his social manner makes him likeable and disguises the reality – the economic and power reality – underneath the social manner. In the last moments of the play when somebody asks if they can keep their job he says 'Yes', and as soon as they go away he just rips up the piece of paper. That's not a likeable person. On the other hand I don't think one ought to present all Tories as hateful, despicable, mindless or in anyway charmless. It seems to me very important that the kind of audience who will see our shows take the ideology that he represents, and the development of Tory ideology very seriously. It is no way to treat it with a figure that is easily written off; no problem, you don't have to think about it – he's just hateful. You've got to present it in somebody you've got to take seriously. What is present in the play is something that I think the Labour Movement has got to get to grips with, which is the fact that the alternative to Jack Browning, to the new Toryism, is an alternative which embraces play, imagination, fantasy, different ways of thinking, different ways of human beings relating to each other, different ways of men and women relating to each other, blacks and whites relating to each other. All of which are in the play.

1984 was the centenary of the founding of the TUC. For many years Norman Willis and the TUC had helped us in all kinds of ways, culminating in their giving us a free office and phone in Congress House. As a small Thank You, I adapted the Miles Malleson/Harry Brooks story of the early heroic days of the Trades Unions and the Tolpuddle Martyrs, Six Men of Dorset.

SIX MEN OF DORSET[55]

Welcome to *Six Men of Dorset*. 7:84 is delighted to present this play at this time. As this government renews its many-pronged and devious attacks on the trades unions and their members, it is as well to remember both the efforts and sacrifices which were made to bring the unions into being, and the conditions of life which the working class suffered without them.

Today we are seeing another great effort and great sacrifice – this time to protect those unions. And we have no reason to trust our present rulers to be any less rapacious or to inflict less suffering if they should manage to do away with them. They have shown themselves willing to return to the 1790s – starvation, child mortality and disease included.

Above all, this play shows what can be achieved by massive organisation, demonstration of will, and the determination of the working class and the allies not to be defeated. The six men of Dorset are an inspiration to us all, men and women, today: the triumph of the movement to release them, in the face of all odds, is just what we need today, to remind us that we can and must win.

Talk of the Labour Movement winning anything must have come as gall to the new, Thatcher-appointed Arts bureaucracy. The show, directed by Pam Brighton with music by John Tams, opened in the Sheffield Crucible, to huge national interest. The battle between Thatcher and the miners was getting bloodier and more bitter every day. During the week in Sheffield, and for performances in Manchester, South Wales, Liverpool, Dorset, many thousands of Trades Unionists came in to see the show. In London, the Shaw Theatre was packed nightly: on the first night the leader of the Labour Party, Neil Kinnock, and the Secretary-General of the TUC, Normal Willis, rose to their feet and led the audience in singing the final song: Raise Your Banners High!

Little wonder Rees-Mogg cut our grant, in the truly democratic spirit of the dictatorship of the majority:

7:84 ENGLAND LOSES ARTS COUNCIL FUNDING
'No Politics Please, We're British'[56]

It is a fact that several miners who had not before been out on the picket-line went out and picketed after seeing 7:84 England's production of *Six Men of Dorset*. It is a fact too, that every review of this production so far has expressed astonishment at Sir William Rees-Mogg's decision to cut this company on 'artistic' grounds, and on his stubborn refusal of all efforts to save it. Tens of thousands of trades unionists in Sheffield, Liverpool, Norwich, Ipswich, Newcastle, Dorset and South Wales have seen their own history on the stage, perhaps for the first time, and the experience led some to the point of taking political action.

Whether a work of art is improved or damaged by a direct political purpose is, rightly, a matter for lively debate. But it is a matter for some alarm when the guardians of our culture appear to have made it almost impossible for a work with a particular political message to be made at all. Especially when those guardians have astonishingly little actual qualification for making artistic judgements of any kind apart from their adherence to the political elite that appointed them.

That this is indeed what is happening will be disputed with all the deadly charm of dry Tory public relations, but that it is the case is now generally wearily recognised. Wearily, since the assault on civil liberties, the bending of the highest principles of the law, the cruelty of the Government's social policy have all been painfully charted by many wise and good people, only to be oiled out of sight with a velvety sigh and a coo of ministerial assurance. If they can get away with the Belgrano, they can get away with political theatre.

7:84 England are not the only victims, nor is Sir William Rees-Mogg the only executioner. CAST, a socialist group sending out to clubs all over the country variety acts that offered something other than strip and racist comedy, had their small subvention removed. Others, like Red Ladder, were 'devolved' – thrown on the mercy of local authorities, who have minimal funds and even more political volatility than the Arts Council.

Socialists, you will recall, wish to reduce all nature's variety to drab uniformity: remember Mao's uniformed millions, Stalin's monolithic architecture, the little brown clones of Ho Chi Minh? And Tories, in case you had forgotten, love individuality, enterprise, independence of spirit – sadly, this is as untrue in the arts as in local government.

In the theatre, the concept of national and regional 'centres of excellence' is the instrument to express the Tory longing for something to look up to. It is also neat, conveniently fundable, and good for absorbing any stray dissent.

The independent theatre companies, apart from being bureaucratically inconvenient, apt to have messy books and to give away tickets to the unemployed, were also difficult to have vetted in advance by 'responsible' people.

These companies, however, attracted a tremendous amount of new talent, who created new and vibrantly different ways of doing things. Any sane, perceptive bureaucrat who cared for the future of theatre would have encouraged such free, intrepid and seminal companies to grow and flourish.

But, alas, we have had no sane perceptive bureaucrats for many a year. Mr Tony Field, ex-Head of Finance at the Arts Council, actually wanted these companies to have the life-span of a butterfly, then rapidly die. There were so many of them, he argued, expecting regular support, that they were becoming a burden, to be chopped off.

The legacy of Mr Field's generation of arts bureaucrats is that 'centres of excellence' – the National Theatre and the RSC, and the new regional elites – buy up all the bright ideas and people from the independent companies put them through the mincer of their production processes, sanitise their ideology and cover them in gooey lighting. Their victims emerge no longer vibrant, different, startling or unique, but conformist, tame and toothless. If politics is to be allowed, it is certain to be the unedifying spectacle of left-wing writers presenting a travesty of their past allegiances.

The reason for this is not, of course, direct political repression. In the case of 7:84 England, CAST and some others, it clearly is: the confusion, self-contradiction and mendacity of their fictional 'reasons' for cutting 7:84 have convinced anybody who has studied them that the real reason is political distaste. Distaste for class politics. Class, after all, has been proved, to the satisfaction of the south-east of England, not to exist. And theatre that supports working-class aspirations, and reminds people of their history and their human potential, is clearly a bit of a bore in 1984, in the south-east of England.

But the urge to centralise and guarantee excellence is, though closely connected, due to a deeper malaise of the eighties: the growth of the corporate-state mentality in general, and its grip on the minds of arts bureaucrats and their committees in particular. As this mentality spreads and the frantic warnings of those who oppose it are swept aside as mere public relations problems, the need for more and more theatre that can bring people together to give voice to our condition, and even move those people to take action against it, grows urgent. That it is to be frustrated by the unscrupulous actions of appointees of this government, and of a bureaucracy now led by a buddy of the corporations, simply makes the need, and the offence against civilised values, the greater.

However we were not without determination, nor without friends. The TUC let us stay in the office; then Ken Livingstone and the GLC agreed to fund a major production with a £70,000 grant. The show was to be done in a Big Top on the South Bank car park. I conceived a show called All The Fun of the Fair:

ALL THE FUN OF THE FAIR[57]

My conception of *All the Fun of the Fair* was that it would be a travelling carnival of socialist politics and values. All around and inside the tent would be
side-shows – Fortune Tellers, Aunt Sallies, Wheels of Fortune with loaded
arrows, Try Your Strength machines, Hoop-tossing over objects just too
large – all the hucksters operating in true Tory Spirit, taking your money,
offering glittering prizes, but making it just impossible for the punter. The
show itself was to be a series of scenes from modern life cast in the mould
of or based on fun-fair or circus images – of Roller Coasters, the Wall of
Death, Freak Shows, Punch and Judy – with a band and songs in between.
I was excited by the prospect, bubbling over with ideas, eager to get it going.
We were pricing Big Tops, finding sites and raising extra cash with GLC
help from the other Metropolitan Boroughs in the North and Midlands –
who were all keen to have us during the summer of '84.

I was advised, and agreed, that I would need a director, as writing and
organising was quite enough. So I approached a good director – let's call
him Rupert. I went to see Rupert who received me cautiously, told me he
was an anarchist-Trotskyist, and somehow, I still don't know how, persuaded me by the end of the evening that I really didn't want to write *The
Funfair*, he certainly wouldn't direct it, but what I *really* wanted to do was
to commission him to write and direct a play to be set in the tent about life
on an oil-rig.

There was indeed a way that the idea of telling the stories of why a group
of men from all over Britain were forced out into the North Sea to survive
could have been quite good. Rupert wanted to flood the tent with water,
build the rig in the middle, and play all the non-rig scenes in the water. It
was to be called 'Britannia Rig'.

My admin team in London, let's call them Bill and Dave, went to see
Rupert, and came back pouring scorn on Funfairs and agog with the thrills
to come on the rig. They plunged in, booking the tent, the transport, the
crews, the sites, the actors, the musicians, the designer – who soon had the
set under way in a yard in Bradford – and the composer. All absolutely
great, but at this point we still had neither money nor written offer from the
GLC. Nevertheless the hard-pressed officials in the GLC were sure, confident, certain, etc. that the first large cheque would be with us – 'very soon',
'next week'.

We went into rehearsal not only without any money, but also without a
script. Rupert had been having a crisis of some kind, and was a bit behind.
With a great show of charisma he united the large-ish cast behind the idea
of creating the show in rehearsal, and soon they were all – or not quite all –
in a state which must have been similar to that in Jonesville in Guyana

before they took the poison, or in Munster in 1533, when the Anabaptists' faith in John of Leyden, also an ex-actor, led them to stand in starvation in the town square with their arms held out expecting on the third trump to be bodily assumed into everlasting glory.

Of course such a movement has to have an enemy. This turned out to be me, 7:84, and Neil Kinnock, in that order. Ken Livingstone soon joined us, as we shall see. By the Friday lunchtime of the first week, the cheque still had not arrived from the GLC. What had arrived was an injunction from the Conservative-run Westminster City Council forbidding the GLC to spend any money at all except that specifically listed in the base estimates, sums identified the year before. We were not so listed. Therefore we could not be paid, at least by any straightforward route.

We could not pay the wages by noon on Friday – the greatest crime in the theatre. With mutterings the company agreed to wait until the Monday. We held a Board Meeting over the weekend, and the Board instructed me that we could not continue to trade unless circumstances changed – i.e. a cheque arrived or a firm, dated promise was given. The GLC officials were still pretty confident they would find a way to release the money by the following Friday, but would put nothing on paper.

On the Monday morning I (Enemy Number One), on behalf of the 7:84 Board (Enemy Number Two), on which sat Neil Kinnock (Enemy Number Three), had to tell the company that Ken Livingstone (Enemy Number Four) had failed to deliver. We were confident that the money would come by Friday, but we could no longer ask them to work for us, as we could not guarantee their wages, and would be trading while insolvent – making the directors personally liable for the whole deficit and liable also to go to prison. Needless to say I was deeply unhappy, and angry – and suggested our anger should not be directed at the GLC who were doing everything to help, but at Westminster Council and the Tory plotters and planners, who were desperate to discredit the popular and successful policies of the GLC.

The company invited me to a short Equity meeting, but as part of management I thought it inappropriate, and went back to the office. At this 'short Equity meeting' Rupert and 7:84's administrators Bill and Dave, told the bemused and angry company that the resolution to their problems was not to attack the Tories, not to protest outside Westminster City Hall (this proposal was defeated with the observation that if they tried that they'd get their heads cracked open – a principled stand!) but by a cunning plan. They would go out the next morning with blankets and fruit and nuts into City Hall, the GLC headquarters, and occupy Ken Livingstone's office!

There is not a great deal to be said about the personal courage involved in this fearless decision. Nor about the political sagacity of handing the Tories a victory on a plate – a source of merry propaganda about the incompetent GLC, and a triumph in stifling a lefty theatre show. Nor about the likely practical effectiveness in getting the show on by embarrassing and betraying those who were already working flat out to help us.

I learnt of this only after it happened. I made my way down the mahogany corridors of the GLC, towards Ken's outer office, where they were – about 15 of them. I met one of the company on my way. Far from the joy of battle I could see only a baleful terror in his eyes, an aura combining nausea and puritanical fanaticism on his face. 'Hi. How are things?' I asked in a friendly fashion. The lips thinned, the pallor grew paler. 'I'm not allowed to speak to you,' he said. 'If you have any questions, you must address them to the whole company, and then go away. We will discuss our answers and elect a spokesperson to convey them to you, or not answer at all should we so decide.' 'Ah' I said, flummoxed. He moved on in a soldierly manner.

When I got to the office, Ken Livingstone's chief aide took me off for a meeting with the Drama Officer, an old friend from Scotland, and they told me of their proposals, well underway before the 'occupation', to present a cast-iron case at the Friday meeting which Ken Livingstone was to chair. They had a chance of lifting the injunction altogether by then, but failing that, their legal people, with whom I also had meetings, were cautiously confident, as were the others involved. One of the problems they faced was that they had what amounted to two administrations in most departments, the new officers brought in, and of course the old bureaucrats left over, who had some seniority, and whose blocking power was legendary. I imagine a similar problem confronts Gorbachev in pushing on with *perestroika*.

Eventually the aide, let's call him Alfred, and I had a meeting, or put a set of questions to the owl-faced throng. Solemnly the spokesperson, given the go-ahead each time by a nod from Rupert, unfolded the replies. They regarded the GLC as morally responsible, and 7:84 as legally responsible, and Neil Kinnock as politically responsible – a point of view that has something going for it. They were to occupy until satisfaction of their demand; their demand was now not for money to do the show, but for money to pay their full twelve-week contract and *not to do* the show.

It was now impossible to do the show, they said, since as 7:84 had broken their contract they were free to find other work, and theoretically they might have. It was pointed out to them that the GLC would find it difficult to vote money to a show that they knew was not going to happen. They refused to reply to this. Little did I know then that Rupert had accepted another job already, to begin on the following Monday, acting in, of all things, a Ben Jonson comedy. This obviously made the whole thing utterly impossible anyway.

The meeting on Friday voted us the money – cast iron, cheque on Monday. After the meeting it seems that the intrepid occupiers deliberately informed members of the Finance Department that they would not allow the show to go ahead. On hearing this, the Finance Director refused to issue the cheque.

The occupiers went off for other work or twelve weeks paid holiday. 7:84 was left with a commitment of £65,000, facing bankruptcy, unable even to pay its phone-bill.

The rest of the story is happier, in some ways. Ken and his people, with encouragement from our supporters, put together a package which enabled us to do a new show – *All the Fun of the Fair*, at last – and write off most of the deficit. I had spent so much time in the corridors and offices that my concentration on writing the show was not what it should have been. Chris Bond directed at the Half Moon, and it suffered from its painful gestation: it should have been a thing of great joy: it became bitty and bitter. The critics, new and old, did not enjoy it – but I was happy that it pointed, in its style, to a way to the future.

WELCOME TO ALL THE FUN OF THE FAIR[58]

When Prince Andrew was asked would he like lots of babies, he and his Sloane Ranger replied that it would be 'Quite Fun' – and laughed. Most of the beneficiaries of the Tory handouts and their immediate families are no doubt finding lots of things in life 'Quite Fun' – and we are being urged by the Tory propaganda machines in White City and Wapping to think of Britain as the land of surging hopes, reviving economy and lots and lots of fun for all to come in the neo-Nippon dawn of the hi-tech boom and enterprising, competitive capitalism.

They are trying to force on us a new definition of fun – something to do with Fergie Fizzes and whooping down ski-slopes and zapping Argies.

Our Fun Fair sets out to show another side of this Hooray Henry Fun Machine, to see the Fun Fair that is life in Britain's Inner Cities today. The imagery of the traditional fun-fair inspired the idea of transforming the theatre-spaces we visit, of using the variety and dislocation of the fairground to try to capture some of the feeling of life in the cities today and of exploding some of the myths of 'Fun' by showing what lies under the fun-fair, and helping give voice to the massive NO that is being felt in the hearts of the vast majority of the population to the appalling gruesome values of the Tory State.

We simply could not believe that 7:84 England could be destroyed by a malignant bureaucracy. Our public support was immense. The worldwide howls of rage that came in to the Arts Council were encouraging to say the least. We made plans to replace the Arts Council grant, we explored moving to Merseyside, where Merseyside Arts were prepared to pay half of our annual grant provided the Arts Council would pay the other half. The Arts Council declined.

The official reason for the cut was 'artistic standards'. Six months after they cut us, they wrote back to one protester that it was no longer a problem of standards, merely a 'change of policy'. The policy presumably being changed to one of not supporting 7:84. The fact that they had been telling lies for six months was never explained.

With the active intervention of the General Secretary of the TUC and several leading Trades Union leaders, we were offered an office and a telephone in Congress House for as long as we needed it.

Although we tried hard to keep going, and my son, fresh from Glasgow University, heroically manned the office, unpaid, we had no joy. Unity Theatre had a trust with a lot of money to spend, and insurance money to rebuild the burnt-out theatre in Mornington Crescent, but after many meetings it became apparent that squabbles and dissension within that once magnificent theatre meant no one would get the money except possibly the bar which stayed open through fire and flood. After a year or two of chasing shadows, we reluctantly wound up the company. When our grant was removed, we were presenting a succession of brilliant shows, highly popular with our audiences throughout England and Wales, successful by any definition. We had not failed: we were defeated.

MEANWHILE, IN SCOTLAND

I wrote a report for the Board on, amongst other things, a detailed plan to move into the under-used building that the Edinburgh Lyceum had as a wardrobe store, but which in fact was a brilliant little theatre, and is now the site of the Traverse Theatre and restaurant and bar. The report went on to more speculative areas, about the need to raise profile by mounting more big shows and touring them more widely in an effort to avoid being cut:[59]

POLITICS & PROFILE: There is no doubt that we are in a somewhat stronger position in Scotland than our comrades in England. But we must never become complacent or over-confident.

What can we do to make their job of getting rid of us harder?

The first thing is to maintain a high, and if possible scintillating, profile in the media, in Scotland, in London, and internationally.

I sincerely hope that Freeway Films[60] will get some form of go-ahead from Channel 4 to make *Blood Red Roses* in the autumn. Although there are complaints that this is taking too much of my time away from 7:84, I think these complaints are mistaken and short on imagination, and that a major TV production of one or more of our shows would be the best thing to happen to the company for a long time.

The Ragged Trousered Philanthropists did us a lot of good in Scotland, and we must pursue this line of work, not to exclude, but to make possible, the other work we do. *Men Should Weep*, and other bigger shows of ours, should be touring in England as well as Scotland, and any chance to get onto the International Festival Scene should be gone for with all our forces. Perhaps we need 7:84 Promos to help all this. We may in the past have been very puritanical about these things, or maybe just inexperienced. While we must never become PR merchants, we must wise up or die. I have put all that first to indicate a change of emphasis that will be difficult to make, and for some of us a bit distasteful.

The other thing we must continue to do, where we feel much more at home, is to strengthen our ties with the Labour and Trades Union Movement, and build on the solidarity of our audiences. There is no doubt that this is the most important in the long term, and the most attractive politically.

If we can manage to generate a circuit in England that is self-financing, perhaps even profitable for the company, then we should see that as another piece of furniture against the door.

In 1986 I wrote and directed a Highland Show called There Is A Happy Land, *which was a history in song and story of the Scottish Gaels, their diaspora and their future. I invited one of the excellent bands playing traditional Gaelic music to be part of the show. Ossian was a five-piece band, the songs were sung by Catherine-Ann MacPhee; Simon Mackenzie and Liz were the storytellers. We had a stage crew of three. Eleven people on a Highland tour charging only three pounds a ticket. This profligacy was later thrown at me by the Arts Council as a major crime. 'You must be mad' – I quote. The show, however, was a great success, and I later taped a version of it for Channel Four, which won the top award – the Spirit of the Festival award – at the Celtic Film & Television Festival.*

My next Highland tour was Mairi Mhor, *the story of Mary McPherson from Skye, a great singer and greater song-writer. We were back to four actors and a piano. The writing, by then, was on the wall.*

I wrote a report for the year 1987:

7:84 THEATRE COMPANY
THE SCOTTISH PEOPLE'S THEATRE[61]

The year between December 1986 and December 1987 could best be described as a year in which the company was not very good at the housekeeping, but excellent at getting out and doing the job. Our Weekly Returns may not always have got in to the Arts Council on time, but our audiences virtually trebled over the previous year, five highly successful tours were mounted, to considerable critical acclaim, our publishing programme continued, we have issued what looks set to become a hit record, the company were invited to Canada and took part in the Canadian Popular Theatre Alliance biennial Festival of Popular Theatre representing Western Europe, and were invited to play in the Berliner Ensemble theatre in Berlin, which we did to a huge reception. Since then two television dramas based on 7:84 plays have gone out on Channel 4, largely due to our association with Freeway Films – *Blood Red Roses* and *There is a Happy Land*.

At the same time we have taken steps to reduce our deficit, which was revealed during the course of the first half of the year to be £33,000, to almost nothing by the end of this financial year, without reducing our touring commitment – indeed increasing it; we have built up our income from local authorities; improved our financial control; and are all set to reorganise our administration.

We are also preparing proposals for an additional programme of work under the supervision of David Hayman, our Associate Director, and John McGrath, to take a more broadly based series of large-scale theatre shows on tour throughout Scotland, to replace the work of the now defunct Scottish Theatre Company in big theatres, and to represent Scottish mainstream theatre to the rest of the world.

The Tours

When we last met with the Drama Committee representatives in December of last year, we were about to open our production of *The Incredible Brechin Beetle Bug* by Matt McGinn. Our aim then was to present this excellent piece of children's Christmas theatre to audiences in parts of Scotland which would not normally receive a professional Christmas show. In this we succeeded – playing to great enthusiasm to large houses in Thurso, Wick, Fort William, The Borders, Brechin and Montrose. The show was directed by John Haswell, and benefited from the first venture into theatre of the popular folksinger Alasdair MacDonald. Since this show, the book of the songs of Matt McGinn, who died in 1977, has been brought out in Glasgow, and there are plans to reissue some of his records. The company formed many associations with schools and other groups which will stand it in good stead in the future.

The show toured for six weeks, and played to good, usually very good houses. Due to some undetected over-expenditure, mostly the costs of touring, particularly accommodation, the show cost more than it should have, and contributed to a deficit which was already growing due to the previous Highland Tour. The show proved so popular that we decided to bring it back this year, but to play for a long run in Glasgow, and only take it to places where the audiences would be large and the touring costs small, so capitalising on a success. In this way perhaps the losses of 86/87 would contribute to recouping the deficit in 87/88.

Our next tour, also directed by John Haswell, was a play we commissioned under the SAC [Scottish Arts Council] New Writing Scheme, from Ena Lamont Stewart, with whose play *Men Should Weep* we had such a great success a few years ago. *High Places*, as it was finally called, was not as good a play, but had some fine writing in it. It was enjoyed by many of our audiences, and toured for eight weeks in the lowlands and the industrial areas, being our Small-Scale Industrial Area Tour for the year.

During February, the company had the extraordinary honour of being invited to East Berlin to play in the Berliner Ensemble theatre, and to participate in the Festival of Political Song. The performance of *There is a Happy Land* in the Berliner was a great success, and the company were in great demand for concerts, official and impromptu, throughout the Festival.

During May, we were invited to the Canadian Popular Theatre Alliance's biennial Festival, held this year in Cape Breton. There were companies presenting popular theatre from India, Jamaica, Zimbabwe, Nicaragua and from all over Canada, where our work has inspired a number of emerging theatre companies. Several of them have sent people to work with us or observe us, and there is now a real friendship developing between the company and the Canadian popular theatre movement, as indeed there is with the Australian.

There is a Happy Land had a particular relevance to that part of Canada, and we had to repeat the performances several times, and take the show to other parts of the Province, where the Gaels demanded it. *The Baby and the Bathwater* was received with respect, admiration and solidarity in the Festival.

Meanwhile back at the housekeeping, things were looking difficult. The Finance Committee had been trying to extract accurate figures from the Administrator for some time, but when they were finally and fully revealed, what he had forecast as a £12,000 deficit transpired to be a £24,000 deficit, which, when added to our accumulated deficit of £9,000 gave a new accumulated deficit of £33,000. The SAC instructed us to completely recoup this whole deficit in the current financial year, and to fulfil the same number of weeks touring. Clearly, those touring plans had been based on a subsidy of £130,000 not one reduced to £97,000.

Fortunately our next show was our Large-Scale Tour, *The Gorbals Story*. This had been one of the major successes of the 1940s in Scottish Popular Theatre, and we had rediscovered it as part of our *Clydebuilt Season*. We had not been able to perform it then, but in David Hayman's highly acclaimed production it proved to be still as popular today, and indeed could have gone on for a long time in Glasgow.

The reviews were excellent, the cast and design very strong, the appeal to the audiences powerful. It was one of our greatest hits, and one of the greatest successes of Scottish Theatre during 1987. It toured all the major theatres of Scotland, playing to very good houses throughout, in His Majesty's Aberdeen, the Lyceum Edinburgh, Dundee Rep, and was invited to Newcastle Playhouse for a week. It took far more in Box-Office than we had budgeted, and is making a healthy contribution to our efforts to elimi-nate the accumulated deficit during this year.

After the run of *The Gorbals Story*, the company went dark until September. At this point the Administrator left, and we decided the Artistic Director would also handle the finances of the next tour, to save money – in more senses than one. This tour was our Highlands and Islands Tour of the year, a new play – NOT commissioned under the SAC New Writing Scheme, because the writer was the Artistic Director, which apparently disqualifies him from being treated as a normal writer.

The play was *Mairi Mhor – the Woman From Skye*, and featured the songs and life of Mairi Mhor nan Oran, the greatest Gaelic songwriter of the nine-teenth century, a woman, and the bard of the Highland Land League in the 1880s – a period of considerable importance but great neglect, in the history of the Highlands and Islands. We could only afford a short tour of four weeks, but with generous help from HIDB, Highland Region, the Western Isles Council and Skye & Lochalsh District, its tour was memorable. We played for a week in the Western Isles, and on Skye, and in Inverness, as well as a week in Aberdeen, and in Edinburgh and Glasgow. The show was very well received, particularly in the West, and as the reviews show, was well received critically, with the critic of the *Guardian*, as usual, the only sour plum. We have received a spate of letters from other parts of the Highlands complaining that we have not visited them this time, and indeed the short-ness of the tour has meant we are neglecting whole areas of Scotland we would normally visit every year. Nevertheless it was thought prudent not to risk further losses. As it turned out, the show cost far less than it should, being written for four performers only, and mounted with impecunity, and the income both from box-office and from Local Authorities was well up on budget forecast, so this production also is making a good contribution to elimi-nating the deficit, as well as being in the best tradition of 7:84 as theatre.

Books & Records

7:84 is continuing its series of publications of Scottish Popular Theatre of the Twentieth Century with two additions to our list. One was a re-issue in May of *Men Should Weep*, with fuller critical apparatus, reviews, etc.

The series as a whole has done a great service to the neglected master-pieces of Scottish working-class theatre, and is selling well. Of our previous publications, *Blood Red Roses* has been made an option for Strathclyde schools, and is virtually sold out.

We have gone into partnership with Greentrax Records to release Catherine-Ann MacPhee's first album. Our contribution to the costs of the recording, etc. was helped very much by the generous sponsorship of Tele na Gael Ltd, a new independent company producing programmes from the Highlands and Islands, whose contribution of £1,500 will be matched by ABSA [Association of Business Sponsorship for the Arts]'s sponsorship scheme.

Organisation

The company has been experiencing a certain amount of administrative difficulty. The strengthening of the Board's Finance Committee, chaired by Robin Worrall, has meant that problems have been identified earlier than usual, but there is no substitute for an efficient, high-powered administrative team in the office. This we have not had over the past year.

There is an appalling shortage of competent administrators in the UK as a whole, and in Scotland in our kind of theatre in particular. This may well be because the opportunities for rapid career advancement are not so many or so attractive as they are in the metropolis, or it may simply be that the money available does not attract the right kind of person. The SAC itself has done very little to encourage Arts Admin training to any high level in Scotland. The option of sending people to the City University seems to produce expatriates by the dozen, who rarely come back, and if they do are no use to touring companies. Perhaps we should recognise this as an area where complacency and recrimination are not in order.

The company has advertised recently for a new administrator. We go into the interviews with optimism, but the level of applicants has not been high. We do not propose to appoint another inadequate person. The solution may well be to headhunt. This may result in a situation where for the first time in its life 7:84 has to pay differential rates. The Board are debating this point at the moment.

The Future

As far as the work of the company itself is concerned, we see no diminishing of the demand for the three main areas of our work: Larger Theatre tours, mostly looked after by David Hayman; smaller-scale industrial area tours organised by John Haswell, who also looks after our Community Programme; and Highlands & Islands Tours, the province of John McGrath, who continues to be in overall charge of all areas, and responsible for Company Policy.

However, plans are now emerging for the next three years, and we wholeheartedly welcome the SAC's proposals to stabilise income for the next three years. We hope this will become a Three-Year Rolling Plan, and that it will bring the chance for a lot better forward planning, and a certain amount of stability and security.

Our plans for next year (88/89) include a new production at Mayfest, which will tour large theatres and then return to Glasgow to the Pavilion Theatre to inaugurate a Three Play Season there to run through the Garden Festival, from July to September.

Also during the coming year, we are planning to mount a major event in collaboration with Freeway – a new production for Channel 4 on Anglo-Scots relations, called *Border Warfare*.

And we plan to present a Highland Tour of a version of *The Silver Darlings*.

For 1989, we are planning an ambitious Promenade Production of Ariane Mnouchkine's play *1789* – and hope she will be able to have some involvement in the production herself.

We are also planning an exchange with a company from Soviet Georgia – the Film Actors' Studio of Tbilisi – and intend to take *Border Warfare* on tour to Georgia and other centres in the USSR.

For 1990, we are planning the third of our Popular Song/ Popular History pieces, about the story of the Clydeside and the growth of the industrial working class of Scotland, to be presented as part of the City Of Culture festivities. [Glasgow was Europe's 'City of Culture' in 1990.]

Expansion of Large-Scale Touring

Due to the sad demise of the Scottish Theatre Company, it looks as though the provision of larger-scale, touring productions to Scotland's larger theatres will be curtailed unless proposals come forward to replace STC's work.

7:84 has for many years actually been playing these very theatres, with a comparatively high level of success. While we do not wish to change the nature of our basic operation, we are now in a position to put forward a series of concrete proposals to the SAC to extend the nature and the scope of our Large-Scale Touring operation to include provision of high-quality, classical and Scottish plays from the main stream of theatre, presented in a way that will make them both accessible to and enjoyable by Scottish audiences.

We realise that the first problem will be a political one, in the sense that 7:84 has taken a clear political stance in its work, and it may be considered unsuitable for the larger theatre-going audiences to have too much of this element. Of course the position we have taken turns out to be that of the vast majority of the population of Scotland, and we see no reason to alter it, but we do understand that in presenting work for a theatre-going audience, we would have to make it clear that they were not going to be ideologically savaged in some way.

David Hayman, who is our Associate Director, and responsible for most of our successes in this area in recent years, has expressed a strong personal commitment to this project, and is very excited at the possibilities it holds for extending the range of theatre available throughout Scotland. He is interested in discussing a three-year programme that will include a continuation of the line of very successful Scottish revivals we have now under way, but will be extended to include also some Shakespeare, Chekhov, Lorca, Brecht, Büchner (specifically a Scots version of *Woyzeck*) and Scots versions of foreign classics.

We have not applied in this area before as we did not wish to get into conflict with the STC. We regret their passing, and feel we could provide something very seminal for future theatre generations in Scotland in their place, as well as making very exciting theatre for theatre-goers now, and provide a continuity of employment for some of Scotland's more experienced and skilled performers.

It sounds as if, and indeed it was, a healthy, productive and hard-working set-up. In spite of the Arts Council, in spite of the operational changes forced on us, 7:84 Scotland was well recovered from the Women in Power *fiasco, and doing good work. But the world was changing. Tory triumphalism was rampant, and the Tory triumph was affecting the whole of the UK, even the Labour Movement in Scotland.*

In 1987 the axe fell. Liz was in the 7:84 office, and noticed a letter from the Scottish Arts Council to our administrator, lying on a desk. As everybody in the company had access to everything, she read it. It told him that 7:84's grant was to be completely cut after the incoming year, and ordered him not to tell anyone until after their press conference – at which they did not intend to announce it. I was in New Zealand at their Writers and Readers Conference. The phone rang in my hotel room in Auckland at 3 in the morning: it was Liz, with the news. We agreed she would picket the Arts Council press conference and hand out photocopied leaflets to the press telling them what the SAC were trying to suppress. It appears there was a near-riot inside, the press demanding answers, the SAC evasive, the Chair apoplectic that their plans had been overtaken by the truth. I later had a meeting with the SAC Drama Director, and managed to get a letter out of her. In a hopelessly optimistic spirit, desperately trying to think positive, I reported to the Board:

CRISIS FOR 7:84 SCOTLAND

Memo to 7:84 Board
re: Withdrawal of Funding[62]

Having now had a chance to examine the letter from the Arts Council dated 18 March 1988, I would like to outline some comments to assist in discussions that may arise in private or in public, and particularly at the Board meeting.

To begin with, this response from the SAC to our application for Three Year Funding is totally unexpected, indeed we were expecting not only Three Year Funding but also extra money for touring in the Highlands and Islands, and extra money for a Six Week Large/Medium Scale tour in the autumn. At the last meeting with the Drama Committee representatives, in November, while we had tried to clear up some misunderstandings that had been in their minds about *Mairi Mhor*, and some complaints about their forms not being returned on time, there was no hint of any action as draconian or as final as this. Therefore to say it comes as a shock is to understate the case.

Detailed Comments

The SAC'S reasons for withdrawing funding to the company come under three headings, with various points in each category. I shall take them in their order.

1. In Terms of the Board

They claim they are not convinced 'that there have been sufficient changes to the Board to enable it to act as a body which has a clear, objective view of the management and operation of the company.'

The Chairman of the SAC has declared that any attempt to say the cut is politically motivated is 'evil nonsense'. So far we have not said that. It was the Press who raised the question, not us. However, to question the competence of our Board clearly has some politically different view of the role of a Board.

The 7:84 Board has traditionally been made up of three strands:

i. People distinguished in public life whose advice, help and support we value, even if they may not always manage to get to meetings. We are always in touch with them, and they have done a great deal for the company.

ii. Representatives of the communities we take our shows to, often people who organise venues, or who are prominent in the life of their communities, from all over Scotland.

iii. Past or present members of the working company, who are on the Board to represent the interests of the 'employees'.

To these, we have added the business acumen of the proprietor of a successful business, the immense knowledge of our kind of theatre of a distinguished administrator and the professional knowledge of one of Scotland's top theatre agents. The Board is also assisted by an experienced accountant, the staff in the office at the time, and by two members of the company who are not necessarily Board members, to report on the current tour.

Amongst the members of the Board are some very distinguished and indeed eminent people, who bring their experience in many areas of life either to our discussions at Board meetings or to personal meetings outside the Board meetings. There is not one whom we would like to lose.

However, we must try to regard the Arts Council's observations in a positive and practical spirit – without completely destroying our own principles.

If there is indeed the need for more 'objective' people to maintain a clear view of the company's management, then perhaps we should consider the creation of a Management Committee, which will not interfere, as some Management Committees have been known to, in the right of the Board and the Artistic Director and his team to formulate Policy, but will bring a knowledgeable and objective group of views to the actual Management and Financial and Administrative problems of the company, and would meet more regularly – on a monthly basis – and would have a broader range of experience of the specific problems of a theatre company than our present Finance Committee.

I would recommend the consideration of this proposal, or alternative proposals, as one way to overcome what the Arts Council perceives as a weakness.

2. In Terms of the Administration and Financial control

The SAC letter states:

'The Committee has been concerned for several years about the quality of the administration and about the inability of the company to retain the services of an efficient and experienced person for the job.'

While it is certainly true that we have gone through a difficult period in this area, and that during the year 1986/87 we did make a deficit due to inadequacies in this area, there does seem to be an unnecessarily fatalistic tone to this remark.

First of all, they must be aware, as the Drama Director was party to our interviews, that we do now have the services of a very competent, experienced Administrator. She will also have been able to inform the committee of the high priority we placed on this appointment, and the vigour with which we pursued a solution.

The bulk of the accumulated deficit of £33,000 we incurred during the problem year 1986/87. Before that, the deficit was £9,000. The SAC comments:

'However, the committee were concerned to learn that in spite of being a condition of grant aid for the last 3 years, the company would not be able to clear its deficit, or the majority of it, by the end of 1987/88, and that it would only be able to contribute approximately £14,000 towards its accumulated deficit due to certain problems that occurred with the winter tour of *The Incredible Brechin Beetle Bug*.'

Obviously we must take this criticism very seriously, although it must be said that the ultimatum that we should clear our total deficit of £33,000 in one year and still do the same number of touring weeks was a very punitive one, and always going to be difficult to achieve. The fact that we may well have cleared over half of it must be considered a success, or at least not a total failure.

The complaint of not receiving weekly returns was one which occupied the SAC a great deal during my meeting with them. This is one which they also agree can be very easily remedied.

There is obviously a need for the office to maintain a steady flow of information to the Drama Department at the SAC, and for Reports etc. to be delivered in good time. This must become one of our main priorities, whether we like it or not.

3. In Terms of Artistic Product

The Arts Council's assessors have views of our shows which we may well not agree with. Reading their reports to the Drama Committee is bloodcurdling stuff. The main complaint in the letter is of *Mairi Mhor*, but every show gets hit hard, *The Gorbals Story* and *In Time of Strife* among them. The assessors clearly have a set of values which are opposed to the theatrical values of the company. What exactly we can do about this is hard to say. There is a level of scorn – not to say contempt – in the collected assessments which I find difficult to react to.

In my meeting with the Drama Director this morning, she said she thought we should apply for Project funding for two of the projects in our set of proposals by September, i.e. *1789* and *The Silver Darlings*, and that we should put in an appeal during October for the November meeting.

The main recommendations she made were that by that time we should have produced the three shows, or two of the three shows that we planned, that they should be artistically very good indeed, that we should have set ourselves up on a firm financial footing, and that we should have a strong administrative team, and have turned our Board into an efficient team like that of a commercial company with its members having a wide range of business skills, and attending regularly.

Either we choose to continue making theatre in roughly speaking the style we have developed over the years, or we change to suit the tastes of supercilious assessors, or we pack it in, or we try to transform our style.

I hope that in addressing ourselves to these demands we can remain true to the socialist inspiration and purpose of our work.

RESIGNING FROM 7:84 SCOTLAND[63]

Scott *You've written at some length about the period when you were forced to resign, first from the Board and then as Artistic Director and then from the Company altogether. How do you feel about that period?*

You mean the period when I was obliged to leave the Company because I would not stomach the changes that the Arts Council were forcing upon it? I think what was going on at that time was a determined move to follow London. Most, as we know, of the arts administrators in Scotland crept up from London during the 1980s and the arts policy in Scotland seems to follow London with a gap of about three years. When the English Company went, Elizabeth actually said to me, 'We've got three years.' She was dead right, to the minute. It was very strange.

Scott *The big difference, though, was that after you decided to quit the Company, the grant was reinstated.*

Right. There was a huge response from all over the world to the idea that we were going to get cut. The Arts Council were saying, 'We will reconsider if certain things happen.' I eventually got an audience with the Arts Council, where I was told three things would have to change. One, we would have to stop touring the Highlands with such ambitious shows because they were losing money. The second was that we would have to abandon our policy of having equal wages for everybody in the Company, which we'd held to for seventeen years, and we would have to have a General Manager at what was called the 'market price', which turned out to be slightly more than twice the wages that everybody else in the Company was on. Thirdly, that I would have to sack all the Board of Directors because they were obviously not being competent, people like Gordon Brown, for example, and Norman Buchan – and people who represented the audiences from all over Scotland, who came to our Board Meetings to feed back what they were thinking and feeling about what we were doing. Members of the Company, past and present, who were on the Board representing the people who did the job, they would all have to go, and they would have to be replaced by people who were lawyers, accountants, business people and people who were, I was told, politically objective about our work. I think it was probably that none of those were conditions acceptable to me, having spent all my life building a company that existed on totally different principles.

I had a choice at that time, either I could stand on the bridge of the ship, salute and go down with the ship heroically or I could take a slightly more tactical view and say well maybe if I resign, somebody else can take over who will be able to use this subsidy to do similar work. Rightly or wrongly – and sometimes I regret it – I decided that it would be better to resign and allow somebody else, who wasn't tied with the commitments I'd made to my principles, to try to move in and operate within what the Arts Council wanted.

When I resigned from the company, my resignation letter to our new chair, Bill Spiers, of the Scottish TUC, was the front-page headline in The Scotsman, *and the SAC, their Drama Committee in particular, were made to look what they were, politically repressive fools, all over the world.*

There was a huge response: from Trades Unions in New Zealand to local branches in Wick, from theatres in Canada to academics in Cambridge, from the Berliner Ensemble to widows in Ayrshire – all too late to save me, but helping to rescue the company from oblivion.

Over the years we had played theatres in Belgium, Holland, Canada, the USSR, Berlin, as well as London and of course all over Scotland. We got letters of support from all of them except the leading Scottish theatres, who didn't think it appropriate.

The withdrawal of the grant was met with bafflement and rage everywhere. It was technically because we had not completely cleared a paper deficit of £33,000 in one year – we'd only cleared £14,000. Given the subsequent handouts to Scottish Opera, the sum of £19,000 – not an overdraft, merely a Balance Sheet deficit – seems flimsy stuff. But as I had resigned, and the pressure on the Arts Council was immense, they told the new 'realist' administrator the company could continue.

I told Robert Dawson Scott:[64]

I was very pleased that the work was carrying on and I felt positive about it, particularly after Hayman and Kelly left and a new young outfit took over. But it was very different from what we were doing. In a way I just wish that they'd changed the name and not called it 7:84, because it is now doing a good job and one that I value for itself, but it's another theatre company. They are very patiently trying to rebuild an audience in various places. They're trying to create a style which is recognisable. They're trying to extend the language of the Company, which I think is very good. I think that they're going in an interesting way but somehow not the way that was central to my thinking. But, why should they?

Scott   *Do you think that if you'd ducked and dived a wee bit, back in the mid-1980s, if you'd perhaps made one or two different choices, that you could still be running 7:84 now?*

Well politicians never answer hypothetical questions. I think actually if we'd done *Border Warfare* one year sooner, the whole attitude towards 7:84 and towards what I was trying to do with the Company would have been very different.

Scott   *You put the vast chunk of your most creative years into this Company and in the end you left under a cloud.*

The way I left the Company was entirely consistent with the way I started the Company: it was sticking to exactly the same attitudes and principles that started the Company going.

Scott   *What I was driving at was that the whole wider political world was just too hostile an environment to survive, and that was not anything to do with you particularly, it was just . . . that was the reality of the time.*

Well the reality of the time always had a lot to do with 7:84. I mean we tried to reflect it in the work we did, and I think that was probably the problem: that we were too close to the reality of the time for comfort. I don't think we ought to subscribe to conspiracy theories, but at the same time I don't think we ought to forget that Margaret Thatcher put her people into every position in the institutions right through the whole of British civil society in order to bring about the biggest social engineering feat since the Mongol hordes invaded Muscovy. It is an amazing piece of social engineering and we were swept aside almost without too much thinking; we were just a bit of an irritant.

The Chair of the Drama Committee, and prime wielder of the hostile axe, recently told a student interviewing her that she thought they had made a huge mistake in cutting me out of 7:84. Again, I am sure we had not failed (except in the matter of the uncleared deficit) – once again, we had been defeated by a government determined to destroy all opposition. As in all these cases, it simply served to intensify the opposition: I took two terms away in Cambridge to write The Bone Won't Break:

THE BONE WON'T BREAK[65]

In *A Good Night Out*, I described the work of 7:84 and other theatre companies in playing to working-class and non-theatre-going audiences, and the
experiences, cultural, personal, artistic, that had led me to turn away from
a career in 'Mainstream' theatre and film and television, and spend my time
writing, directing and organising shows to tour round the places where
working people usually went for their entertainment, shows which had
direct relevance to their lives, and the story of their class. One of the main
planks of the work was the need for 'class-consciousness' in the working
class, that is, knowledge of, solidarity with those with common interests and
roles in society. Through the 60s and 70s this concept of 'class-consciousness' raised no problems: people knew what it meant, and knew it existed,
and could chart its growth. Now, ten years later, the concept is unfamiliar,
a word for something that no longer exists, something that failed.

Mrs Thatcher recently went so far as to question the idea that we live in
a thing called a 'society'. 'What society?' she asked, with fearless intellectual
rigour, 'we don't belong to society, we are all just individuals, doing the best
we can for ourselves.' And what could be fairer than that? Far from being
class-conscious, we are now not even conscious of being part of society as a
whole! I presume the concept of patriotism transcends this argument, but
otherwise she has no doubts that people should see themselves as belonging
to groupings no larger than the family, and the only things we have in common with others is the desire to do well for ourselves: this we have in common
with everybody – some may have succeeded, indeed some spectacularly, others
may have had less success – some none whatsoever – but we are all trying,
that's what keeps us both together and apart.

This magisterial refutation of Marx, Weber, Lenin and the whole of
sociological thought in the twentieth century would be laughable, if its purpose were not so plain, and its effects – as imposed on the self-perception of
a great many citizens of the USA – so palpably beneficial to the forces of
reaction.

So there was I, basing my whole artistic practice on the concept of 'class-
consciousness', and there was the leader of my country telling me it didn't
exist. What is more, she was going to make certain it didn't exist, by telling
people, over and over again, very slowly, that it didn't exist. And this was
only the first method of disintegrating the nation. There were many others.
All of them played a major part in the way I was able to work.

The second, and most obvious method was the systematic destruction by
a series of governments with large majorities of all the *institutions* of the
working class, the very embodiments of class-consciousness. The trades
unions obviously had to go, or be refashioned in the image of American

unions – providential societies, offering discount mail-order sales, pension- and private health-care schemes, old folks Christmas parties and holiday packages on the Costa Brava. So ASLEF was humbled, the teachers brought to heel, the AUEW under Gavin Laird turned into a toothless, compro- mised, strike-free zone, the Electricians under Hammond not even fit to stay in the TUC, and the doughty miners under Arthur 'the Horned Serpent' Scargill beaten into submission, physically smashed, sacrificially slaughtered by the media, and finally split in two, in a move that Frank Kitson must have savoured. With the unions smashed up, the TUC itself had little to sustain any militancy it might have had; it is now split, and largely ignored. It plays no central role in public life.

The Labour Party itself was subject to a succession of splits and natural disasters, not to mention a media black propaganda campaign that made the Dublin cinema bombing look amateur. The creation of the SDP, so earnestly supported by Norman Tebbit, made sure that the Tories would be able to keep on slipping in between the SDP and Labour. If Labour had ever embodied working-class consciousness, both were seen to be humi- liated throughout the 80s.

But the third reason for the disintegration of this very consciousness was the Labour Party itself. In common with almost every Social Democratic party in Europe, and Australia and New Zealand, it has undergone a dramatic, or some might think suspiciously well-co-ordinated change in its purposes. The old Parliamentary Labourism made endless compromises in a desire to show it could make capitalism work better than the Conservatives; the new-ish Crosland/Gaitskell revisionist tendency, based on the quietist assumption that most people really can't be bothered with politics and should be allowed to dig their gardens, led to a fear of mobilisation of any kind. In the 80s the Labour Party had capitulated almost entirely to the smart efficiencies of the market economy, which of course leads them to an acceptance of an individualist, competitive ethic. They justify this by their need to attract the middle-class and professional-class vote. They end up no longer the expression of the class-consciousness of the working class, but as 'the party for all the people'. Of course their emphases are different, and some policies, including their arts policy, are very conscious of the needs of the working class, but their philosophy has shifted crucially from collective to individual action, and motivation, and so from class- to individualised consciousness.

The fourth contributory factor is one that has long been a feature of the British working-class – the 'self-improvement' ethos, which has now become an extreme reluctance in many if not most working-class people to call themselves 'working-class', indeed to regard being called that as something of an insult. Apart from the sturdy yeoman tradition of not wanting to be pigeon-holed, stereotyped or dismissed, this self-perception is also based on a sense of the possible inferiority implied by the phrase 'working-class', and a desire to assert that 'we' are as good as 'them'. Nevertheless these same people also have long held a great loyalty to the institutions of labour and to the local 'culture' of the working class – the pride in being Yorkshire, or Scouse, or Brummie; the pride in local dialect, traditions, places; the fanatical pride in the football team; the clannishness, exclusiveness, distrust of strangers; the love of local jokes, songs, comedians, pubs – all these still unite people in an ambivalent way: at times purely local, at others symbols of solidarity. A great many theatre companies around Britain drew on just this sensibility to draw in the crowds, and to present them with longer per-spectives, wider horizons, unexpected connections.

Of course the working class has undergone a very significant change in the last ten years: unemployment has split it in two, creating a sub-class of very young and older people mostly, who no longer see the name 'working' class as meaning them. In some ways they see themselves 'opposed' to and by those in work, who pay tax to keep them housed, clothed and fed. New, UB40 culture, is growing up with all the dangers of aimlessness and political instability traditionally associated with the 'lumpen' or 'ragged' proletariat.

Sixth, there is the new ideology associated with Euro Communism of the *Marxism Today* variety: the 'identity of interests' of many minorities will together create a major force. How often have they been glibly lumped to-gether – blacks, women, Asians, the disabled, the jobless, the gays and les-bians, even 'kids'? Often these groups have nothing in common *except* being a 'minority' – which of course 'women' are not.

This ideology – based on the revision that abolished the 'dictatorship of the proletariat' – is a serious, thought-through set of ideas, and has split the Communist Party in fragments: one part clinging to the idea that the working class will lead a socialist revolution and so create a classless society, the other apt to characterise the actually existing working class as sexist, racist, brute macho dim-wits who belong with Tory backwoodspersons, indeed can be demonstrated to be locked in a mutually dependent, endless negotiation with the ruling class. Needless to say, this belief, now wide-spread, has further diminished the role of the working class, and its central-ity to revolutionary struggle, and so has made class-consciousness secondary to gender – and racial struggles.

The absence of any clear and obviously relevant development in Marxist or Socialist political, social or philosophical theory in the past decade has led to an air of staleness and repetition in the writings and exhortations of the left in general, and of Labour politicians and Trades Union leaders in particular. Having been put on the defensive by a series of massive defeats, the ideologists of the British working class have failed to respond with much more than rhetoric, clever devices or a masochistic glorying in the outrage-ous triumphalism of the right.

To this I need not add that the immense propaganda machine of the Tory party and government, financed with tax-payers' money as well as the cash from big business, and the associated onslaughts of the press, have not made the presentation of working-class perspectives to the public any easier. Indeed there is a case to argue that without this image-factory working full-blast against it, the class-consciousness of the working class would never have declined as sharply as it has. In Scotland, the main newspapers are not in the pocket of the Tory party; this could well be a crucial reason for the almost total success of anti-Thatcher politics in Scotland, and the relative strength of the Scottish TUC and the unions.

It is in the context of the decline in working-class consciousness I have just outlined that I have been working for the last ten years. I have been working as a writer and director in theatre, film and television; as Artistic Director of two political theatre companies; as Producer and Executive Producer in films; I started and now run an independent company making programmes for television; I have worked as Chairperson of the Independent Programme Producers Association in Scotland, and on its Council in London through the negotiations for Access to ITV and BBC; and I've been a fairly active member of ACTT, the film and TV union, the Writers Guild, the Directors Guild, the British Academy of Film and Television Arts, and of Equity, the theatre union. I am not a member of any political party, but am of the libertarian socialist left, and have led a moderately active life in politics in Scotland, particularly in cultural politics, or the politics of culture. More importantly, during the last ten years I have written at least fourteen full-length plays for the stage, one opera libretto, seven television plays, one documentary and two feature films, as well as directing most of them and a few by other writers. It has been a period of almost continuously frenzied activity.

The crucial questions for Marxists are those connected with the revolutionary role of the proletariat – which itself has been a subject of great contention. To many of you it may well have a quaint and rather scholastic air – and indeed one could well be forgiven for asking, in late 80s Western Europe – 'Which revolution? What role? Which proletariat?' – as none of these is even remotely on the agenda. To suggest that the correct organisation of the coming revolution should be the primary concern of socialists in Britain today does display a certain vagueness about reality, and a criminal neglect of other, more pressing priorities.

Nevertheless, the fact remains that an Establishment controlling Britain does exist, made up of powerful men (and a very few women) in the financial, industrial, military, and multinational sectors, which finds allies throughout our civil society. Clearly in political circles, but also in the legal, judicial, police, Special Branch network, in the educational establishment, among many top professional people of all kinds, among the large land-owners, and, crucially, in the Civil Service executive. This mighty and altogether unselfconscious set of people – just individuals doing well for themselves, as Thatcher would say – is ably and vigorously supported by the various American levers of pressure – NATO, the US Embassy, the CIA, and the World Bank – as well as the now very effective pressures from the altogether unelected officials of the Common Market.

It can scarcely be denied, given the spectacle of Tory Party Conferences, that we do have a ruling class. Interestingly, they are not at all ashamed of *their* class-consciousness, they are almost exemplary in their class loyalty, in their self-definition and projection, in their internationalism and solidarity with their comrades in difficulties – Pinochet in Chile, Somoza in Nicaragua, the charmless rulers of El Salvador and Guatemala. But at home, they are not often ostentatious, prefer to be seen as family-men sharing homely problems with their employees, nice to meet, sharp, intelligent and able to afford to be kind and considerate.

If this then is the 'ruling' class, whom do they rule? Or if we choose to see them as managerial rather than proprietorial, whom do they manage? The preferred answer is that they merely regulate their own small area of other lives, including each other's, that they have no community of interest, merely serve their own imperatives in a small segment of the capitalist economy, and so are not 'ruling' anybody.

But this won't do. We have seen their collectivity of interest expressed in government activity for ten years; we have seen their class-consciousness expressed in the ideology of the radical right, now dominant. And we have seen that while 'they' and those close to and supportive of 'them' have flourished in the last ten years, others have seriously declined, have suffered actual hardship – physical, social and psychological – and that these 'others' do have certain common characteristics.

A great many 'others' exist whose whole lives are in part – in certain vital parts – ruled or managed by the ruling class; whose interests may not be identical, but who have strong common interests; who may not have an adequate, shared ideology or set of assumptions, but who have opinions and priorities which oppose those of the ruling class to some extent, and which are constantly under attack; who may not be very articulate or sophisticated in a literary sense, but who have an experience of life which they need to express or participate in the expression of; who may not perceive themselves as of any particular class or group, who may certainly not experience their lives as 'oppressed' or see any other group as 'oppressors' – conscious or unconscious – but who when looked at objectively are not able to experience the same fulfilment in life that others clearly are: who are, objectively, oppressed.

This is an attempt to identify the people in our society – who are I believe in the majority – who make up the opposition to the new dominant ethos, who are economically, or in other resources, net losers in the thrusting entrepreneurial society. I shall simply call them The Resistance, and note that they undoubtedly exist, and are almost certainly a majority of the population of the UK.

They are both the subject of and the audience for the kind of theatre, film and television which my colleagues and I are trying to make. It is their life-experience, needs, values and aspirations that I and my colleagues in 7:84 and many other companies have been working to articulate.

The alarm at the blatantly repressive tactics of the Thatcher government was being felt by many sections of society. As for the theatre in general, there was some horror at the antics of the Arts Councils as carriers of the Thatcherite torch. New Theatre Quarterly *convened a Symposium:*

'NEW THEATRE QUARTERLY' SYMPOSIUM[66]

On 7 May 1988 a meeting was held involving a number of theatre practitioners and academics on the left, to discuss the current state of British theatre under Thatcherism. The meeting was organised by Vera Gottlieb and NTQ Editor Simon Trussler. Also present were Clive Barker, Pam Brighton, Colin Chambers, Trevor Griffiths, Peter Holland, Kate Harwood, Albert Hunt, Nesta Jones, John McGrath, Paul Moriarty, Rob Ritchie, and Juliet Stevenson.

VERA GOTTLIEB: First of all, do we believe that there is a crisis of the theatre and for the theatre, beyond the economic - an ideological crisis? Secondly, if there is, would a national conference help to concert opposition? Thirdly, if that's the case, what would be the issues to put before such a conference?

CLIVE BARKER: I've a feeling that in some ways you have to go back to parish politics. There's been a meeting of people in the Warwickshire area, for instance, to discuss the provision of theatre right through from education to the professional and touring areas. It's surely a question of setting up forums like that to work through particular local demands. If you shut down the National Theatre, everyone can see you've shut down the National Theatre. If you shut down 7:84 England, it's two years before you realise that they haven't come round as they used to. Consequently the steam goes out of the opposition.

PAUL MORIARTY: It seems to me that the problem with parish politics, or parish theatre, is its almost Thatcherite assumption – that you get on with it in isolation, and do what you can.

JOHN MCGRATH: I think we have to be careful not to find what Raymond Williams called 'long-term solutions to short-term problems'. I've a slightly different perspective, living in Scotland. Everybody says, 'This country is finished, Labour are wiped out.' They're not at all wiped out in Scotland. Every time I come to England I sense that people are sinking lower and lower, and feeling that everything is absolutely finished for ever – that there is no solution to this except going into some sort of vortex, where you're constantly chasing yourself in a kind of ideological purity that has no relationship to what's going on in the rest of the country. Either that, or you give in, which is what an awful lot of people are doing.

TREVOR GRIFFITHS: It's called 'new realism'.

JOHN MCGRATH: The Scottish situation, for the sake of argument, is different. We do have a huge majority of Labour and oppositional forces not only in parliamentary representation but also within local authorities, and certainly the working-class movement is not dead either. When the Scottish Arts Council threatened 7:84 Scotland, for example, the first people to get involved were the chairman of the Scottish Labour Party, the General Secretary of the Scottish TUC, and the leaders of all the unions. Which implies to me that we shouldn't go around saying that these people are finished, whatever we think of their politics and the compromises they're prepared to make.

It's certainly a mistake to think that there will never again be a Trades Union Movement in England. It's a ludicrous concept, because the working class do not go away. They may become transformed into machines, and consequently unemployed, but they still remain human beings who require voices and representation. I know it does appear that 80% of the population of England has taken leave of its senses, but that's a site of struggle, and it's wrong to begin the argument from a basis of defeat.

COLIN CHAMBERS: It would be a great antidote to whatever pessimism we do feel to have a centre, particularly if it was to implement some form of manifesto. We are all together, we're not taking it lying down, and let's begin that process of saying we're going to fight back.

JOHN MCGRATH: On the economic front, which you can't avoid, the most important movement is towards replacing state aid with business sponsorship. We know all the arguments about this, I'm sure, but it should be articulated again and again that this is a criminal procedure and is actually disempowering people. The whole idea of selecting what will survive – the survival of the fittest, the definition of the fittest being those companies which attract Rothmans – is utterly irresponsible in terms of cultural activity.

It's the most dangerous thing that's going on. The central part of the Arts Council's three-year plan for theatre funding is the three-part ratio: public money, your own income from box office, and sponsorship. You have to predict these ratios for three years, and if your forecast doesn't show a significant increase in sponsorship your chance of getting funding is considerably decreased. This is a monstrous form of interference.

There has also been a terrible process of erosion brought about partly by the Arts Council's specific anti-new play policy, which has been outrageous over the last ten years and ought to be slammed. This erosion, though, has on the whole been led by artistic directors who have felt the pressures from boards, managements, and funding authorities towards bringing in a mass audience. They've slipped very imperceptibly from the popular – in a political sense popular – to the populist, equating big working-class audiences watching silly shows with some sort of political statement. They're now using the old forms of popular theatre just to get the bums on seats.

VERA GOTTLIEB: Shall we turn immediately to the question of what we do?

JOHN MCGRATH: One of the things that I would like to say about a conference, if there is one, is that one of the ground rules should be that it is for a plurality of theatres. We're not in any position at the moment to exclude anything that's moving in remotely the same direction as we are. I've always felt that political theatre and oppositional theatre are in a sense pre-political, and should make people want to do something politically.

KATE HARWOOD: It seems to me that there is ambition, anger, and vision in a lot of new writing, while it is possibly less polemical and analytical. There's a large group of younger writers who send me plays – men, women, working class, blacks – who do not have the language of analysis but do have the language of protest in their writing. They are part of our theatre, and just because they are not putting forward particularly well-argued socialist ideologies doesn't mean that they shouldn't actually be brought into the fold.

JOHN MCGRATH: There is a logic which says that you have to line up and defend the new play, irrespective of the political content of individual examples, because if we allow the institutions and the companies that exist to collapse, that whole very precarious way in which new plays get on to stages breaks down. The number of new plays being done now is a third of what it was ten years ago. The new groups that are coming together and establishing some kind of prominence on the scene are now doing classics.

We all know this. So we are faced with the dilemma of whether to back institutions going down the commercial route because they need to earn their money. There are practitioners who will say that running *Serious Money* for six months in the West End is the only way to enable other forms of work to take place. These are old arguments, but you can't just step over them and say there's an easy way beyond them. It's a fact of life: people who get commissioned from the National also write for 7:84, occasionally. It's *not* just a matter of earning a living: people are working in those places trying to find a way to connect with other people. If it's all pushed aside in the gathering rush to commercialisation we must cut away from that – although that is a very dangerous option, because we close off a number of people who may not have the kind of vision that we want, but who are in their way fighting.

One could identify very clearly the absence of any organisation attempting to co-ordinate the activities of what must be over a thousand grass-roots or ephemeral companies around the country. Simply having a data-bank or a record of those people would help. They don't need to come together in conferences, but there is a need for some form of communication between companies like that. It's quite possible that some companies have resources which they'd be willing to pass on or lend to others. At the very least you'd have a thousand companies who knew of each other's existence and who'd derive some sort of strength from knowing that there are many others. People wanting to start up would know about that as well, and there would at least be a sense of solidarity between Newcastle and Southampton, which would be good.

Another gap is a large contestatory theatre of some kind, which is able to present a strongly-worked out, ideas-based onslaught on the present Tory consensus. Whether that comes through a building or a touring company, and whether that building, if there was one, is in London or not, are all to be discussed, but there is certainly nothing which does that on a large scale and a top level. I wouldn't want to put that down as hierarchical: it's just very important on a national level that the consensus is attacked.

Another huge lack at the moment is of new and directly involving work being taken to audiences around the country. I do feel that people from all over the country must keep saying as you did, Clive, that it is important that more and more of it must go to audiences all over the country. Again, that's not contradictory to having a centralised contestatory theatre, and it's not contradictory to grass-roots theatre, which is working as best it can.

If we added a broader perspective of the presentation of images of society today, and included television and film, there might be a very good session on that. I don't think we could separate our preoccupations from other people working in the creation of images of society. The growth of video and independent production has meant that a lot of theatre can be tied in with a lot of television and video distribution. The coming of cable and satellite means there'll be fifty-odd channels, and in some legislation which has been passed, notably in Canada, one of those channels has to be a community channel. They are going to want material to put on it. If we could move towards trying to affect the legislation in Britain so that, on a fifty-two channel direct broadcasting-by-satellite set-up, one was for community purposes, then all the thousand theatre companies that are around the country could find a huge audience, and might even get the money to carry on and do more.

I don't think it's entirely right to exclude funding from the areas of debate. One of the most appalling things about the Trades Union Movement in England is that the TUC does not have an Arts Officer of any description, and never has had. One role that the Arts Officer plays in the Scottish TUC is that of knowing all the people who are likely to be interested in the arts in the Trades Union Movement, and putting them together with likely companies. Creating such a role would be a possible way not for the TUC to give us money, because they don't have any, but of making contacts with unions who may have a campaign going, or who may want a theatre company to do something. There are resources other than money: letting them use an office or a telephone or suchlike.

There are other ways to look at raising funding, which we shouldn't exclude. Who else is likely to want an oppositional form of theatre? That would be a useful thing to discuss properly.

I also did an interview with Peter Arnott for Discourse *which raised several key issues:*

THE PROCESS AND PRODUCT OF THEATRE[67]

PA: Why has theatre been attracted to the left this century, is there something in particular about theatre that is susceptible to thoughts about re-organising society?

JM: I don't think there is anything inherently socialist or antihierarchical about theatre; there's nothing particularly co-operative about the processes of theatre which would make it by definition or structurally more susceptible to leftwing practice. The whole essence of twentieth-century industrial procedure and Taylorism is actually right here in the large theatrical enterprises. The thinking, the planning, the creation, is removed from the factory floor, as Fred W. Taylor advocated and is moved into the planning department where you find plays written/finished/finalised and discussed before any of the actual performers get near it. In order to keep the machine rolling, if one falls out or if several of them fall out, others are simply put in, and their actual personal contribution to that is minimal. There are other elements of contestation within the theatre: the content and the processes and I suppose when you are in theatre you are part of a social event and the images you put up are for critical, social analysis.

PA: There is a close connection between what kind of theatrical event you are trying to end up with and what kind of process is employed to create that theatrical event. The kind of community theatre work that I do is participatory from the very beginning, entirely based upon an idea of enabling. More than teaching a particular kind of theatre, it involves getting a group together who have a certain set of experiences and personal histories, and the role of the political drama tutor is on the one hand to get people to be able to say what they want to say effectively and on the other to relate, through political mediation, that experience to broader experiences in class terms and international terms. That kind of educative approach of enabling is I think where the future of progressive culture must lie. What the 'democratisation of culture' means to me is participatory cultural democracy.

JM: One cannot automatically assume that a community venture is going to be more sensitive to the actual experience of that community than a good writer going into that community, or ideally coming from that community, with a depth of experience, and with a set of skills acquired over a period of time, who will speak of that community in a very literary way. You cannot assume that one will be actually more sensitive or representative than another.

PA: Participatory theatre is simply a different type of theatre, and that's not just in its process, it is a different thing to watch. If we're talking about theatre becoming part of the life of a community, of a city, of a country, in the way I think it could be, then the processes as well as the product of theatre have to become accessible to more people. One thing community theatre does is build an audience, it builds an access which is participatory. What happens in the theatre is never as simple as active actors and passive audience.

JM: I agree. The meaning of a piece is not what you can read. What you can read is what you see after it has happened; the trail of the snail; it's been and gone. One of the problems when talking about theatre is that so many people only have access to the trail. So a whole set of conclusions about what theatre is about are created upon inadequate evidence.

I've been thinking about postmodernism and what it means in terms of theatre. I've come to the conclusion that I'm actually pre-modernist. I've attempted to ignore the whole of the modernist movement, and have tried to relate to popular culture which modernism, I think probably mistakenly, rejected. Of course such generalisations require many qualifications. For example one can't write much without T.S. Eliot or Ezra Pound having some vestigial twenty-fifth hand effect on what you're doing. At the same time the communication of modernism does seem to be rooted in just that: the alienated intellectual posture. It was bound to lead to a dead end. Either the intellectual became so alienated that no one wanted to listen to what they had to say, or else it leads to the intellectuals forming smaller and smaller clubs, which seems to me to be what's happening. It's a form of relationship with the audience that's ultimately stultifying. The modern movement did not ignore the world of popular culture, but it suppressed it. It made it third or fourth in the order of priorities from which it drew cultural sustenance. This has led to the dead end out of which postmodernism has sprung, with a kind of brutality and brutalism about its relations with its success and directions, which I find if not fascist, at least pre-fascist. I find that the popularism inherent in a lot of this work is also springing from the failure of modernism to adequately encompass that cultural fruitfulness, so in a sense the kind of theatre I'm interested in is pre-modernist, is not chasing the modern audience, which has become the International Cultural bourgeoisie. That whole creation of cultural commodities seems to me to be the end result of an alienated elite in the bourgeois world. What you're talking about by your community theatre, and what I'm talking about in my version of community theatre, is a rejection of that approach to theatre, art and culture as a commodity. It is an experience which people are involved in or it is nothing.

PA: It is partly a rejection of a way of looking at art. I think it's a way of looking at the experience that modernism had, a kind of celebration of defeat. It negates any reliability of language, making it impossible to tell anyone something straight. The mistrust of meaning, and of the perspicuity of language, are key characteristics of postmodernism. It does also seem foreign to any *collective* activity, purpose, or meaning. On the other hand, it rejects the tradition of modernism which sets itself up as revealing some sort of absolute truth behind appearances. It abandons the idea that for art, and science, there is a way of getting such a revelation of something beyond the language, beyond the signs. The interplay between these signs is all there is.

JM: This is the problem with postmodernism, that ultimately it is as negative as modernism, in the sense that it takes life as a series of contingencies. It seems to me that this is very dangerous, and very similar to the intellectual fashions in Germany in the twenties and thirties. Why it's fashionable here and now is because of this horrible sense of impotence to change anything. For instance, recently someone asked me for support for a campaign against Clause 28 of the new local government bill, on how it will affect a theatre company's portrayal of homosexuality. To my horror I found myself not thinking 'Yes, I'll go along and support that campaign', but thinking 'It's not going to make any difference anyway'. That kind of fatalism that you find yourself slipping into from time to time is really the root of Nazism. It's very dangerous now, in this country, and it relates to this postmodern philosophy, if you can call it that, quite closely. It's a defeated way of looking to the future: pre-defeated.

PA: Yes, there is a modern pleasure in despair and defeat, but that relies on a positive mask you can strip away to reveal the worm within. But it seems with postmodernism that the worm is on the surface. I'm now writing a series of poems on 'fundamental values', and one of them is called 'Solidarity'. I'd have been *embarrassed* to do this six or seven years ago. But now such things as solidarity are almost secrets, of a culture being driven underground. Critics are for ever complaining about sloganising in theatre, but I think we have to reassert socialist values positively at this particular point, even at the risk of being accused of being naive. There is now a polarisation occurring such that we can talk of a cultural separatism. The official culture is a lot less self-conscious about being official than it used to be, it's much less self-conscious about being oppressive than it used to be.

JM: It's not at all self-conscious, it's proud of itself as oppressive. It relates to a global situation, in the sense that Stalin saw Soviet society as he was creating it as the end of history and the dialectic. Now what's happened is that there is a multinational capitalist organisation, which sees *itself* as the end of history. We are now facing up to what the Soviet people faced up to in the middle of the thirties: a power structure which thinks that it has got there. The consequences of both are defeatism and a sense of powerlessness in attempting to influence the future in any serious way. If you do you're a joke, some sort of idiot, either naive as you say or you're hopelessly lost, old fashioned, fighting 19th-century trades union battles, or you're sloganeering etc. simply because you have an interest in your future. It's a deeply dangerous ideological impasse that people have got into. Therefore we're approaching the end of history, the end of the dialectic. I think one thing the theatre can do, and should be doing now, is actually reasserting, as you say, that things move; things change. There is a future, and the basic emotional imperative of solidarity – that what happens to other people matters, that the solution to problems is not simply the market, which is *not* adequate to deal with contemporary civilised life, these things the theatre can actually embody: in its content, and in its processes.

Conferences were held, protests staged, many outraged voices raised, but if Thatcher could crush the miners, she could brush us aside without a thought. However, she was soon to outdo herself, in her arrogance she lived out her own hubris. But that was not the end of the story. The egregious John Major stalked the floor. And words lost their meaning.

We did a week's workshop on Language, inspired by the Thatcherite ability to take words and make them have exactly the opposite meaning from what they seemed to mean. Like 'freedom' and 'opportunity.' The threat was not only to language – it was to democracy:

DEMOCRACY CONSUMED BY JARGON[68]

Most people who bother with the matter at all would admit that the English language is in a bad way, but it is generally assumed that we cannot by conscious action do anything about it. Our civilisation is decadent, and our language – so the argument runs – must inevitably share in the general collapse. It follows that any struggle against the abuse of language is a sentimental archaism, like preferring candles to electric light or hansom cabs to aeroplanes. Underneath this lies the half-conscious belief that language is a natural growth and not an instrument which we shape for our own purposes.

The subject of this lecture, which I have chosen with those words of George Orwell clearly in mind, is: language and human well-being. Or more specifically: the way language is increasingly put to use to deprive human beings of their basic human rights, of their dignity, of their rights as citizens, of their livelihood, and from time to time their lives.

Of course we must recognise that it is not the words themselves which cause the damage: it has got to be the desire of the word user for power, profit or the satisfaction of an ideological imperative which drives their agents, who actually commit the crimes against humanity. Their task is made possible by the manipulation of language to confuse, obscure, deceive and ultimately disempower the victims.

I am not simply talking here about the occasional weasel words of a politician squirming to get off the hook – those of you who saw Michael Heseltine closing down and opening up coal-mines, like so many mouse-holes, will know what I mean. No. I would like to reach beyond the weasel words towards an entire culture of deception, brought about, I contend, by the attempt to uphold the completely untenable values that now have become the dominant values of our society.

We, as intellectuals, have a responsibility to safeguard the integrity of the language. This we are daily, hourly, failing to do. We have allowed politicians, journalists, advertising copywriters, TV and video makers, to mangle the language until it has become devoid of recognisable meaning.

We also have a responsibility to develop our own critical language in a way that will allow us to engage effectively with the startling changes in almost all areas of society. This we have also, on the whole, failed to do. In the study of the key areas of change – science, social life, political life, individual psyche, culture, international affairs, industry and industrial relations, indeed in semantics itself, and above all in semiotics – anglophone academia has fired off a mighty barrage of polysyllabic neologisms – but very few of these ponderous missiles have hit the moving target. If I may extend the metaphor, which is from the world of anti-aircraft artillery, reality has chaffed, and moved on. The verbal missiles explode in the empty air of learned journals or amid the chaff of career-oriented conferences.

I very often disagree with the curious prejudices of George Orwell, but for his fanatical concern for the integrity of the language I have nothing but admiration. But Orwell of course grew and lived in a world – though it may have experienced violent divisions between nations and classes – which nevertheless had a sense of security about community, human relationships, the serious things in life, and in a shared, unquestioned sense of words having meanings which refer to real objects or ideas. Rhetorical politicians of course abused language, but the great leader of the English, Winston Churchill, was a man who had used words for a living, was aware of the history of the language, the disciplines of syntax, the structures of sentences, paragraphs even. His rhetoric had self-confidence, elegance, clarity, and was immediately meaningful to the whole of the nation.

I do not posit a linguistic golden age. Those days are gone for ever, and I for one don't want them back. Nor do I elevate Churchill to any great height – many of us have reason to dislike him intensely. But his speeches, and the writings of Orwell, form a useful benchmark, to compare with the vacuous maunderings of John Major.

So what has happened to language, more specifically to public language? I have suggested that its decline as a meaning-bearing medium has as its prime cause the increasing, now overwhelming use of words in public life to sell the unsellable; to deceive the public, the consumer, the voter; to promulgate the set of untenable values placed at the centre of our public life by a ruthless ideology of competition, enterprise, survival of the fittest and sending the weakest to the wall.

It was Margaret Thatcher's bright boys who perfected the game of appropriating words with a long-established radical meaning, and using them to mean their very opposite. Let's look at some of them. 'Radical' itself – the word used to describe Shelley, Tom Paine, the Chartists, the Paris communards, the millions of working people some of whom gave their lives to win some justice from precisely the privileged few whose interests Thatcher served. Suddenly she and her Keith Josephs and Heseltines and Willie Whitelaws, and their teams of eager right-wingers had dubbed *themselves* the

Radicals, hoping, I suppose, to drag a little of the heroism of Che Guevara into their arid lives, and to wipe out the memory, the presence in history, of those great reformers – who would have cheerfully thrown these 'heirs' into the tumbrils.

Let's look at 'Freedom'. For centuries the rallying cry of the dispossessed, the disempowered, the poor, the underprivileged. Suddenly Thatcher's word-smiths are using the same word to describe a process that reverses the slow gains of the dispossessed, takes away power from the disempowered, in order to give greater opportunity to those who already have wealth and power. So the Health Service was impoverished to give tax cuts to the rich, in other words health care – in the case of my own mother, life itself – was taken from the masses in order to give the few the money to take suites in the London Clinic at £5,000 per week. And the word used to describe this process was 'Freedom'.

We all know how the word 'Caring' was used on all occasions by Thatcher to mean 'depriving'. We may have noticed the subtle change in the use of 'community' – to mean its exact opposite, a gathering of atomised, warring individuals. When we put the two together: 'Community Care' we get the concept that drove tens of thousands of mentally-ill people out of the security they had found, and either onto the streets or into the houses of relatives where they became a volatile presence. Of course for some it was an opportunity, and indeed if the programme had been carried out in the spirit of R.D. Laing and not of Dotheboys Hall it might have produced interesting results. But 'community care' meant that the large Community, the state, which had the resources, no longer cared, and the people we once cared for became a string of individual tragedies, to be swept off the streets at dawn.

Perhaps the single most disturbing feature of Thatcherite jargon was its pain-fully careful air of *sweet reasonableness*, its patent *clarity* underlined by its heavy emphases on *key words*, its tone of hushed awe at its own inspired rationality.

Let's look at 'Enterprise', the great shibboleth of monetarist conservatism. 'Our people' – another favourite phrase describing who knows what kind of possession in the pronoun – our people must be 'set free', as it were, to enter the marketplace and prove by their 'enterprise' that Britain can be great again. This not untypical Thatcherite sentence contains more blatant deception of the public than Stalin's 'Pravda'. But let us take the use of the word 'enterprise'. It conjures up images of New Frontiers, of intrepid explorers hacking through the jungle to discover untold treasures – what a wonderful word – Enterprise. Inspiring.

What it has really meant is now being counted in the 50,000 bankruptcies per annum, the repossessed homes, the broken lives.

And the very, very rare success, who sold out in time to a multi-national corporation.

In the Arts, Thatcher's egregious lieutenant William Rees-Mogg brought about a national calamity in almost every area of the performimg arts: and called it a strategy. In 1980 Roy Shaw, then Secretary General of the ACGB, was forced to stop the Annual Revenue grants to 40 companies. Poor old Roy called them *cuts*. What a naive chap, to call a cut a cut!!! There were demonstrations! This was not the way to do things. Shaw was driven out by Mogg, and of course in 1984 we had more cuts: but this time they were called *The Glory of the Garden* – and words like 'regionalisation' and 'devolution' and 'standards' were bandied about to the press like so many lollipops, which were duly consumed. I was at that Press Conference – not invited, even though my company was being 'projectised', but infiltrated. I stood at the back, next to two of Saatchi & Saatchi's chubby foot-soldiers; Michael Billington asked a tricky question. As Mogg opened his mouth, one Saatchi said to the other: 'Oh I do hope he uses *my* answer.' He was gratified when Rees-Mogg duly trotted out the slippery words the Saatchi man had penned, and poured his balm over the most gullible set of journalists.

Since then the possession of a mealy mouth and/or a forked tongue has been a necessity for any artist, and certainly the leaders of any artistic organisation, who wish to survive into the 1990s.

There are other key-words of the Thatcher period that are worth close scrutiny. 'Choice' for example – a sound reason for transferring a monopoly from state to private ownership – the real reason for the sell-off being the need to raise cash for the Exchequer, i.e. to further reduce taxes. The 'choice' being, if anything, narrowed. Thatcher's famous denial of the existence of 'society' certainly shifted the meaning of that word – the very use of it branded the user a hopeless leftie dreamer, or a slave of the Kremlin. In foreign policy 'Aid' came to mean its exact opposite – 'Aid' meant 'Burden', an obligation to buy British goods then bankrupt the poor nation trying to repay the loan. 'Aid' also gave the donor a right to interfere via the IMF directly in the internal affairs of the recipient country.

There is a clear pattern here to be discerned in the motives for this manipulation of language. If the stark facts of the case were to be clearly presented to the people of this country, they would certainly be opposed to them. There would then be the problem of winning them over with argument or some logical demonstration. This is the way of a genuine democracy. But politicians have no great respect in the 1990s for the intelligence of the people who voted for them. As Groucho might have said, if they voted for me they must be stupid!

They know their values are correct, so to hell with democracy. Of course no politician ever thought the problem in quite those words – but that is the effect: democracy consumed by jargon.

Let us look at another aspect of our verbal culture or lack of it: the dominance of the 'visual' media – television; the movies; comics; photography –

in journalism and advertising; videos; and who knows what next. In the performing arts, the growth of dance, 'performance' art, sub-verbal naturalism, which are now replacing verbal theatre; not to mention the growth of musicals that dominate the West End. What this adds up to is a massive assault on the value of words as a means of communicating.

With so much in our culture being so volatile, it's not surprising that the status of words has been undermined. And it's not surprising that the semiotics industry, in differentiating signifier from signified, opened up a gap between word and meaning that proved both fashionable and seductive. The further cynicism of postmodernist attempts to show that all words and forms are now devoid of 'content' and have become merely echoing vacuities, is yet another nail in the coffin of astringent verbal communication.

But of course the most effective weapon of suppression of opposition is silence – in Thatcher's phrase, 'to starve them of the oxygen of publicity on which they depend.' Here Thatcher was ostensibly talking of 'terrorists and hi-jackers', but clearly the kind of governmental control of the media meant such suffocation techniques could and would be applied to others deemed 'subversive' – other traitors and enemies of the state. Perhaps words are not the most powerful weapon.

As we move into a new era, with our leaders less self-confident, less able to impose their will, less able to befriend the media, we should not imagine that the basic values of our public life have changed in any way – they are simply applied with more incompetence and less profit. The approach to language consequently has become more obtuse, more devious. Whereas 'rationalisation' had been seen through, 'restructuring' carried the Saatchi technique of emphasising the positive in essentially negative actions into the 1990s. It means the same – sacking people, providing worse services, or cheaper-to-make and nastier products, closing down whole communities. But it made the process sound as if there was a future, as if it might 'enhance' people's lives. It was only when Michael Heseltine proposed to 'restructure' the entire coal industry that the population began to question its benevolent nature.

The really new words are more disturbing, more visibly anti-democratic. The word 'sovereignty' has always been a bit of a joke in the European context. We live in a country whose industry is increasingly owned or controlled by US, Japanese or other multinational concerns, whose foreign policy coincides as if by magic with that of America, whose whole economy is toiling to keep out of the hands of the IMF. Yet we prate of 'sovereignty' when we are talking about the residual prejudices of a small group of nationalists. But the sovereignty fantasy is now opposing another set of fantasies called, collectively, Maastricht. Maastricht, we are told, is hugely complex, far too difficult for a democracy to grasp. There will be no referendum, because the voters can't understand the problem. And anyway, the problem will be solved by another complex, ungraspable word: 'subsidiarity'.

The purpose of this kind of language is not the Thatcherite one of forcing the voter to assent to governmental policy by a crude appeal to better things; now the purpose is to baffle the population into a humble apathy, into the realisation that they can't possibly know anything useful any more – they are too ignorant of hi-tech systems, global economics, international power-play, to be capable of holding an opinion.

I believe that the mass of the people of this country do *not* really want the kind of world based on ruthless possessive individualism that they are being sold. I believe that while they can see the point in a certain amount of competition in areas of business, they would rather live as co-operating communities with an ethic of mutual support than as loose assortments of individuals trying to rob and cheat each other to make as huge a pile of money as possible, to achieve a spurious sense of security.

I believe that in business people do not want to see human relations warped and the currency of human exchange debased and devalued in the interests of fanatical efficiency and the ultimate maximisation of profit.

I believe that in the Arts, the public and the practitioners would choose to prioritise creation of good work and making that work widely accessible to the current obsession with smooth bureaucratic operation, marketing and cost-effectiveness.

In industry, we can't avoid a long and painful process of global 'rational-isation' – finance capital has achieved its dream of absolute freedom to roam the world looking for the cheapest labour and raw materials. All the same, I believe the people of this country would rather their Prime Minister did not make deals for coal produced by child labour and evilly exploited miners in Colombia. I believe we would want our government *not* to join so keenly in the rat-race of global exploitation, and to provide much greater safeguards for workers and their jobs at home. Democracy is about society being run according to the will of the people. The use of what I have called 'Jargon' is essentially one of the most effective methods of preventing the people from considering what their will may be. It is profoundly anti-democratic.

What can we do about it? We, as intellectuals, can begin to address the question with some urgency. And we can begin to cut the 'jargon' out of our language, make the effort to think buzz-words and neologisms through and express them in ways that are more accessible, more usable.

And on a broader front, we have to activate ourselves to democratise the media. Just as our parliament has to be a representative one, with account-ability of those representatives to the electorate, so those who control our media and so exercise such enormous power over our lives should them-selves be seen as representatives, accountable and recallable. The concept of public service broadcasting should be extended to all areas of the media. The BBC should fight to remain fully public service, with the right to a critical distance from politics and from government. Rupert Murdoch's

News International should be subject to the same Select Committee parliamentary scrutiny, and if necessary have its licence revoked. With a bit of luck Andrew Neil could end up a bare-knuckle prize-fighter and the editorial staff of the *News of the World* running illicit cock-fights, or training pitbull terriers, or some other less objectionable way to exercise their aggression and lust for sensation.

Before I am accused of crypto-Stalinism I should point out that that was a joke.

More seriously, the ownership and control of the media, *all* the media, needs a certain plurality of approach. They cannot be left in the hands of either State apparatchiks or megalomaniac tycoons.

We are fast developing a non-verbal culture in which our critical awareness of the power of words is being eroded. We need also to use the disciplines provided by semiotics to develop an even finer critical awareness of the power, and the power to deceive, of the non-verbal sign. Having worked recently on two party political broadcasts, and scrutinised in the process many others, I have become aware of the elusive power of the non-verbal innuendo.

I'll end with a quotation from a very unexpected source: Friedrich Hayek. In 1960 he wrote: 'The greatest danger to liberty today comes from . . . the efficient export administrators exclusively concerned with what they regard as the public good.'

Little did he realise that by 1992 they would all have embraced his nonsensical notions of 'freedom' – and that their main weapon of control has become: words.

Democracy is in danger when jargon replaces language, and sells the unsellable by seducing, deceiving and consuming the openness necessary for the democratic process.

THE 1990S AND BEYOND

The 1990s began in 1989. Clearly the political and social situation had changed dramatically from the heady days of the 1960s and 1970s. Clearly I needed a new strategy if I was to be allowed to continue working in the theatre at all. Clearly, try as much as I could, my days running a theatre company in the way I believed in were over. Equally clearly I needed to transcend the gloom and negativity all around me, and get on with it.

Fortunately, there was Wildcat, formed in 1979 from the 7:84 Band, still, at that time, un-axed. It was led by David MacLennan and Dave Anderson, both ex-7:84, and close allies. For them I was able to write and/or direct a series of large-scale new shows:[69]

Whereas in the past I've used panto, *ceilidh* and the concert party, what I wanted to do with *Border Warfare* and the other promenade shows, was to try and use theatre in a different way that allows people to move from one thing to another. I've always loved *1789*, a play that Mnouchkine did a long time ago. I'd done that with *All the Fun of the Fair*, the last show of 7:84 England, where people had to move from one stall in the fairground to another. It creates a different relationship and I think it's a kind of political statement. If you want to you can sit down, go and buy an ice-cream . . . it's all part of you making the decision, to see what you're interested in, what you're getting from it. *Border Warfare* was a massive show that took four hours including intervals. It involved the audience completely, they didn't have to stand all the time, we had two hundred beautiful red benches . . . half way through the second half, just about when the audience were about to faint, we brought them on and recreated the Scots parliament and they got to sit down and were very grateful.

Border Warfare *was a huge success in Glasgow. After the run, I wrote about it:*

SCOTLAND: THE WRITING ON THE WALL[70]

It is truly amazing that, in spite of seven hundred years of strenuous efforts, England has still not managed to turn Scotland into a part of England. Every invasion, from Henry II, Edward I, Edward II, through Henry VIII's rough wooing to Cromwell, was increasingly intended to reduce Scotland not merely to a tributary nation, but above all to 'incorporation' into England: to reducing a nation to the status of a province, or county. By a stroke of genius the architects of the Act of Union of 1707 simply renamed England 'the United Kingdom', which made it a lot easier for Scotland to become part of it. Of course, through the world the UK is still called England, and in England the UK is called England, and Scotland is pretty universally seen as a part of England. But amazingly, in all the important ways, it isn't. Yet.

The glaringly obvious difference is political: the apparently total rejection of Thatcherism in Scotland. This is, however, only one manifestation of a deeper difference: the survival in Scotland of a hope for the future; of the belief that it is worth struggling for a better society; the survival in these cynical years of a widespread sense of the value of every individual person; and the confidence that efforts to enrich and extend the life of every person are worth paying for. It could be said that this is simply a projection of my well-known political naivety on to a nation of which I am not a member. But it is based on the contact with many people, and on many public expressions of such feelings in Scotland. It may well be that in the public life of any 'subject' nation, the possibility of self-achievement at some point in the future nourishes the habit of aspiration, validates Utopian speculations. Or it may be the strength of the belief in socialism in the Scottish working class over the last hundred years or so that simply will not go away. Or it may be something in the so-called 'national character' that ruggedly insists on the individual's responsibilities – and so must insist on rights, freedom and justice as well.

Whatever it is, and there are many manifestations of it, there is that about Scotland which says it is definitely not 'a part of England'. But I think that now the writing is definitely on the wall. The present political crisis is one cause for concern. The achievements of the mass media in standardising cultural differences, and in manipulating tastes and desires, is another. And, the power of the Persuasion People, the army of PR men, administrators, experts, consultants and managers who consciously or unconsciously are set on remaking the image of Scotland, are a third and most insidious cause for concern. The English public schoolboys who think they run Scotland have no real grasp of the way people think or feel about anything, and so far their strategies to whip Scotland into line with England have produced only a massive resentment.

The loyal Opposition, on the other hand, can't decide whether it wants devolution as a device to strengthen the Union, an Assembly as a launching pad for a socialist Scotland, or just to be allowed to get on with its role in Westminster as lobby fodder in a nightly Valley of Death. The Fearless Fifty, as the Scottish Labour MPs are known, arouse the same pity and fear as the doomed heroes of Greek tragedy, and the same sense of the inevitability of their fate. Everywhere in Scotland there is the groan of concerned Labour voters wondering whether they can ever bring themselves to vote for the Nationalists. The Nationalists, while arousing hopes with Jim Sillar's success in Govan, also arouse concern at the opportunism of their tactics, the splits within splits over 'Independence in Europe', and above all, as to how many more candidates of the calibre of Jim Sillar they can field at an election. To many people, they have identified nationalism as a middle-class whim rather than a popular need, and have, unlike Plaid Cymru, no class or even radical platform to offer. Unless this changes, the SNP will not provide a house for socialists in Scotland looking for escape from Thatcher. And while Donald Dewar chirrups on about something called 'independence in the United Kingdom', Labour in Scotland won't do much for those with a genuine fear of the ultimate incorporation: a Thatcherite Scotland.

The centre alternatives – Liberal Democrat-SDP – are not taken too seriously, their support coming mostly for individual MPs rather than the belief in their hazy policies. And the Communist Party, which once played such a seminal role in the culture as well as the politics of the Scottish working class, can no longer claim any electoral strength. There does seem to be a dilemma, even a crisis, in the politics of Scotland. The fact that the country is now ruled by a bunch of suave brigands whom nobody voted for and nobody can do anything about, could cause some disenchantment with the uses of politics. While Scots are still capable of hope, they are therefore still capable of despair; and many I meet feel a kind of despair which no party is adequately responding to. Labour is wrong not to take a bold step against the Union. There are many who would see such a step as the beginning of the real revival of Scotland.

My show, *Border Warfare*, which ended its run in Glasgow a week ago, was packed out every night with people of all ages and classes. As a history of Anglo-Scottish relations, it seemed to touch a nerve in Scotland, to judge by the mighty standing ovations and enthusiastic comments after the show. In it, we recreated the Scots parliament that voted itself out of existence in 1707, and invited the audience to vote for or against the Union. Every night the result went the same way: at least 10 to one against the Union. It's only a piece of theatre, but some 10,000 voted against, and not 1,000 for union with England. But this government has set out to change the culture of Scotland. It feels it must act to undermine the basis of opposition that humiliates it electorally and turns it into a bad joke north of the Border. The insult of the poll tax, the utterly repugnant concept of the 'core curriculum', the Tory redefinition of 'patriotism', the destruction of the welfare system that Scots built, enjoy and still passionately believe in: these are only the beginning of a long list of Tory devices to humble Scotland and make it 'part of England'. Developments in the media recently are not designed to reassure those worried about a non-commodity like Scottish culture. Figures now regularly produced show that whereas Scotland has 10% of the BBC's viewers, less than 3% of the BBC's network programme is actually made here. Commercial television from Scotland likewise has a hard struggle on to the UK airwaves. And Channel Four, while trying harder, maintains the same imbalance. This is bad news, but it is as nothing compared to the likely effects of the Tory broadcasting White Paper, which is intended to unleash on us all the full levelling-down frenzy of market-place broadcasting. It is a rejection of all responsibility for cultural identity, growth, development; it will open the door to a flood of cheap US rubbish and close the door to serious programme-making in Scotland. The burning zeal for the purgative powers of market forces has combined with a truly English ruling-class contempt for the values of Scottish – or Welsh, or Cornish or Liverpudlian – culture. In a splendidly hypocritical gesture, William Rees-Mogg will guard the moralistic fetishes of the pious and the petty, while a monstrous crime against our cultural inheritance is allowed, even encouraged.

As the market forces rationalise globally and integrate the UK into the multinational entertainment empires, so national cultures will survive only as dead emblems to bring artificial charm to a non-comprehending world: a living source of richness reduced to a commodity to titillate. This integration is intended to happen in all areas of culture: publishing, education, newspapers, music. The language itself will become globalised. Should we mourn this? Surely enterprise Scotland is there to launch us into the next century – and surely it looks like that – globalised? For many this is a repellent prospect, and by no means inescapable. Diversity in nature, in human experience, in the language of living, in peoples, is one of the great sources of joy. A culture that is lived, guarded, and developed will tend to have more subtlety, more specific reference, more density than a demotic that has to serve the needs of half the world. It becomes functional, but diminished.

Scots have seen Gaelic culture almost extinguished, the Scots tongue largely ironed out, and the Doric marginalised. But the Gaelic language now has fierce champions, and the regions of Scotland are developing a conscious sense of the value of their own tongue, songs, skills and history – and Doric is far from dead. There is a sense of identity in Glasgow now that is producing music, art, theatre, films, fashion and poetry, and will resist not change but destruction. If the global entertainment and information corporations succeed in reducing the mass media to grunts and Midwestern monosyllables, there is much that will be lost. There will have to be a battle fought; but the problem, as before, is: where is the battlefield? The administrators and managers of every large Scottish cultural organisation – the Scottish Arts Council, Scottish Opera, the national gallery of Scotland, the Edinburgh Festival, Scottish Ballet, among many others – are now English. This is not a problem about any individual's place of birth. But it is worrying when so many and such powerful people take decisions based on assumptions that are not those of their audience, and create policies that do not grow from the specific potential of Scottish artists but from the need to compete in a cosmopolitan bazaar. This is not a chauvinistic rejection of 'foreigners'. That has never been a Scottish tradition. Glasgow welcomes Peter Brook because he offers a new artistic experience that excites and invigorates. Cautious, self-conscious arts bureaucrats with careers to protect and the values of Rees-Mogg and Peter Palumbo to put into practice, however, have an insidious, wasting effect on Scottish culture. They are symptoms of the Management Culture which yearly grows in power and pallor. The rows of grey suits and black document cases that shuttle to and from London increase, even as the prices go up remorselessly.

It is the arts bureaucrats and the management clones who are bringing Mrs Thatcher's values to Scotland: not directly, in content, but pervasively, in style. From them and their power bases in the institutions and corporations comes the profoundest threat to Scotland's individuality, culture, nationhood. The assumptions of the radical Toryism of the South-east of England are brought back with them on every trip: it is a one-way traffic.

The rampant ideology of competition and confidence trickery and reassuring lies has a band of apostles: Beware Picts, the Christians are coming. Perhaps I exaggerate, even caricature: but a caricature works only if it points to reality, and I think these incidences do. If people in Scotland become frustrated by the politicians' inability to speak for them, and so give up hope; if the mighty media moguls reduce Scotland's culture to a few jokes about kilts, and destroy the ways for Scots to present themselves to themselves as well as to the world; and if the Enterprise Culture grows as it looks set to do, with English yuppies yelling round Edinburgh and Scottish trendies smoothing their paths round Glasgow; then there will be no battlefield, nowhere to place a cairn. And England will have won another victory.

However it was not only in Thatcher's England that Unionism sought hard to discredit what I was trying to say. Brian Wilson, once supporter of and source of endless inspiration and information to 7:84, but soon to become a junior cabinet minister in Blair's government, seriously attacked me for a crime I had certainly not committed: he, and the rest of the Labour hierarchy in Scotland, had one version of history, and it wasn't mine.

I wrote to The Glasgow Herald:

'BORDER WARFARE' AND JOHN WHEATLEY[71]

Your political gossip columnist Brian Wilson accuses me of 'chic jibes' at the expense of John Wheatley in my play *Border Warfare*. These accusations would carry more weight if Mr Wilson had actually seen the show.

For the record, in this and in several other plays I present John Wheatley, whom I admire greatly, in a totally sympathetic way. David Anderson shows him here, and showed him in *Little Red Hen* in 1975, as a practical, ingenious but highly principled socialist, a Catholic who stood out against the Pope on social issues and suffered for it, and a great achiever of real improvements in the living standards of the Scottish working class.

Mr Wilson, like his political leader Donald Dewar, sneers at John Maclean, whose extraordinary sufferings and death he writes off as 'went to jail, died young and never made the mistake of being elected to anything'. This contempt is scandalous.

He sneers at 'the literati' – amongst whom he clearly does not include himself, oddly enough – for admiring Maclean rather than Wheatley. I personally admire both these men, and find no conflict in doing so. Maclean taught, fought and died for his socialism, an intellectual who refused to compromise in his beliefs, even in order to get elected to Westminster.

Wheatley also fought and went to jail for his principles, but was enough of a pragmatist to know that to achieve results in the short term he must 'not go too far ahead of the mass of the people'.

Surely Mr Wilson and Mr Dewar can see the need for both approaches within a large and developing movement?

Perhaps it is Maclean's refusal to compromise with Westminster that sets their teeth into a growl? Perhaps it is my quoting, in *Border Warfare*, Wheatley's own call, in 1922, for 'a bold socialist lead' that leads the Unionist right wing of the Scottish Labour Party into ignorant, gossip-led abuse, and abysmally low journalistic standards?

I also admire Mr Wilson and Donald Dewar for many of their skills and achievements. But I hope they are not going to make a fetish of compromise.

Which, of course, is precisely what they went ahead and did.

JOHN BROWN'S BODY [72]

John Brown's Body is named after John Brown's Shipyard in Clydebank, which is now virtually closed and was one of the great centres of shipbuilding along the Clyde. It's a symbol for what's been happening to all the massive industrialisation that happened during the late 18th and throughout the 19th centuries in Scotland as a whole and particularly along the Clyde. John Brown's body does lie pretty much alone in the grave, but the point of the show is that his soul goes marching on. It presented the history of the Scottish industrial working classes, but we did it in a slightly different mode with a kind of helter-skelter around the walls. Pamela Howard designed both, and she's terrific to work with. Under the helter-skelters were little stages and at the highpoints of the helter-skelters there were trap doors so that people could clamber down. Again people were free to follow, but I got this daft idea that we'd have a platform in the middle of this area and somehow it inhibited people from moving. It was weird actually, because in *Border Warfare* we had these trucks which came on and we could make a platform in the middle and then take them away again or have one platform end to end. I don't know why I wanted this thing, but we had it and it inhibited the audience. I loved the roller-coaster up and down the walls and used this a tremendous amount. It looked great as it rolled up and for the coalmines it was fantastic. That really worked.

WELCOME TO JOHN BROWN'S BODY[73]

It's about the industries of Scotland, the people who worked them and the way they had to work. And it's about how a very small number of people, the ship owners, the steelmasters, the coal owners and such, managed to persuade a great many more people to maintain them in power, opulence and riches, while they, the workers, lived in misery and degradation beyond belief.

And of course it's about how these workers had to organise to defend themselves, and how their organisations had to become political organisations, and confront the power of the owners where it mattered – where it was built into the power of the state, the apparatus of Government and Civil Service, into the dominant ideology.

And so Socialism was born – from hunger, exploitation and desperate need.

And now they are trying to tell us Socialism is dead and gone. Now the mistakes and criminal oppressions of 'Communist' regimes in Eastern Europe are being used to pour scorn on anybody who advocates any co-operative effort to make a better society not based on the profit motive. This will fail.

At the same time, as work itself changes in so many unexpected ways, a whole new set of problems has been thrown up that can't be answered with the old rhetoric. No wonder a lot of Socialists are bewildered, or demoralised. But, the need for working people – and the unemployed – to organise, to defend themselves remains. While the rich pickings of the technological revolution are funnelled into a small set of pockets and not spread through society as a whole, there is still a need for Socialism.

Perhaps this is a good time to look at why the working class had to organise itself, why so many working people in the last 200 years fought, died, were imprisoned or transported, why the fruits of so many hard-won victories cannot simply be taken for granted, and why the fight, like the soul of John Brown, goes marching on.

Wildcat also boldly put on the first professional production of The Cheviot, the Stag and the Black, Black Oil *since 7:84. It had been done by many amateur companies, and many schools, but this was a full-scale revival, directed by one of the original team, John Bett:*

A CHANGE IN THE WIND[74]

The re-launch of *The Cheviot, the Stag and the Black, Black Oil*, in a big and beautiful production by John Bett, seems to have opened up a wonderful new view of speculation about the awful gap between 1973, when it first toured Scotland, and the bland and tittering 1991.

Even before it went into rehearsal I was told that it wouldn't be the same, that some toothless, insincere travesty would certainly be the result. I was told that all this fire-in-the-belly stuff wouldn't go down in the 1990s, and sympathy was expressed for the actors required to perform this anachronistic task.

David Hayman, the current director of 7:84 (Scotland), the company whose name was made by the play, publicly rejected the play for the 1990s as a 're-hash', and denounced the use of what he called 'the red mallet of ideology'. ·

But the public thought otherwise – and the production has, happily, been quietly packing in enormous houses at Clydebank, Glasgow Citizens and now on the fringe of the Edinburgh Festival.

I had been given the courage to agree to another professional production by seeing two recent non-professional productions. One was at Queen Margaret College, where the drama students gave it great enthusiasm and energy, and the other was by students in St Etienne, where some of the young Algerians had made a different kind of sense, and created quite another theatre language. Both were unlike the original, but the audiences responded with the same feeling.

And in the carnival atmosphere of the Big Top in the fun fair on the Meadows, it's doing it again, to very mixed audiences. And I began to wonder why.

It lacks the spectacle of Ninagawa, the newsworthiness of the East Europeans, the trendiness of the alternative comedian: but it appears that the public have been staying away from these events. Not, I hasten to add, because they are inferior to *The Cheviot* – far from it. I begin to wonder if it isn't due to some quite unexpected swings in the public taste.

The audiences for *The Cheviot* have ranged from schoolchildren to pensioners, and from all ages, particularly teenagers, we've been getting the same reaction. People love the comedy, the music, the variety, but particularly they love the fact that it is saying something about Scotland today, something direct and passionate.

When pundits try to define the 1990s, they see them as an extrapolation of the 1980s, materialist, amoral, greedy, self-seeking. From the accumulation of reactions to *The Cheviot*, I feel that people, especially young people, in the 1990s have already leapt to a totally different base for their attitudes.

The Thatcherite triumphalism of the 1980s has put them off the 'left triumphalism' of much of the quasi-revolutionary rhetoric of the 1970s. The dismal failure of 'enterprise' economics to produce a better life or a happier country has put them off ideological dogma. The revelation of so-called 'communism' as a system of repression run by power-crazed old criminals – something we on the left had known for years – has made them very cautious indeed about easy responses to calls to the class war. But it would be wrong to assume that people in the 1990s therefore only want spectacle, titillation and silliness.

As the tanks roll into Moscow, Lithuania and Georgia, before we have even recovered from the anxious nights and the horrific images of destruction of the Gulf War, we in the 90s are looking for something with a bit more weight, more rooted in reality, more thoughtful and thought-provoking. The pundits hail postmodernism, the withdrawal of art from consideration of the 'real' world, replaced by a series of games with symbols emptied of sense, as the style of the 1990s. But this is too logical and clever a progression. The new generation will start from its own feelings and premises, not from what it's told to do by art critics.

The cultural engineers of the Arts Council, press and television have coaxed, guided, tried to manipulate public taste away from theatre with social purpose, even with social content. Fashionable disdain has elevated chic cynicism, art-school hollowness, the coy, the cosy and the whimsical into the icons of the 1980s. By a relentless process of attrition the arts media have tried to create a public seeking nuance, exoticism, ambivalence or evasion. But the world begs to differ, and seems to want content, passion and thought: as much from the Leningrad Symphony Orchestra as from the *Thrie Estaitis*.

I'm delighted the audience have taken *The Cheviot* the way they have, as something rooted in the tragedy and comedy of the people of Scotland – of course because I wrote it, but much more because of what the response says about at least a part of the nature of the 1990s.

At least in Scotland. And it was, after all, in the 1990s that Scotland got its Parliament back.

In Belfast, they had a bit of a problem: a theatre company there had discovered the work of Thomas Carnduff, who was not only a Protestant, not only a member of the Orange Order, but also in solidarity with the Catholic shipyard workers subject to sectarian abuse in the yards, and generally in favour of peace and reconciliation: an awkward maverick. They wanted to try a public reading of the work of Carnduff. The problem was that there were not many people in Ireland they could ask to do it, for obvious reasons. So they asked me to come over and direct the readings, which I did with great pleasure, and give a talk on working-class theatre:

WORKING-CLASS THEATRE[75]

There are several things that could be called working-class theatre:

1. Plays written by working-class people aspiring to the nature of West End or boulevard theatre; i.e. for all I know, Noël Coward could have been born the son of a bricklayer. Clearly that does not qualify his plays as 'working-class' in any meaningful sense – on the whole they are plays about, and for, a smart metropolitan middle- and upper-class theatre-going audience. This conditions all their modes of operation, and while never excluding working-class people from the Box Office, or from being represented on the stage – plucky little comic figures that they are – such plays do actively exclude the majority of working-class people, and certainly do not present their experience as central, or share their perspective on life.

2. Do we mean plays written directly for mass audiences like Brian Rix farces, or the melodramas like *Ghost Train* so beloved of community drama producers? Or even music-hall sketches, Christmas panto, stand-up comedians and such? My answer to this is yes, of course. This is the bed-rock of popular theatrical entertainment.

3. Do we mean theatre written by working-class people simply to express or show the way they live, with a variable degree of sophistication in its presentation? Where the audience is anybody who cares to pay attention, including their own people? Again, yes of course. Here we find many great works of the working class in the industrial period: in the novel, Tressell's *Ragged Trousered Philanthropists* is the classic example. In Scotland, Ewan MacColl's plays and Joe Corrie's plays and poems, and many others in England, in Ireland a wide range from O'Casey to our hero of this year, the rediscovered Thomas Carnduff. This is theatre that bears witness, that is known from personal joys and sufferings, that celebrates and commemorates the otherwise neglected lives of countless millions of people, generations of the unseen, the unheard, therefore supposedly mute and invisible.

Why is it important? Often it is naive, theatrically behind the times, clumsily constructed, with awkward patches of dialogue and lapses into sentimentality and/or melodrama at the rise of a curtain. But not always. The literary establishment has chosen to emphasise these aspects to dismiss, groan and titter at the plays of working-class life, and to consign them to the rubbish dump of literary history. And the underlying reason is not hard to find: they not only have no interest in it, but have much politically to fear from the public awareness of the life their paymasters consigned the working class to lead. Maxim Gorki in Russia was not doing the Czar any favours by simply telling of his own experience. As Gramsci put it, simply to tell the truth is revolutionary.

Joe Corrie was a Scots miner who came out on strike during the General Strike in 1926. The miners were out for eight months, and went back defeated. During the strike Corrie wrote sketches performed by and shown to the people of his own mining community, Bowhill, in Fife. They were short, funny, and pungent, and must have cheered folk up a lot. When the strike was over, the coal owners insisted the men renounce the union. Corrie refused to go back on these terms. Instead he wrote *In Time of Strife*, a great play, about the strife in his community when the strike was being lost. We played it during the 1984 miners' strike, and it more than stood the test of time.

But this great play had lain for 35 years unperformed. Why? Because of the class enmity between James Bridie, Scotland's leading theatrical power broker, and the Fife miner. The net result of this was that Corrie's work was impossible to get hold of, and never seen. He had ceased to exist, and the realities he put on the stage were out of sight and out of mind. Bridie, on the other hand, was the first chairman of the Arts Council Drama Committee, had his whimsical, insipid comedies on in every big theatre in Scotland during the 60s, is set on school syllabuses, university drama courses, has a Collected Plays in print, and a bust on show at the Citizens Theatre.

The same Bridie played a significant role in the career of Ena Lamont Stewart. Her play, *Men Should Weep*, a truly great play, is the story of women in the Gorbals in the 30s. The Glasgow Unity Theatre commissioned the play in 1947.

Ena then wrote another play, about the Highland Clearances. She showed it, with great trepidation, being a woman of a very nervous disposition, to James Bridie. He said, patronisingly, that she should stick to comedy. When I asked if we could read it, Ena said she'd gone home and burnt it. I don't want to fetishise Bridie's role in all this: he was a successful Glasgow doctor and merely representing the views and interests of his class.

Carnduff puts the case for working-class writing succinctly in his poem 'A Worker's Philosophy':

> I have done with my Omar Khayyam,
> I have laid it back in the case;
> I am studying life, not by culture,
> But meeting it face to face.

Although Carnduff, Corrie and Ena Lamont Stewart all refuse to be reduced to a party political position, and deny they were politically motivated, the very truth, the very face-to-face meeting of life in their work, has profound political resonance. The attempted denigration and dismissal of their work has a large political dimension. Inevitably, the fight to keep their work alive, to record it as an important part of theatre history, and to make it available today, is a political struggle.

And now you are looking out for Thomas Carnduff, another worker/playwright. The fact that his work not only was never published, but also can only be found in fragments speaks volumes for the values of the literary and theatrical hierarchy he clearly displeased. Even though he had huge success not only at the Abbey in Dublin, but also here in Belfast, the 'working-class content' that the manager of the Empire Theatre objected to also had him kicked out of history.

I congratulate you on your efforts to give him his place, and through him the forgotten lives and now distorted beliefs of his fellow workers and their families. I'm sure the spirit of Carnduff is one that will help to bring a new perspective on the tribulations of today's working class.

Industrial society has changed, almost beyond recognition. The old class characteristics have on the whole shifted with the shift in the production processes. The relationships between classes have changed, and the emergence of women's struggles for female equality and emancipation has rewritten not only what we were once fighting for, but also how, with what methods and structures, we fight.

The working class has not gone away. There are writers like Carnduff down a few streets not far from here still. But thanks to generations of struggle they now, I hope, feel there is an easier road to acceptance, performance, help, from people in some parts of the theatre.

The problems we face now, in an age of ever faster-changing and subtler modes of hegemony from a cleverer, more confident and renewed ruling class, are not so easy to deal with. What we need now are more writers, like Carnduff and his working-class brothers and sisters, who will 'study life, not by culture, but by meeting it face to face'.

In 1992 Wildcat commissioned from me a large-scale adaptation of Neil Gunn's The Silver Darlings, *which was well directed by John Bett and designed by Wendy Shea. It toured all the major theatres of Scotland.*

One of the strings to my theatrical bow was simply to write plays, and send them out to the theatre managements. Since 1987 I had been writing, very slowly, a play for London, a 'community' play for the theatre-goers of the South-East. I was becoming increasingly obsessed with the personal values of the beneficiaries of the Thatcherite free-market policies, of the people who kept voting her back in. I had conceived, and worked very hard on, a Molière-esque story of the way I saw these people's values: as a conflict between Lust and Greed.

In the early 1990s I began the soul-destroying process of posting off copies of a non-solicited play: The Wicked Old Man. *It met with a curious response: the readers and the dramaturgs all wanted to do it, the theatre directors all rejected it. They must have known that it could offend their audiences mightily to be so represented. Also, many of them were dependent on corporate sponsorship, and could not afford such a dubious piece of writing. And it was not written in any recognisably fashionable style, indeed from their point of view might seem badly written. Plus it was outrageously and deliberately politically incorrect.*

Thank God for Jude Kelly. The West Yorkshire Playhouse was as near as the play got to London. Jude did a brilliant production, again designed by Pamela Howard. It showed absolutely no sign of transferring to the West End.

THE WICKED OLD MAN[76]

The story of *The Wicked Old Man* is not for me to expand on, or excuse: while not a documentary, it aspires to plunge into the depths of one group of people to entertain and seek truths about how at least some members of the 'Contented Majority' live together, about the change in our values since we threw out the baby of enlightenment with the bathwater of patriarchal socialism, and about what the new values are doing to us as human beings.

The publicity of *The Wicked Old Man* carried a West Yorkshire Playhouse health warning: grit your teeth to meet an odious bunch of nineties nasties. And indeed the play doesn't go out of its way to see any of its characters through rose-tinted spectacles, be they man, woman, child, black or white: that was not the job of this particular play. But every one of the characters acts perfectly reasonably in their own eyes, in the given circumstances, with their own acquired values. Indeed, to themselves they are all honourably motivated – except Harry, who has in his despair, grown into a wicked irony. What the play invites us to look at is the overall set of values of this group of people, and to ruminate on the social engineering that has created them and now continues to justify them with the mildest of tolerant oppressiveness, to regulate our alternatives out of sight with the lightest of touches.

I hope that even if none of these considerations means a thing to you, you will find a good story to enjoy, and let me leave the last words to J.K. Galbraith, whose *Culture of Contentment* I cannot recommend too highly:

> The present age of contentment will come to an end only when *and* if the adverse developments that it fosters challenge the sense of the comfortable well-being. As well as a strong and successful political appeal to the disadvantaged, there are three other plausible possibilities as to how this will happen. They are: widespread economic disaster, adverse military action that is associated with international misadventure, and the eruptions of the angry underclass.

Have fun in the nineties.

Nadine Holdsworth, towards the end of the 1990s, asked me:[77]

Holdsworth   *Throughout the 1990s you have remained steadfast in your commitment to a politicised popular theatre. How do you counter the critics who suggest that it is old-fashioned to maintain that position?*

There is no such thing as a de-politicised world. What they mean is that they prefer a politics which is bland and faceless and appears as if things happen in a passive way. That is the way the world goes, but it is still crap to talk of a depoliticised world, it can't possibly mean anything at all. The politics are harder to disentangle due to the jargon, newspeak and the dreadful confusing PR language that is employed. So, the public is less interested in politics because it feels it's nothing to do with them. It is more difficult to talk about the political dimension of commercial life than it was through the 1970s and 1980s when people were very much aware of what was going on.

It has gone on a long time, this attack on writers whose work evokes a political dimension. This view holds that theatre ought to be what Brecht called pre-prandial theatre, something that is just an entertainment that won't spoil your appetite, and that mildly stirs your intellect. That is why Tom Stoppard is so successful, because of his specious ability to mildly stir the intellect of the middle classes. I can't believe what I see when I go to a Stoppard show, in a sense that the audience think they are being intellectual listening to this vapid sixth-form philosophy, or rather references to philosophy, not even philosophising. Stoppard is now, I'm afraid to say, being rapidly joined by David Hare in that massaging of the middle classes' intellectual pretensions.

Now class is a word that went out a long time ago, but I'm afraid it exists and there is a cultural class war, just as there is an economic class war. The so-called depoliticisation of society is simply a way of trying to conceal the existence of conflict and I'm afraid it is the job of writers to tell the truth. If they look at people's lives they cannot say it's de-political, you've got to keep your eye on the ball and say what's going on. It is to me a kind of criminal deception to talk about the de-politicisation of society.

Holdsworth   *Another aspect of theatre, which is now predominant, is a much more visual, physical theatre. Alternatively, you have always worked with text, in particular the monologue form . . . .*

Well, I think one of the main struggles in our society is the struggle for language. Language which means something and words that have resonance and at the same time precise meaning. It is true that most of my work has been text-driven or character-driven, situation-driven, but I think these words are much more powerful than icons, more precise than icons. What's happening now I think is a visual dumbing down of society, which is going on through the replacement of words with graphics, icons, moving images.

At the same time what is happening is a reorganisation of nationalities and the old guardians of the English language, whether it be Oxford English, or Yorkshire or Lancashire. So, of course, just as the movies in America reflected the melting pot of all those nationalities to form a terrific art form, so here, I think, the growing melting pot of our linguistic communities is leading to a visual rather than a verbal culture. I think that is how society has changed and that's fine, but I do think it is still necessary to fight, even if it's only for the use made of icons in order to clarify that more precisely.

Monologues are where language really counts and I have always employed them since my very first play and I have always loved the power of the monologue.

And there was Liz, my partner Elizabeth MacLennan, a strong, intelligent and resourceful presence on the stage, loved by Scottish audiences for her many perform-ances with 7:84: together, without the benefit of subsidy, we toured one-woman shows – essentially monologues but in fact complete plays – written and directed by me for Liz, which said just what we wanted to say, and didn't have the heavy hand of the Arts Council anywhere near them. I wrote a piece for Liz to do called Watching for Dolphins, *which is about somebody who has spent their life as a militant, as a socialist, as a feminist, who has reached her early fifties and is begin-ning to look around and see what's happened to the world and trying to come to terms with it. [Part of John's luck, it began life as a rehearsed reading put on at very short notice in the Assembly Rooms in Edinburgh.]*

WATCHING FOR DOLPHINS[78]

I was working on revisions to my work-in-progress, *Watching for Dolphins,* when the Junta ordered Soviet tanks onto the streets of the cities, their guns turned against the Soviet people. The outcome was fortunately a happy one – but I felt impelled to rework the play once again, and to ask the per-former, Elizabeth MacLennan, to give a public reading of the play as soon as possible.

Anyone who has felt inspired by the vision of a socialist world, a world of co-operation between individuals, of equality, and of love for human life will share with the heroine her bafflement and outrage at what that word 'socialism' has come to mean in the 1990s. This very week, in the name of socialism, the tanks rolled again to repress and kill.

Reynalda Ripley has dedicated most of her life to action, to passionate commitment to socialism and feminism. But in 1991 she finds herself batt-ling to open a bed-and-breakfast bungalow in North Wales. As she burns the home baking and drops the geranium pots, she has to explode – or at least explore how and why and where she has to go – and so is launched on a farcical-comical-satirical-tragical evening, grim at the thought of who exactly might come into her house, never bitter, but deeply sad at what has happened to her hopes, her own life: but never giving up.

I was interviewed by Lizbeth Goodman about it for a BBC programme:[79]

The story is about a woman who has spent her entire life as an activist either for socialism or communism or feminism, and she finds herself now at 52 with all or nearly all the things she's dedicated herself to, discredited in some way by forces beyond her control. It doesn't mean she doesn't think they are still true or they still have validity and what *Watching for Dolphins* is about is her position looking out for signs of fresh political life which would mean something to her, which would answer to her needs, demands for a better world.

One of the games that we play in *Watching for Dolphins* is a game with the audience about how we should tell this story. It starts of as a kind of frothy comedy about a woman who can't quite get it together in the cooking division. Then she asks how would the postmodernists do it, and she creates this film noir with an American film director, and the other way she says we could do this is a C4 documentary. Liz plays all the women in a documentary about her life.

I was also very obsessed by events in Guatemala, particularly by the book I Rigoberta, a fantastic book. I wanted somehow to find a way to make that work without people coming on in ponchos! We devised this idea of somebody working in a garden centre where there were plants, hanging baskets, trees, snakes in the form of hose pipes that could evoke an exotic jungle and at the same time still be the back room of a garden centre, which were eventually all got together by our long-term design collaborator and friend, Jenny Tiramani. Liz played a woman who'd seen a bit about Rigoberta on the television, got intrigued, went to the local library and got the book, had her lunch-break and started to read to herself. It was a way of relating Rigoberta to us, and it was very powerful. Of course one bright critic complained that it wasn't an original play, apparently able to ignore the meta-language of the performance and the production completely, but it alerted audiences to the abuses of humanity going on in Central America, the USA's backyard, with the connivance of the USA. And Elizabeth gave a great, moving performance.

Of course to stay alive I had to work also in film and television: I wrote and directed some nine hours of television for Channel 4, then was appointed to its Board and was never commissioned again. I produced or co-produced four films, including Carrington, *which won two prizes at Cannes, and* Half the Picture, *based on the Scott Inquiry into arms for Iraq. I wrote a film produced by the BBC called* The Long Roads, *which won various BAFTAs and the Writers' Guild Lifetime Achievement Award. And I continued to hold forth from time to time:*[80]

Forsyth   *You wrote the screenplay for the film* Mairi Mhor, *a story of a woman from Skye who in 1871 at the age of fifty began to write songs. This started life as a 7:84 production?*

Well, it started life as a real story, and my involvement came when I was trying to find some songs of resistance to the clearances in 1973 and couldn't find any. Through playground contacts of my children we encountered an old lady from Achiltibuie, then working in Hammersmith Hospital, who sang us verses of Mairi Mhor's songs that were normally left out. I got very excited by what she was singing and borrowed some of Mairi's songs for *The Cheviot* and have been heavily reliant on her ever since. So, I felt that I owed her a bit of a debt. When it came to 1987–1988 I began to think that we could do a show about her life and how relevant it is today. We did that show, but I felt that there were various things wrong with it, so when I had the opportunity with the Gaelic Fund to make a film in the Gaelic language Mairi was the first thing that came to mind.

Forsyth   *Your forthcoming television film,* Half the Picture, *which you've co-written, also started life as a stage play. Did you always think they would make good films?*

Not with *Half the Picture*. One of the things about Mairi was that during the staging of it I projected subtitles in English onto landscapes of Skye. It just looked so fantastic and it seemed to work so well with the songs that it was a basic impetus for making a film of it. In the case of *Half the Picture* the impetus came, oddly enough, from the press. Television cameras had been denied access to the Scott Inquiry because Lord Justice Scott, whom I admire enormously, thought television was purely for entertainment and therefore that television cameras should not be let in. When we did the stage play the press said why on earth has this material not been exposed to the public, why hasn't it been seen on television? So, the BBC, in their wisdom, decided it would be a good idea to make this programme to coincide with the report of Lord Justice Scott on the whole question of Arms to Iraq, which raised massive questions of constitutional importance, like the relationship between civil servants and ministers of Government, like the use of presenting 'half the picture' in parliamentary replies so that what was said would be accurate, but only give half the picture. Other questions, which are tremendously important to democracy, were brought up, I think for the first time, by the Scott Inquiry. Everything that is in the programme was said at the inquiry, except I also introduced into it some of the people who were not called to give evidence, i.e. the victims, the Kurds, some of the Arabs and the man who was in charge of Matrix Churchill, who lost his job, and 600 of his people, who lost their jobs. They are dramatised, but basically what happens and what forms the bulk of the programme is the actual detailed statements, the dialogue used by Major, Thatcher, Heseltine, the senior civil servants, lawyers and treasury solicitors. It is dialogue you could not invent. Richard Norton Taylor, the *Guardian* journalist who sat through every single bit of the Scott Inquiry, did the reduction, the preparing of the evidence, cutting it down; as a journalist his instinct is to be absolutely fair and not to misrepresent anybody.

Forsyth *You have been co-producer of the film* Carrington, *like* Mairi Mhor, *another film about a remarkable central woman character.*

That's true. Christopher Hampton had written the film in 1977 about this remarkable woman, and it had been knocked about and not made for a very long time. Christopher said to me he thought it was the best screenplay he'd ever written. As he'd won an Oscar for *Dangerous Liaisons*, I thought we'd better try to rescue it from oblivion.

Forsyth *Who was Dora Carrington?*

Dora Carrington comes into the movie as an eighteen-year-old art student, a brilliant art student at the Slade with connections in the Bloomsbury Group, and she meets Lytton Strachey, who is much older than her and she falls in love with him. But her Lytton is gay . . .

Forsyth *Bit of a drawback . . .*

Well, it is and it isn't. She chose that relationship as something that pleased and satisfied her. Also, she was a remarkable painter. This is the thing which is very important about her. In her own right she produced a wonderful collection of paintings. Her attitudes are of the twentieth century, and in her own way she lived a sexual revolution against the mores of the Victorian era and dragged the Bloomsbury Group, and behind it England, into the twentieth century.

Forsyth *Why the move into producing?*

I have been producing with Freeway and before that when I was working for the BBC in the 1960s I produced thirteen movies, but I was happy to do that because I felt that at the time television was taking a lot from cinema and not giving a lot back. I was also interested in people in television being able to work on film, on location, which in the 1960s was very difficult, so I was happy to push television drama in that direction towards location filming. To do it I had to produce, and really producing cinema or television is terribly easy compared with running a fringe theatre company.

Forsyth *You're as busy as ever and diversifying as much as ever. This is made all the more remarkable given that a couple of years ago you were extremely ill.*

Just under two years ago I found that I couldn't move around. I was stuck in bed on a remote Greek Island with no doctor, and I began to feel poisons in various parts of my anatomy. It got very painful. I was actually writing a three-part mini-series for Channel 4 which was set on a remote Greek island . . . that was my excuse . . . I got into terrible trouble, and I went to see the only available doctor, who was a heart specialist from Athens on holiday. He said to take some antibiotics. I managed to get back as far as London with a lot of help from the family and went into hospital to find out what it was, and they kept me in for three months. I have a manageable form of leukaemia. It is never cured, but it is now at so insignificant a level that I never think about it. I feel better than I ever felt and six months of chemotherapy is wonderful for all kinds of ailments. I had a duodenal inherited from the *Z-Cars* days, which never went away, and the chemotherapy zapped it completely. I used to get terrible migraine and now no more migraine, no more pills, nothing. So, I do recommend it for minor ailments.

Forsyth *You've obviously made a good recovery, but did you suffer a psychological battering. Has it changed you at all?*

It has changed me, but not through psychological battering, because the hospital was fantastic. The main thing they did was give me information, told me exactly what was going on, what they were doing, why they were doing it, what it was going to do and what it was going to feel like. One of the earliest things they said when I went in and they analysed what it was – they said, 'We can deal with this. It is going to be long, painful, a real drag, but we can manage it and you're not going to pop your clogs just yet.' Given that, when they come along with the needles, you just hold your arm out and see if they can find a vein that still works.

Forsyth *So many theatre companies across Britain, indeed across Europe, are developing a different kind of theatre using, for example, video, dance, a lot of movement, choreography-based pieces rather than an emphasis on text. What do you think of this development?*

Sometimes I think of it as part of a general movement away from meaning, and as somebody who was brought up in a text-based society, with a text-based education, I object to it. I feel very strongly it's a dissipation of meaning; it's making meaning rather more amorphous, rather more difficult to pin down. Dance, it could mean this, it could mean that – it's vague.

Forsyth *Is it an easy way out – it's easier than commissioning someone to write a play?*

No, I think that's a bit philistine. I was going to say, on the other hand, that a lot of what is coming up in movement particularly is very exciting, interesting and, although it moves more towards music as a form than it does towards what I would consider to be theatre or writing, it's still entertaining, it's got a lot of power and a lot of passion in it, and it's got a lot to say. Some of the movement pieces I've seen I'm very excited by, but on the other hand I believe theatre is where specific character and the use of words by those characters is terribly important.

Forsyth *What do you make of the phenomenon, the whole flowering of Scottish literature concerned with working-class themes? Why is it happening in literature and not in theatre?*

You'd better ask the drama committee of the SAC.

Forsyth *They're to blame? Clearly there is an audience for it.*

Wildcat and 7:84 do theatre with working-class themes and they get huge audiences. Clyde Unity is trucking around with it. I don't think it has died out, but what I'm sad about is that this type of theatre hasn't developed into the really sizeable popular theatre with ambition, big ambitions that I was hoping we'd move into with 7:84 and the company that had the disaster with *Women in Power*. If ever I have a regret it is that that whole development was stifled.

Forsyth *This year sees the 13th Glasgow Mayfest, a festival which began as an extension of the Mayday festivities and which had a strong identity as a festival of popular theatre and music. You were one of the original board members but you resigned, I think, because it was starting to embrace business sponsorship, to get away from its roots. Do you see it that way?*

I think latterly it has moved in the direction of being part of the international festival scene. I think the jury is still out. To be fair to Paul Bassett, who has just taken over on the next one, we'll have to wait and see. I was talking to the Scottish TUC in 1978–1979 about the idea of week-long popular festivals that we would do in Glasgow and then take to Edinburgh, Aberdeen, and possibly other places. The Scottish TUC has always amazed me by its involvement in and commitment to cultural activity, certainly compared with the English TUC. It's had Arts Officers like Alex Clarke, Christine Hamilton and now Mary Picken who are very active in that area, and so when the Mayfest became a reality it was very much a commitment to popular forms. I thought it was great, and I was very proud to be part of that. I think what happened was what happened to everything in the 1980s: it became privatised, it moved towards business sponsorship and satisfying business sponsors. I've always been very suspicious of the international festival product like the Ninagawa lot, Peter Brook and all those things which make up an amorphous festival product floating round from Avignon to Edinburgh. I've always thought there was something curious about these floating spectacles.

Forsyth *Thinking of a piece that was not amorphous:* Watching for Dolphins. *In this play you tackle the whole problem of socialism in the 1990s and how that crisis of socialism is a crisis for individuals. I'd like to quote something from Vaclav Havel. He says, 'My rejection of the word socialism is derived from my traditional antipathy to overly fixed and therefore semantically empty categories, empty ideological phrases and incantations.' He goes on to say, 'There have been periods in history when everyone called himself a socialist who was not on the side of the oppressed and the humiliated – I too was such an emotional and moral socialist. I am still today, the only difference is that I do not use that word to describe my position.' 'Socialist' really has become a taboo word, hasn't it and it's a problem for cultural agitators like yourself?*

If you'd lived through what he lived through in Czechoslovakia, it's not at all surprising that he had that reaction. I think one of the great moments of twentieth-century history was from 1966 to 1968 in Czechoslovakia, in Prague where Dubcek was slowly beginning to get rid of the Stalinist idea of what socialism was. To try and create what they called socialism with a human face, or the Third Way. That experiment, which still has tremendous resonance to us today, was stifled by, as we know, Soviet tanks. So, Havel is quite right to reject that style of socialism that was imposed on Czechoslovakia from without by an imperialist regime in the Soviet Union. That is quite straightforward, and I absolutely agree with him. On the other hand, in this country, there has also been a squabble, which is still going on, over what's called socialism. Maybe what's been called socialism here is the other side of the coin – is it capitalism in disguise, is it simply being nice and capitalist? What I tried to do in *Watching for Dolphins*, which is really about that old-fashioned concept 'commitment', was to say that people who have experienced a commitment of that kind towards a human kind of socialism could never give it up for ever; they are always watching for the dolphins to break the water and create this exciting moment.

Forsyth *Are you as idealistic now as you were when you were thirty?*

Well, in spite of everything, yes. I don't believe in idealism, but I do believe in pessimism of the intellect and optimism of the will; that's still a motto I inherit, and I still think that there will be dolphins and things will move forward despite all the brutality that goes on in the world. I still think that you have to look to the future as something positive, otherwise you end up with cynicism, and I hate cynicism. You can't live by cynicism. You end up producing something that adds to the miseries of the world rather than subtracting from them. So in that way, yes, I am optimistic, I believe you have to believe in the future.

I even wrote a 60th birthday wish to Harold Pinter:

HAROLD PINTER ON HIS SIXTIETH BIRTHDAY[81]

What was exciting about Harold Pinter's plays as they first hit me in the 1950s and early 1960s wasn't the boring old 'mystery', it was the language and the laughs. I'd like to say Thank You for both, on his 60th birthday.

The language. I think it was Cocteau who said that whereas poetry is made like a spider's web, theatre poetry must be made of rope. Pinter's theatre language created its effects by bold, even crude juxtapositions of words and images; by encasing startling phrases in silence; by gonging out the bizarre rhythms he heard in the utterings of the inarticulate; by the sounds of unspoken violence that surround us.

Some of the feel of this language maybe came from Beckett's radio plays; from low-life Dickens; a bit of Dylan Thomas, whom very few avoided; and some from the vast verbal experimentalism that flowered at the Royal Court as writers struggled to bring new voices, new poetry, into the theatre. But of course Pinter heard his own music, a private sound that he has given up much to remain true to. I couldn't hear it much in his later plays, which I have not found much joy in.

And the laughs. Not the heavy humour of *The Birthday Party,* but the wonderful explosions of invention of *The Caretaker,* and the giddy whirls of those early short pieces. When his plays lurched towards the symbolic, I lurched the other way. When they tried to be menacing, I was not impressed. When, in later years, they moved up-market, I found them less interesting. But this new lease of laughter, this hempen poetry that worked *as theatre,* this relish for the language of the linguistically deprived: great.

And now his more direct involvement with 'issues' and 'causes' is earning him sneers. Those who praised his 'nuances', his evasions, cannot abide direct-ness. He himself seems to find a conflict between his secret, private crea-tivity, and the linear logic, the insecure rhetoric of political utterance.

It is my birthday wish for him that he can resolve that conflict, in a way he almost did in *Mountain Language,* and go on to create yet another theatre filled with the energy, the language and the laughter of those early plays that meant so much to us in those dark days. For a new darkness, of cowardice and confusion, could easily descend. Harold is one of the few who could strike a light.

At about this time I was brooding on the whole concept of nationhood: living in Scotland at that time, you couldn't help feeling it in the air you breathed. In 1993 I did a talk on the subject from the perspective of the theatre:

THEATRE AND NATION[82]

In modern society, the idea of Nation, anyway one created by kings and barons and earls, is meaningless unless England is playing football against or actually at war with another nation – in which case, loyalties are created by competitive instincts, and hysteria overtakes cultural diversity. 'National-popular', however, is the accumulation of the diverse popular cultures forced together in one 'Nation'. It embraces the Cumbrian clog-maker on one hand, and the yuppie commodity-broker on the other. It is aware of class, regional, ethnic and gender diversity: it does not insist on monopoly, unity or coherence.

In Ancient Athens theatre had several roles: to present poetic images of behaviour, of excessive obsession, and of its consequences, all of which serve vividly to exemplify the deeper values of the society, its quasi-religious bonding morality, its 'Social Imaginary'. Also – in comedy – to lampoon the mighty, to undermine the overweening, to set limits on power – or try to. Aristophanes could tear shreds off Creon in the theatre, to great acclaim, but Creon could still be elected to power a week later.

But has the Royal National Theatre anything to do with this role of theatre in society? Is it not merely a place where the English show the world that they can compete internationally in terms of production values, not nationally in terms of moral values?

Here's Ken Tynan, most vociferous proclaimer of the English National Theatre, speaking to the Royal Society of Arts, in 1964, one year after the Old Vic became the National Theatre under Olivier:

> The notion that an ideal playhouse is a place where you can see a permanent company of first-rate actors appearing in a large and varied repertoire of first-rate plays is generally accepted: but the notion that such a playhouse must inevitably incur an enormous financial loss, even if it plays to capacity, is less widely embraced. The formation of the National Theatre Company was a step towards sanity – towards placing the theatre on the same footing as art galleries and public libraries.

However in the same talk he revealed that of the National Theatre audience, only 0.3% were manual workers, a figure he found 'most distressing, demonstrating as it does that live theatre is socially beyond the desires and financially beyond the means of working-class audiences.' However 89% of the audience came from the Home Counties. Tynan concludes, 'Obviously, we must tour as much and as widely as we can if we are to deserve the epithet "National".'

Clearly this theatre is about theatrical excellence: no bad thing in itself, I'm all for a bit of it here and there – but it doesn't seem to have too much ambition to fulfil a major self-reflective or image-creating role in English society.

It should be said that David Hare's sequence of plays on the Church, the Law, etc. has made an attempt to air matters of 'national' importance. The night I saw the play about the Anglican Church, however, the spectators felt more like a synod than an audience, and even more than 89% came from the Home Counties. It was nevertheless a kind of step forward – but towards what?

Where the 'popular' is amongst all this, I don't know. The 'demos' i.e. the rabble, who make up the word democracy, are nowhere.

In the words of my favourite Scottish judge, Lord Braxfield, in 1796, sending Thomas Muir to the convict hulk:

> A Government in every country must be just like a corporation, and in this country it is made up of the landed interest, which alone has a right to be represented. As for the rabble, who have nothing but personal property, what hold has the nation of them?

This may sound shocking in terms of the right to vote, the right to be represented in parliament, and so it is – but if we examine the theatrical 'nation', not in 1796 but today, we can see that the 'rabble' has even less right to 'representation', in our National Theatre. They may be on the stage, or at least some acceptable version of their lives may be on the stage, but they're not so often in the auditorium.

Scotland

It should be clear anyway that Scotland has even less claim to attention than the Cumbrian clog-maker, in terms of a UK 'Nation'. It is itself a nation of over five million people with distinct cultural, social, and political differences from England, and the so-called 'United Kingdom'. It also has within it a great variety of cultures, at least two languages, and a great range of ways of expressing reality and real feelings in the theatre.

Now there is a certain movement towards establishing a National Theatre of Scotland. The aspiring classes of Scotland look to Ireland, see the Abbey Theatre, to France and see the Comédie Française, to Norway, Sweden, Iceland even, and see those proud nations strutting their stuff in glorious buildings with hugely subsidised companies, competing on behalf of their nations with Peter Brook, Peter Stein, Giorgio Strehler, giving their nation's theatre industry status, prestige, a flagship. And Scotland has nothing.

I was urged recently to join the committee for the Scottish National Theatre, so I have been giving this matter of national theatres quite a bit of thought.

The late great Scottish Constitution Convention, killed stone dead for the time being by the English inability to stop voting Tory, was debating many interesting ideas for a new Constitution for Scotland. In the first place it was to be written down so it could be invoked when necessary, unlike the UK's accretion of corrupt custom, bad practice and worse precedent. Also on the agenda was the idea that every constituency should have two members – one man, one woman – to make sure the new Assembly really was representative.

It occurred to me, and I must say to a few others, that if the Convention could begin to re-think the entire Constitution, maybe the theatre should at least question the concept of a 'national theatre'. Maybe we all ought to be doing that.

The Nation States

The nation states of Western Europe were created basically to make bigger gangs of robbers, to fight off the other gangs of robbers and if possible beat them to a pulp, take their gold, and rape their women. In parenthesis, these nations set off and conquered the rest of the world, drawing lines across deserts, through jungles etc. to divide the rest of the world into nation-states too. Perhaps Scotland failed dismally to build an empire; but its formation was of the classic kind: the enforced union of several very disparate elements into one country strong enough to drive back the endless succession of English thugs marauding over the border. It gave and took bits of Cumbria, Northumbria and the Isle of Man until a border was settled, but it remained a nation of many parts.

The main parts are:

1. Shetland & Orkney.
2. Western Isles & Skye.
3. Pictland.
4. Grampians.
5. The Northern Highlands.
6. The Central area.
7. The 'Industrial Belt'.
8. Ayrshire.
9. The Lothians.
10. The Lowlands.
11. The Borders.
12. The South West.

I'm far from familiar with all of them, but there are profound differences between nearly all of them, in fact several would have great difficulty understanding each other.

But from Edinburgh now transponders bounce messages off the satellites, and the BBC speaks in the same accent, to all of them, and the movies on TV and the videos in the Post Office stores of Sutherland, the late night garages of Skye certainly don't sell Gaelic or Highland culture, ancient or modern, to the eager youth – and if they tried, the eager youth wouldn't buy it.

And the population is in perpetual motion: the demographic changes in Glasgow are minor compared with those in Easter Ross, and the country-side is being emptied of its indigenous crofters and farmers and shepherds, and re-populated with retiring couples from Oldham, window-cleaners from Woking who've sold their houses dear in the south of England and bought cheap in the west of Scotland, and pubs go from bankrupt natives to men from Sheffield with redundancy money.

I can't paint you an image of a static, monocultural peasantry, or even of a stable city culture, for there are whole areas of Glasgow removed to breeze-block tenements on wet hillsides, and there are new nations, new cultures coming in all the time, the Asian, the Caribbean, now the immi-grant workers from the south of Europe, soon perhaps the Rumanians, the Ukrainians, all moving around on this ceaseless crusade to equalise the world's oppression – to import and export exploitation, and the burden of wars.

And all of these parts of the Scottish nation, from Shetland to Dumfries, are changing in ways that are quite reckless, challenged only by nostalgics; they are forging new languages, losing old ones, adopting rootless, bland neologism for rootless, bland experiences; they are sloughing off genera-tions-old prejudice, to reveal the pristine new ones underneath, the same snake at the heart of it all; they are abandoning moral structures of social intercourse built over countless centuries, with no more thought than they would spend on choosing a route for a motorway.

Do I sound bitter, resistant to change, another nostalgic? I'm not. I have enough faith in people to know that novelty becomes humanised in the warmth of usage, and in turn becomes the object of nostalgia, enriched by time and memory, invested with a density and significance it was never born with.

Why I am concerned is that the self-reflective institutions of our society are allowing all this turmoil without any adequate attention being paid to it.

If we go back for a moment to Greece in 5th Century BC, to the decision to send off an imperialist expedition to invade and colonise Sicily, not only was this decision argued over by every Athenian in the Assembly – and all male Athenians went to the Assembly – but also it was the subject of some of the finest, wisest, most perceptive writing from the historians, and was the subject of comic and satiric pieces in the theatre, and even became the source of a shift of values criticised in Euripides' tragedies, notably *Women of Troy*.

Don't let us forget Athens, or Attica as a whole, had at that time a popu-lation no larger than 250,000: the average size for one of the parts of Scotland

I've outlined before, or one quarter of the size of Birmingham. So how did one quarter of Birmingham cope with the Falklands expedition? Or the shift in moral values during Thatcher's reign? What are the ways we can examine our society as it changes? What plays the role in our national life that the drama, the *agora* and the *ekklesia* played in Athenian democracy? To return to Scotland briefly – would plonking a well-heeled outfit in Edinburgh that resolves to tour as often as the money is forthcoming to the four other big cities, and which 'distressingly' has 0.3% of its audience from the 60% of society known as the working class and 0.001% from the unemployed – would this possibly fill the role the drama played in Athens? No. It would not. And *pace* Ken Tynan, such an outfit, no matter how professionally competitive with the Abbey Theatre, would not deserve the epithet 'National'. I leave you to decide whether the one in London does.

So what *does* fill that role?

I made a four-minute film on the Gulf War. Channel 4 carried it on Easter Sunday last year after the Gulf War finished. It's from a poem written by Hamish Henderson called 'Elegy for the Dead in Cyrenaica: Elegy I'. With the help of ITN's archive footage, we made an *Elegy for the Dead in the Gulf War*.

Most of the British soldiers killed in that operation were Scots. Hamish lives in Edinburgh, where I also live, as does John Bett, who read the poem, as do the fiddler, the editor and the co-ordinator. We were looking at Iraq, but meditating on our own society. Surely, in its very tiny way, this was fulfilling the role of the National Theatre?

Perhaps television is capable of playing this role. Certainly the 'nation' looks at it. The most profound look at England's part in the Falklands expedition was Richard Eyre's film of Charles Wood's *Tumbledown*. Where in the theatre is there a commentary on World War II to match Jeremy Isaacs' *The World at War*? Where among the countless RSC value-added productions is one that will tell us, in the way Bleasdale's *Boys from the Black Stuff* did, what Thatcherite values applied with such grim determination really did to our society? By far the bulk of our theatre investment goes to trying to make old plays have new relevance, which is in itself no bad thing, but it leaves very little for new plays penetrating into the core of the 1990s malaise, or even tearing it open with Aristophanic savagery. Yet there, every Sunday night, is *Spitting Image*.

What does that do to those of us who try to make theatre?

On the one hand, it leaves us marginalised, incompetent and irrelevant. On the other hand it presents us with the biggest opportunity theatre has had since Molière came to Paris.

Let us look again at the concept of the nation.

Could not, should not a National Theatre for Scotland be there to bring to life, to theatrical vitality, *all* those areas of Scotland? If the nation was created to centralise power to give strength – should not theatre now use this idea to make a centralised bank of skills, talents and enthusiasm which cannot replace but which can inform and teach and galvanise into action the dormant skills, talent and enthusiasm of each region?

And why stop at the stage? If video is the form of the future, then why not help new creators in all the regions to use video to report, to make documentaries, to make dramas, series, movies eventually, that will be motivated by the need to reflect, to challenge, to satirise, to assert individuality. Not the need to debase popular taste, to standardise the diversity of popular culture, in order to sell more soap. Or shares in the next industry to be privatised.

Why not look at what Field Day have achieved in Northern Ireland, and publish books and pamphlets? Why not find and encourage poets, painters, sculptors, people with new skills?

Why not use the very unprofitability of theatre to create a network of bases, workshops, skills centres, in which *all* of our society could find a home, an incitement to participate, to speak, to express.

The real guarantor of democracy is not in the words of class-bound judges or venal aristocrats, but in the active participation of everybody in civil life, in the institutions, the organisations where we learn to live in a democracy, and practise democratic processes, where the Social Imaginary is created, the Democratic Personality.

Democracy is above all about the realisation of the individual's happiness and ambitions in society. Our society has created a need in many of our most imaginative and bright children, a need to realise their happiness inside their very private heads – tuned in to a Walkman, turned on to coke, or crack, or ecstasy, and soon wearing TV specs, seeing the world through an endless re-run of Michael Winner comedies – driven inside.

Of the many things it tries to be, what theatre can be most triumphantly is a public event, an assertion of common humanity, and a celebration of a shared culture.

If we can even begin to move towards that kind of National Theatre, we will be making a society fit to live in: a society alive to itself.

The globalisation of culture, and its dominance by US film and TV production, was something that occupied me a great deal during the 1990s. I drafted the resolution signed by 40 UK film producers at the festival of British film in Dinard which we hope went some way to strengthening, in the GATT negotiations, the EU's resolve to exclude the 'audio-visual', i.e. film and television culture, from the global free market being imposed by the US-based multinationals on the whole world.

I also worked for a time in the European Commission in Brussels on a High-Level Think Tank advising the Culture Commissioner on future policy. I reported on it in Edinburgh in the National Museum of Scotland's series of European Lectures:

EUROPEAN MEDIA POLICY[83]

Since 1959, I have been – artistically speaking – leading a double life. On the one hand, I've been a playwright and director. But at the same time, throughout my theatrical career, I have worked, often very hard, in film and television, writing, directing and producing films and television plays and even series, like *Z-Cars*. Recently I met Neil Jordan, the director, in Paris. After we'd been introduced and talked movies for five minutes, he told me there used to be a bloke with the same name who worked with the 7:84 Theatre Company. I expressed my indignation at the existence of this impostor, and didn't disabuse him. God knows what he'll say when he meets the other bloke.

I'm afraid I've a reputation for being somewhat literal-minded, so I decided to talk – very seriously – about how the European Commission and Parliament have impinged on my world as a film-maker, and rather more about the roles they could and should play in protecting and encouraging the creative and industrial potential of European cinema.

More specifically, I'd like to give, if I can, a flavour of the debates going on in those parts of the Commission and the Parliament that deal with 'Culture', and particularly film and television production – what is known in an unlovely phrase as 'the Audio-Visual'.

I was asked to be a member of a 'High-Level Think Tank' set up by Commissioner Oreja, of Directorate-General Ten, which has responsibility for, among other things, European cultural well-being. We were set up to help formulate future cultural policy, with particular regard to the Audio-Visual. The context was said to be that of the dawn of the Digital Era, but the real context was of course political.

There is in Europe the kind of struggle going on that we were familiar with in the 1980s: the Free Market, so-called 'liberalising' ideology, red in tooth and claw, promoted by the large multinational conglomerates like Kirsch, Rupert Murdoch's News Corp, Bertelsmann, Berlusconi and the major Hollywood film studios, which wants to destroy any regulation of television, to outlaw import quotas on the audio-visual, to allow, in a phrase, profit-driven market forces to have free play to dominate the media of Europe.

On the other hand there are those who regard the media as different from the cosmetics industry, who do not see the production of film and television as the same as producing bottles of Coca-Cola, who see value in culture and who refuse to see Public Service Broadcasting as disposable.

Let me turn to look at the Global Situation, to try to characterise the situation of the European cultural industries, with special reference to cinema, in the global audio-visual economy:

In fact the main features of this relationship are plain to see and incontrovertible: the US audio-visual factories, with truly astonishing ruthlessness and efficiency, dominate the cinema and television screens of Europe, and they are only prevented from destroying the indigenous industries and cultures by national and EU legislation. This Jack Valenti and the Motion Picture and Television Association of America scream at as 'restrictive practice' and worse than Stalinist protectionism.

At this point, I ought to say that I was asked to research and make proposals for a new Media Programme. The Commission has implemented Media I, which ran to 1995, and is currently in the middle of a review of Media II, which will run to the end of 2000.

The Media Programmes are the instruments by which the producers, distributors, cinema-owners and film financiers are encouraged by financial incentives to develop the European film industry along the lines of European policy. There are no straightforward grants or loans to produce films. The policy concentrates on three main areas: Development, i.e the difficult phase of taking a good idea, a good first draft of a movie, through to being a world-beating screenplay, well cast, scheduled and budgeted, with a reputable director, all ready to attract the right kind of finance. The other areas are Training, in which policy emphases can change, and Distribution – the process of getting the movies to the audiences, and making a return on the investment – a highly specialised business.

After many individual submissions, and many hours of often heated debate within the group in Brussels, a Report was produced. It does not fully satisfy any one member of the Group: we were a very diverse bunch, from the ex-Prime Minister of Portugal, who wanted to kill off all Public Service Broadcasting – having suffered under Salazar, then the Portugese Communist Party, he had his reasons – to Bolek Sulik, the Chairman of the National Broadcasting Council of Poland; from Jan Mojto, MD of Taurus/Kirsch, to the President of the EBU [European Broadcasting Union]: but it at least opens perspectives on the debate which are not simple 'Free Market' mantras. And it will, we hope, inform this debate in years to come.

In my own particular area, Media III, we agreed that the programmes need to run on a much longer-term basis, and to have a massive increase in their annual allocation. Their task is monumental, and its importance cannot be over-estimated in terms of European industry, commerce and culture. They need to be given the resources, financial and human, to complete it.

If they fail, and the US majors come to dominate the audio-visual through-out Europe and the industries of Europe lose out on one great expanding sector of the world economy, unemployment in the audio-visual rises and our children learn what Hollywood wishes them to learn, and come to think, in time, in the way the US wants them to think, then it will be contrary to the values that Europe has created and come to cherish, and will diminish Europe's contribution to the world, and its ability to control its own destiny.

Emanating from the New Ireland came a fresh attempt, hugely successful, to exploit the entertainment culture of the lower orders: Riverdance *was massively popular. Before it came to Edinburgh, I was asked to write a preview for the* Scotsman *newspaper.*

GO WITH THE FLOW[84]

There's no doubt about it: *Riverdance* is a hit. It began as an interlude in the 1994 Eurovision Song Contest, serving up a bit of Irish local colour in-between the 57 varieties of overcooked soup. Apparently the 300 million viewers loved it. Two Irish television producers and a Chicago choreo-grapher seized the opportunity, and now almost two million people have paid a lot of cash to see *Riverdance,* and over two million have bought the video.

Good luck to them: the show is the apogee of Light Entertainment, pro-fessional, hard-working, and effective. The musicians are excellent, the dancers exciting, and drilled to perfect synchronisation. It's all high-class show-biz, at times brilliant razzmatazz, and hugely successful.

It was Brian Friel's *Dancing at Lughnasa* that first put together the themes of Irish set-dancing, the invocation of Ireland's pagan past and the natural trauma of mass emigration. This play also was massively successful, playing around the world to delighted theatre-goers. It was an inspired piece of theatre writing – moving, probing and beautifully crafted.

Now along comes *Riverdance,* popularising and exploiting with a born-again commercialism the same themes, and again they flock in their millions. Why? The sheer physical exhilaration of the thunder, an electric storm of thrilling energy that can't fail to stir even the dullest stumps.

Audiences of several thousand people a night sit and listen to the New Age poeticising invocation of 'the primal quest to come to terms with spiri-tual and elemental forces', of 'the sun's great power', of Cuchulain, 'hero of many an epic battle, who fought the sea itself', of 'the circle of the seasons . . . the first shoots of spring . . . Summer's ripening and the gathering of Autumn's bounty.' It tells us 'the key to everything is love.' All this just under the Hammersmith flyover, where you can get strawberries all the year round, and the key to everything is money. Facing the theatre once was the flat where Dennis Potter did battle not with the sea, but with rheumatoid arthritis. *Riverdance* in Hammersmith was a phenomenon, but a distinctly odd one.

It isn't just a dance show. It has become an event, claimed to be 'a redefinition of Irishness' – and perhaps it is. What is new about it is its realisation of the appeal of a mythical peasant past to 1990s audiences in danger of losing not only their rural ethnic roots but also even their urban identity as the industries that brought them together in the cities fall apart.

Mansholt was a Dutch Socialist working for the old EEC in the 1970s. He drew up the Mansholt Plan: a proposal to depopulate Europe's countryside, to turn agriculture into a capital-intensive industry, remove the surplus population to the industrial areas, and leave the countryside with enough farm-labourers to keep the place tidy for the tourists, vacationers and retired townsfolk. Although this plan was howled down at the time, it has become the hidden agenda of the EC, and a reality for us all.

Even as the landowners were evicting and exiling the Highlanders of Scotland, the middle classes were passionately warbling parlour arrangements of their songs, and codifying their dances and their dress. So now as we democratically empty the countryside of Scotland and Ireland, we seek our entertainment in elements of the cultures which are being destroyed, made palatable for our mass-entertainment parlours on stage and television screen. And the commercial savvy of the new, hard-eyed Ireland makes sure it is professional, satisfying on one level, and most efficiently marketed.

Perhaps audiences flock to *Riverdance* for deeper reasons - perhaps all this vatic nonsense about primal quests and autumn's beauty expresses a deeper lack in post-industrial society. In film, the influence of Joseph Campbell's popularising work on the narrative structures of the world's cultures has been immense, and consciously used. Spielberg learnt everything from it. Campbell died on George Lucas's ranch. The huge popularity of their films again draws on a deeper need in fragmented, distracted consciousnesses.

The question we have to ask ourselves is whether these shows are merely exploiting that need, leaving us with an even greater lack, or exploring and clarifying and creatively fulfilling our needs, even inciting us to do something. Maybe *Riverdance* doesn't exactly do that, but it leaves us with a warm glow – and an empty glen.

Throughout the 1990s, I was also very involved in writing plays for the new generations, both plays to be performed in schools by professionals, and a huge play to be performed by the schools themselves. Their subjects were: the media; the trades unions; and the Universal Declaration of Human Rights.

Media Star *was written for Edinburgh's Theatre Workshop, and showed in a fairly comic way how one misunderstood event could be taken and dealt with by the press, then television, and finally the movies. It was toured all over Scotland, and led to many discussions in secondary schools about the nature of the media: a subject sadly absent from the 'core curriculum'. Later, we made a New York version of the play with drama students at Columbia.*

Subsequently TAG – Theatre About Glasgow – asked for a play to celebrate the centenary of the Scottish TUC to take round schools.

The greatest challenge however was presented by a group of headteachers in England and Wales, who asked me to research and write a play for all seventeen schools they represented to make their own production of. Liz and I did a series of workshops in the schools, to find out the general level of the students' awareness, and were very impressed by their strong desire to explore the notion of Human Rights, which seemed to tie together a lot of their preoccupations with the injustices of the world, and hold the potential to open their eyes to a few more. After the workshops, I wrote the play, called The Road to Mandalay. *Not all seventeen schools did a production, for various reasons, but we then went round and did more performance-oriented workshops with the thirteen or so who did. I wrote a piece to point the school students in the general direction of the kind of performance the show was written for:*

THE ROAD TO MANDALAY[85]

Notes for Directors and Performers

The Road to Mandalay is a piece of Rough Theatre. It is therefore neither Posh Theatre, nor Agitprop, which is a different thing altogether, usually made in times of upheaval, war or revolution, to persuade people to take sides in action. Rough Theatre, however, has its demands if it is to work properly. Among them are:

1. RESEARCH: Firstly it demands of the performers a kind of commitment that comes only from a full understanding not only of the character they are playing, but also of the whole situation the character is in, and the attitude to it of the production.

Find out the facts, think about them, use your imagination to feel what the people in the scenes felt, but do not identify with them in a sentimental or uncritical manner.

Show the story, as well as the character, and the reason for the scene being in the play will come clear to the audience.

2. WORDS: Use the words. There is a style of television acting taking over the world in which the words are not so important as the face of the actor.

In Rough Theatre, the words are a major contribution to the meaning and the enjoyment of the play.

Some lines of course can be 'thrown away' for effect, variety, or comedy, but even they must be clearly articulated. Learn to take pleasure in the words, and the audience will have an added dimension of enjoyment.

3. COMEDY: Many of the scenes have elements of comedy, some are pure comedy. This should be explored in rehearsal and played for an audience to the full. Plunge in, try ways of doing things, ways of walking, ways of talking, ways of dressing - if you feel a comic urge, go for it.

Don't be afraid to be tasteless, or to end up unfunny – that's what directors and rehearsals are for.

But don't let your comedy be cruel, or inhumane, even if it gets cheap laughs. Let it be anarchic, rude, mocking; let it take the mickey out of pomposity, conceit, lies, hypocrisy; let it smile, laugh, giggle, groan or get hysterical; let getting your laughs be a skill you learn, and are proud of; and let your punch-lines never droop.

4. MUSIC: Another skill to be proud of, singing, playing – a great source of enjoyment for you and your audience.

5. VARIETY: The music and the comedy are only two of the elements that provide the variety that is the hallmark of this kind of theatre. When the play is essentially about something that everybody knows is serious and important, there is all the more reason to tell the story by chopping styles and forms, by showing one problem as a sad song, one as a slapstick comedy, another as a comic or satirical song, another as a straightforward acted scene, another as a monologue to the audience by a slippery character, and still keep a framework that does not trivialise or fritter away the essential gravity of the subject.

6. STYLE: I've mentioned changing styles through the play. This sounds, in the abstract, quite wrong and woolly.

In fact, it means playing some scenes as the Marx brothers would play them, singing a song as a Harry Enfield character would sing it, basing a character on Morecambe or Wise's performances, or on Kathy Burke's style, or as Wells or Fortune would play it, or as a stand-up comic would approach it. Obviously the material is never pure comedy just for giggles, but the secret is to decide on a style for a scene, then try out every trick in the book of that style.

7. URGENCY: The subject of this play, and of many Rough Theatre plays, is one that profoundly affects the future of the human race, which can kill

people or bring happiness to their lives. In reality all we can do is share a few thoughts with and ask a few questions of our friends in the audience, and give them some entertainment on the way.

At the same time, the thoughts we share are urgent, and matter. Without preaching a sermon or being solemn about it, we need to convey this urgency, and to say that we think these questions matter. Here, it is vital not to talk down to the audience or treat them as dimwits: they will grasp the story far more quickly and fully than we realise. The act of sharing these thoughts and sensing a response is the most rewarding thing in theatre, to be worked for and treasured.

Working with schools is a very rewarding occupation. During this time I also started an organisation called Moonstone, at the instigation of Robert Redford. This runs workshops to train new screenwriters and directors under the guidance of experienced screenwriters and directors. It, too, is most rewarding, but is a different story.

I digressed from the set of One Woman shows I wrote for and toured with Liz. The third, but by no means the last, was a play called The Last of the MacEachans, *about the changing scene in the Highlands, with the indigenous population being driven out by the White Settlers, just as the Mohicans had been, and the need for changed attitudes, and for a new spirit of adventure. We opened again on the Edinburgh Fringe, played the Citizens Theatre, Glasgow, and tried to tour the Highlands with it, only to discover that the venues we had opened up in the teeth of official disapproval, were now organised into a formalised circuit, run by a committee of the very White Settlers the play was satirising. Needless to say, we were discouraged from touring the Highlands of Scotland.*

But we did tour. A friendly company in Belfast, Tinderbox, fixed up a tour round the north of Ireland, both sides of the border, and gave us a van, and a brilliant driver-technician. We were on the road yet again. We had finally come back to where we started, with everything we needed packed into a Transit van, and fit-ups and get-outs and B & Bs and immediate contact with the audiences. We were extremely happy. In Dundalk, my mother's family turned out in force. In Coalisland we narrowly missed a shooting. We ended up on the far, bleak Atlantic coast of Donegal, in a tiny arts centre that had been the Workhouse in days not long gone. The audience was large and full of recognition of their own situation. As I was wrapping the cables at the end of the show, and the audience was having a few drinks before taking us to the pub, a Donegal woman watched me for a time, then approached me. 'Now, see this er John McGrath . . . would he now be the same John McGrath I used see in the Abbey Theatre in Dublin, and the Dublin Theatre Festival?' I hesitated. 'Er, yes . . . he is . . . er, in fact it's me.' She looked hard at me: 'Well now –' and she took a deep breath and gave me an enigmatic stare, 'well now, you've come a long way.'

What she maybe had guessed was that I was as happy in Dunfanaghy Workhouse that night as I would ever be at any old National Theatre.

The same year that The Last of the MacEachans *opened on the Edinburgh Fringe, Wildcat had set me up with a huge show to write and direct in the centre of the Official Festival. Dave MacLennan had suggested, some time before, that I might be interested in making a modern reading of Lindsay's festival favourite* Ane Satyre of the Thrie Estaitis. *At first I demurred, as I always do when someone suggests a subject. But it was a great idea, and it grew on me. It ended with a massive sprawling piece about the future of Scotland, and how the forces of post-industrial society, particularly the media, could negate by their powerful cultural and political imperialism, the benefits of independence or even of devolution. I called it* A Satire of the Fourth Estaite.

A SATIRE OF THE FOURTH ESTAITE [86]

I was persuaded to do *The Fourth Estaite* in the newly built International Conference Centre in Edinburgh. What was intriguing about that was that in the foyer there were hanging television screens all round and when people came in I played the electronic version of the marketplace, QVC from Cable, so people were bombarded by electronic sales pitches for cheap trinkets and cars. Out of this atmosphere of kitsch bazaar, there emerged a Seville Easter procession with statues of Blair as The Saviour, Thatcher as the Virgin Mary and John Major as John the Baptist, followed by a crowd of self-flagellants. They lead the audience up escalators into the theatre, while outside there were third world figures trying to get in, staring in through the window. When you finally got into the theatre, there were three people on stage trying to sell you something.

It was a hard job breaking down what was ultimately a conference venue, but we built out the stage and we used a lot of music, and the story was very strong. The form was not traditional; I used a lot of elements from traditional theatre and subverted other elements of more conventional theatre. We did use a lot of popular devices, but it wasn't a kind of 'this is a ceilidh play', because I think forms have become more eclectic, and you have to try and develop them. I did use the basic verbal structure of *The Thrie Estaitis:* it was written in verse and the verses all rhymed. I tried to emulate the original's excoriation of the venality and corruption and abuse of power with characters based on medieval stereotypes: Lord Merde, Sir Righteous Indignation, Ersatz Sensualitie, King Humanity et al.

It was a play about Scottish Devolution, independence and how independent Scotland could be as part of a global economy. It made a kind of symbolic figure of Scotland being born again and meant a great deal to people in Scotland. It was well received and I think, on the whole, I was pleased with it.

The show was extremely popular with festival audiences, packing the 1,200-seater every night. Predictably enough, the big wheels of the London press found it offensive, but it was hailed in the Scotsman *as 'a triumph,' leading to an interesting article in the paper about differences of perception.*

REACHING THE STAGE OF OPTIMISM[87]

When Nicol Williamson was invited to the White House to perform some of his highly acclaimed *Hamlet,* the then President of the United States (alas, it was Richard Nixon) sent an aide to greet him and his distinguished company of actors and musicians. 'Are you the entertainment? – Follow me!' – and off they were whisked, away from the real people who graced the court of Tricky Dicky.

Perhaps all the 'Scottish' shows invited to the Official Festival felt a sensation similar to Nicol's, or indeed to Hamlet's friends come to entertain the court at Elsinore: that the real drama is going on, or being cancelled, elsewhere. And just like the Players, we were kept in the servants' quarters, and excluded from any of the grown-ups' festivities. Certainly presenting *The Fourth Estaite* to the English press was not unlike presenting the Murder of Gonzago to Claudius.

Nevertheless it was for myself and Wildcat a very happy experience. The audiences were huge and enthusiastic, the critical reception in Scotland and from the saner parts of the English press was very good, and we had a lot of fun doing it.

Of course, since we attacked the more right-wing and evil sections of the press with wit and vigour, we were given a witless mauling from them in return.

I feel no call to defend the show against them. Several Scottish commentators have already noted the impoverishment of their concept of theatre, and the age-old English failure to understand, and so to scorn, things Scottish. And, of course, I am prepared to believe that they alone, out of the 1,200 people cheering on opening night found nothing of interest or value in the show. I believe it because they simply don't speak the language of Scottish concerns, or indeed of Popular Theatre, being deprived of such a thing by the depredations of the English Arts Council – which are shortly to be pursued by the Scottish Arts Council. Presumably that is what Seona Reid [the new director of the Scottish Arts Council] is here to achieve.

Yet there was one feature of all this that struck me as having a wider, sadder resonance. It has to do with optimism. It seems that Scottish audiences today are looking for something with some hope for the future, some optimism in it, while these poor English critics and intellectuals seem to find the whole notion of 'optimism' rather objectionable, rather like whistling at a funeral.

The urge to write *The Fourth Estaite* came when it became clear that, no matter how many second thoughts Blair may have, no matter how hard the Scottish Labour Party may try to make the Scottish Assembly powerless, they could not wriggle completely out of their commitment to some sort of constitutional change for Scotland. Now the people of Scotland want to make sure that the change is for the good, and is really what they want – a taste of democracy even.

It struck me then that England has very little possibility for change to anything but another right-wing Labour government, at best. Optimism has never been a central feature of the pragmatic English character. At the present moment it is clearly repugnant to both right-wing theatre critics and radical intellectuals alike.

I have long argued that theatre alone cannot achieve any social change. At best it can voice the demands of forces already in motion, or strongly desired. Perhaps that is the basic reason for the distaste for *The Fourth Estaite* and other Scottish pieces in the reactionary bits of the English press: they can see nothing to look forward to, and can't understand why anybody else should. Without that desire to look forward with some hope for the future, shows like mine must seem callow indeed. All very sad.

So I have come to the conclusion that we in Scotland are all very privileged, not only in having a rich, coherent and developing culture, but also in having a future to look forward to making – in having the obligation to be dragged, kicking and screaming, into some form of optimism.

I shall certainly continue to anger the right-wing press with optimism, and to fight against the old fools and vested interests here in Scotland who will be trying to take that future away and turn us into a minor, hopeless, version of England.

Then two things happened. The Scotsman *was bought by some billionaires and handed over to the Conservative Party in the egregious shape of Rupert Murdoch's ex-lieutenant, Andrew Neil. It was exactly what the play was about. Certainly there was no longer any chance that such a play would be hailed by that paper as a triumph. It belonged to the multinational mentality, and all that implies culturally and politically.*

The other thing was that the Scottish Arts Council cut Wildcat's grant. This was a body blow to David MacLennan, and to the rest of the company. To me, it felt almost personal. Indeed, my show was given as one of the reasons for the Arts Council's distaste for their work. After she came out of the show, Seona Reid, the SAC's Director, was heard to say that this sort of thing was disgraceful, and had to be stopped. She maybe had not noticed the other 1,199 people having a thoroughly good night out. I wrote:

THATCHER'S LAST TWITCH[88]

The damage Mrs Thatcher and her followers have done to culture in Great Britain is incalculable – and by that I mean incalculably great. The practice of rule by centralised authority dispensing its wishes through layers of managers, of disregarding the will or even the intelligence of the creators of culture, the punitive downscaling of grants to organisations that cannot function properly already, the PR assault disguising cuts based on ideological repression as 'enhancements' and the redefinition of culture as something for the chattering classes to chatter about – all this, and more has led inexorably to a climate of fear and negativity among the creative forces, first of England, and then, as night follows day, of Scotland.

What never ceases to astonish me – not to say alarm me – is the silence of the artists. Either they are cowed by fear of financial reprisal, or believe that speaking out is a waste of time, that their opinions should be kept to themselves. They no longer even organise effectively. This must surely be the product of years of impotence under Thatcher's tyranny, her crushing of all organised opposition. Forgive me if, having nothing now left to lose, I dare to speak out. I would welcome more voices to be heard – I'm sure there are many people feeling the same way.

The SAC's latest exercise in 'enhancing' Touring Theatre in Scotland reveals startlingly clearly that the spirit of Thatcher lives on and is embodied in the Director of the SAC, Seona Reid, who came up from the harsh world of London's Arts Board to sort out Scotland, and remake its culture in the image of the devastation she left behind her in London. The question we, the newly devolved, must ask ourselves is: Is this what the new Scotland really wants to dictate its Arts policy?

We are told that the decisions to cut Wildcat and reduce Borderline's grant, to ignore the work of companies like Raindog and Lookout, and to celebrate the addition of £42,000 of extra money to touring theatre is really 'to ensure that the very best of touring drama is available to audiences throughout Scotland'. It is nothing of the kind.

What it is really doing is making sure that 'the very best' is defined by a handful of bureaucrats, that the vibrant culture of the Highlands, Grampian region, the Borders, not to mention the huge mass of working-class people all over Scotland, will be ignored. They will be served up, if they are lucky, with a cut-price version of what the Traverse or the Tron audiences might consider trendy.

The theatrical expression of the specific cultures of Scotland is dead, after ten years of SAC ideological intervention. And the sad thing is, they won't even understand what I'm talking about. Not that they ever did. They have now successfully disenfranchised, taken away the theatrical voice of many millions. When we look at the methods of reaching these latest decisions, we cannot be surprised. A decision was taken about the amount of money available to touring before the demand was assessed. Of course the Arts Council has constraints, but it also has priorities. These were not apparently open to question.

Then a 'specially selected' (by whom?) sub-committee was set up consisting entirely of theatre bureaucrats and managers. Not one artist, actor, writer, certainly not one representative of the Stornoway audience, the Wick audience, of the Glenrothes club audience, of the Easterhouse audience, of the people of Hawick. How's that for representative democracy, Mr Blair? How can a group of managers, whose main job is to satisfy the theatrical leisure time of the tourist trade and the regular middle-class theatre-goers of their area, have the slightest comprehension of or concern for the needs of rural audiences in Ullapool or working people in Govan? How can they understand that the people of the Highlands have their own traditions, their own language, their own demands of touring theatre?

No wonder they agreed to cut Wildcat's grant completely.

Perhaps, as they so coyly put it, Wildcat's 'artistic proposals as a whole were less compelling'. Let us look at them: a Tramway piece based on William MacIlvanney's *Docherty*, new work from Liz Lochhead, Marcella Evaristi, John Bett and of course David MacLennan and Dave Anderson, a new translation by Joe Farrell of Alessandro Barrico, co-productions with the Royal Lyceum (of a musical I intended to write on the early life of Sir Walter Scott) and further collaborations with the Citizens Theatre. Hardly stuff any civilised funding organisation would wish to reject unseen. In amongst it is the material that will draw thousands of non-theatre-goers into halls and spaces all over Scotland, that will inspire dozens of young working-class entertainers to join the profession, and train new young writers to work in ways that relate to their own background, rather than some alien concept of 'culture'.

The SAC in its wisdom has seen fit to present Wildcat with a special grant of £50,000 to present Liz Lochhead's version of the opera *Carmen*. This alone indicates its abysmal priorities. Would they offer Scottish Opera £50,000 to present *Carmen*? It would scarcely pay the conductor's fees and travel. The scorn for Wildcat's audiences is underscored by this crass gesture. The priorities of the wise sub-committee are self-evident.

And what of the work of Raindog, ever enterprising and surprising, of the brilliant new company Lookout – are they now condemned to the scrapheap of Scottish Theatre, doomed by a bunch of bureaucrats to eternal damnation?

This sub-committee was said to be judging 'against a set of artistic, managerial and cultural criteria'. Would the SAC now please publish these criteria? May we ask which set of bureaucrats drew them up for their own convenience and to represent their own taste and priorities, and to whom they are answerable?

Where is the Scottish Office in this debate – or set of instructions? Until a few months ago the Minister currently in charge of the Arts, Sam Galbraith, and the Scottish Secretary himself, Donald Dewar, sat on the Board of Wildcat. Were they such fools as to know they were supporting a company unworthy of showing its face in Scotland? I think not, and sympathise with their present position. They are lumbered with the methods and institutional practices of an outdated dogma.

Seona Reid is not, it is to be hoped, the face of New Labour, but represents the last twitch of a long-discredited Thatcherism. The people of Scotland never subscribed to that punitive creed, and suffered under it for seventeen long years. Surely we are not now going to face a future dominated by the same sterility?

I must apologise if I bang on in this way. Unfortunately I've had quite a lot to bang on about. One of the problems of consistency is that it's very easy to be accused of inflexibility: [89]

Holdsworth   *Your political position has always been fundamental to your theory and practice. Has that position been modified during the 1990s?*

The basics of my position haven't altered at all, but it clearly has to take account of the world it lives in and so the means to achieve the objectives that I believe in obviously have to be modified. The first element of my political position is that the world isn't changing of its own accord. The use of the passive mode, or mood, in terms of what's happening to the world, is to me the most troublesome aspect of what is happening today. I still believe, first, that the world is changed by individual decisions and, second, that co-operation between human beings is better for everybody than competition.

Thatcher came in at a time when co-operation, which the Labour Party ostensibly stood for, was failing miserably, and Thatcher then set about liberating the market forces, the competitive spirit, the entrepreneurs. It appeared for a time that Thatcher was actually winning intellectually and politically, certainly winning *that* argument. The world was convinced that the free market was the future of mankind, and Fukuyama had declared that history was at an end.

Seeing the failure of Labour to provide a genuine third way, to create a co-operative society, has clearly made it more difficult to be optimistic about the kind of basic beliefs that people involved in 1968 held, that inspired me throughout the 1970s and right through the 1980s. However, I think I now see in Europe that the overall policies that the European Commission is interested in do achieve a certain balance between liberating the entre-preneurial spirit which drives the economy and, at the same time, regulating it and forcing, in a contradictory way, a kind of humanity and humane practice on that. Now I think that is the best practical way forward, and it's one reason why I think some aspects of what New Labour is trying to do are positive, although I think a lot of what they are doing is retrograde. Some aspects of what Gordon Brown, as Chancellor, has been able to put in place have been positive in the sense that they don't begin from the idea, that Thatcher held, that there is no such thing as society. They begin from the idea that there is a society and that society has a responsibility to all of its members. Of course I would like to see a lot more done, but the Govern-ment is constrained all the time by a population which has been led by Thatcherism to believe that anything that interferes with the freedom of the entrepreneurial competitive spirit is going to land us back in 1978, the 'Winter of our Discontent'. The population is terrified; they've got long memories, and they don't want that.

I also believe that people should have the maximum share in the benefits of technological advances. It is not enough when two huge companies merge, or one takes over the other, to increase their profits by laying off 15,000 people. That means that 15,000 people are on the dole and maybe 400 people, maybe 40 people, double their income. The big problem is now that technological advances are being made by multinationals, because they can afford the research and development budgets, they are now not only able to merge, buy-up and take over, but they are also inventing the labour-saving devices, the ways of making do with an even smaller workforce, to do the same work by electronic means. Again, this might sound naive, the individual nation state can no longer cope with the power of the multi-nationals, and it takes something like the European Union to be able to have any impact at all, although we have been discovering some of the corruption evident within the European Commission. So, I'm not saying that the Euro-pean Union is in any way a united force that is able to control the multi-nationals. But you can take something the size of the European Union and, you can, with the political will and the political power, actually control, humanise and make the multinationals regard something other than their profit margin.

The one thing I am sure about is that we have constantly to remind people that these things do not happen in some passive way, but that other human beings create them. *People* make decisions that end up with the dole queue, with people living on or below the poverty line, with people living in sub-standard accommodation, with people of the world ripping each other off, just as much as Ethnic Cleansing in Kosovo is the result of a set of deci-sions. Every multinational has its Milosevic.

Holdsworth   *You've always talked about the importance of a vital counter-culture. Where do you think that counter-culture exists in the contemporary context?*

Obviously the dominant culture is post-Thatcherite, of the West End and the values ingrained in the Arts Councils. I think *that* culture needs serious questioning. It is more insidious, expensive and insulting to ordinary people than it ever was. There is the broad idea that the whole working class vanished in a puff of smoke around 1980. The working class hasn't vanished: they've gone away from settled communities, but they're still somewhere and I think the challenge is to reflect their experience. They have a point of view, and they are forming new cultures. You only have to go into playgrounds to get informed: kids create new formations – cultural community begins here.

The other element is the non-working class, the unemployed. What you might call the *Big Issue* counter-culture. *Trainspotting* was a prime example. Jimmy McGovern is writing wonderfully for television about that counter-culture. In television and film there does seem to be a new kind of dynamic. There are a lot more movies being made, and we are able to make movies in areas which were previously inaccessible. Whatever you thought of *The Full Monty*, it did come out of a very real working-class experience, however commercialised it may have been, the experience of people being thrown on the dole. The movies are exploring, they're open, searching here and there.

There is a sense in which a great many things that are interesting and exciting are happening in European theatres. Ariane Mnouchkine is still one of the best, one of the most demanding and challenging directors in the world. She is not mainstream, even though she gets big audiences every night in a suburb of Paris. We can, I think we are, slowly learning a great deal from the European companies that have the support to experiment, to make mistakes. A company like Complicité, which I like a lot, has drawn on many European traditions that we were ignorant of, or didn't think we could do twenty years ago. That is another source of a kind of renewal of British theatre.

In a conference organised by David Bradby at London University, I was asked to give a keynote speech. I used the opportunity to try to put together my political and artistic philosophies for the twenty-first century:

THEATRE AND DEMOCRACY[90]

There can be few more devastating moments in recent theatre history than that created by the sight and sound of Ekkehardt Schall's savage rendition of Brecht's *The Anachronistic Procession, or Freedom and Democracy*. Written in 1947, it is Brecht's mordantly bitter welcome to the new rulers of

Germany, and rips apart their claims to represent either Freedom or Democracy, using as its basis Shelley's equally savage *Masque of Anarchy,* written shortly after the massacre of Peterloo:[91]

Spring returned to Germany.
In the ruins you could see
Early green birch buds unfold
Graceful, tentative and bold

As from many a southern valley
Voters left their house to rally
Forming a disjointed column
Underneath two banners solemn

Whose supports were all worm-eaten
Their inscription weatherbeaten
Though its gist appeared to be
Freedom and Democracy . . .

Keeping step, next march the teachers
Toadying, brain-corrupting creatures
For the right to educate
Boys to butchery and hate.

After them behold the former
Editors of Streicher's *Stürmer*
All set to protest unless
We get Freedom of the Press . . . .

Through the streets resounds the lash:
SS men flogging for cash.
Freedom needs them too, you see –
Freedom and Democracy.

And those Nazi women there
With their skirts up in the air —
Legs, they reckon, are what gets
Allied sweets and cigarettes . . .

Cold winds blow a requiem
From the ruins over them
Former tenants of the flats
That once stood here. Then great rats

> Leave the rubble in their masses
> Join in the column as it passes
> Squeaking 'Freedom!' as they flee
> 'Freedom and Democracy!'

One of the great services theatre can perform for the people of any country or region or town or village is to be the instrument of authentic democracy, or at the very least to push the community as near to authentic democracy as has yet been achieved.

Brecht's verses and indeed Shelley's *Masque of Anarchy* fulfil one of the major responsibilities of any citizen of a democracy – to draw attention to false democracy.

We live in a world where every crime a nation can commit is excused by false claims to democracy. Throughout the twentieth century, democracy has been the universally acceptable, authenticating concept in the pursuit of public relations, and the most abused system in reality.

But the theatre can and has played many other, deeper and more important roles in the quest for authentic democracy. As we look at the constituent elements of democracy, it will become very clear where theatre can and has played a variety of roles.

What is Democracy?

I would like to consider the person who has provided perhaps the most fecund interface between Democracy and Theatre, Cornelius Castoriadis.[92]

But first we must look for a few definitions, or, at least try to capture some of the qualities of authentic democracy. We must examine the workings of the Athenian democracy, its architects, Solon and Cleisthenes, and the keywords – or concepts it produced to define its values.[93]

Of course democracy takes many forms. The form we in the West live under, and are now busily exporting to the rest of the globe, is called Liberal or Representative Democracy. Its main current purpose is to provide the global legal framework for the multinational corporations to increase their power and profit. In this, it is succeeding *con trionfo*.

Castoriadis lobs a grenade at this form of democracy:

> Nowhere among the political philosophers – or among those who claim to be such – has there been any attempt to provide a reasonable foundation for representative democracy. What is this theological mystery, this alchemic operation that makes of your sovereignty, one day every five years, a fluid that spreads over the entire country, enters into the ballot boxes, and comes out again that same evening on the television screen, on the faces of the 'representatives of the people'? This operation is clearly of a

supernatural character, and no one has ever attempted to provide a foundation for it or even to explain it. People limit themselves to saying that under modern conditions direct democracy is impossible, therefore that representative democracy is necessary.[94]

Participation by the body politic was essential under the Athenian regime, and laws were established to facilitate such political participation. In the modern world, we witness an abandonment of the public sphere to specialists, to professional politicians, interrupted only by rare and brief periods of political explosions known as revolutions . . . .

> There was in the Greek world an explicit recognition of the power and the function of Government. In the modern period, where Governments are nearly omnipotent, we notice that in the imaginary sphere and in political and constitutional theory the Government is hidden behind what is called the 'executive' power. This term is tantamount to mystification, it is a fantastic abuse of language, for the 'executive power' does not 'execute' anything. The lower echelons of the administration do engage in 'execution' in the sense that they apply, or are supposed to apply, pre-existing rules. When the Government wages war, however, it does not 'execute' any law; it acts within the very broad bounds of a law that recognises it has this 'right'. And this we have seen in reality, in the United States with the Vietnam war, Panama, Grenada, and now we are probably going to see it again in the case of the Persian Gulf, after which time Congress will be unable to do anything but approve of the action.[95]

To this we can now add the use of nuclear-tipped shells on the civilian populations in and around Basra, and the destruction of Serbia.

Democracy has been severely distorted by this multinational form of Representative Democracy. There are surely more health-giving fruits of democracy, of humanity's attempts to find a way to live well together. Let us look first at some of the basics . . .

1. First of all, a democracy needs *Borders:* a *demos* or community seeking to run itself on democratic lines draws a boundary, and almost all those within are citizens with rights and responsibilities. Those excluded are non-citizens. Exclusion however is both geographical, i.e. those outside the borders, and internal, i.e. certain people within.

The boundaries geographical are always being contested, and defended: e.g. Europe and national sovereignty, the great debate now being conducted.

The boundaries, limits, to the demos are used to defend the demos from tyranny from without, and to define the limits of the population; but attitudes to 'foreigners' and immigrants living within the borders vary. Who is included, who is excluded, is a site of contestation, now as it was in Ancient Greece.

It cannot be assumed therefore that anybody who manages to live in a demos automatically becomes a citizen. Things are a little better than in England in the 18th century, when Lord Hardwicke declared in 1757: 'Our men of property are our only freemen'.

Clearly the demos needs to defend itself from would-be tyrants from within, and there must be limits for definition of the qualifications for citizenship to have any meaning. Nevertheless, the boundaries within can be used for anti-democratic ends, can be used to exclude women, the young or landless people from the franchise, to disempower the inconvenient.

Of course the voices of the excluded have to be heard, and the values of the included celebrated, upheld, and scrutinised. The borders of democracy, especially the internal, have to be constantly contested.

2. Within the borders, every citizen is part of the decision-making process. To make reasonable decisions, every citizen needs one thing: accurate, un-biased and full information. Without it, their decisions are based on lies, misunderstanding, propaganda and prejudice, so are worthless.

If we pause to consider the sources of most of our population's information today – *The Sun* and the rest of Murdoch and its rival press, television news, the fruits of the Government's spin doctors' labours and the advertising industry – we can have little doubt that the foundations of infor-mation upon which today's consumers/voters take action are distinctly shallow.

3. One essential element of Cleisthenes' reforms that lead to Athenian Democracy was the concept of *isegoria,* literally the equality of freedom of speech. This was not theoretical, or gestural, but meant that every [male] citizen who chose to was given an equal time and opportunity to speak on the affairs of the city.

Today, the story goes that Tariq Ali and Howard Brenton wanted to speak, in a play, on the affairs of the City, and sent it to the Royal National Theatre. The Director was delighted to receive a play from these two controversial writers, but when told the subject was Tony Blair, he rapidly passed on to the next American musical.

Perhaps it is naive and utopian to try to recreate the Athenian parliament in our mass society, but democracy demands a climate where the freedom to speak one's mind is granted equally to pro and anti government voices. It remains a concept central to the operation of authentic democracy.

4. Democracy implies that the will of the majority prevails. Yet this can rapidly become a tyranny of the majority, as in Northern Ireland, whose majority was deliberately manufactured, a majority who for many years chose to tyrannise the minority in the name of democracy.

Solon saw this situation coming, even before Athenian Democracy. His notion of *demossion kakon,* or public evil, saw that injustice to a minority would infect the entire community, and saw its avoidance as a prime human responsibility.

The device used by most modern countries to ensure the rights of minorities is a written constitution, to which any group or individual may appeal. It is indeed a matter of growing concern that Great Britain and Northern Ireland does not have one.

5. The cornerstone of democracy everywhere is equality of justice: *isonomia* – Equality before the law for every citizen. It was an essential element in Cleisthenes' reforms. This was related to two other concepts: *dike,* which was really a sense of right and justice and, by extension, the defence of the weak in society; and of course *dikaiosyne,* justice itself. Aristotle observed that 'the determination of what is just is the ordering of the whole of society'.

In a society whose laws have been created for centuries by blatant class interest, and which doesn't even have a written constitution to appeal to, can we claim a true sense of right and justice? Can we claim every citizen is equal before the law when rich individuals and corporations can hire for huge fees the most devious barristers? When the police condemn a poor black before he gets to court, then he has to meet the magistrate's prejudice?

Of course, when trust in the equality before the law breaks down, people see violence as their only resort. Then that 'violence' is contained and condemned, and a vicious circle of repression sets in, and democracy goes out.

6. The most vaunted attribute of democracy is that it means equality for all. Yet everywhere we see inequalities: not only before the law, but inequalities of gender, age, influence, access to power, opportunity, even of life expectancy. Then there is the major inequality between rich and poor, within our society and globally bolstered by birth, education and social contacts. What do the opinions of the voters of Rochdale matter, when the City and the media have the ear of the Prime Minister? Some, as Orwell noted, are more equal than others.

7. On a more positive note, the concept of *isotimia* helps bind together a society. Meaning literally 'of equal honour', it refers to the equality of every citizen's political rights (and responsibilities). Citizens are not just taxpayers,

nor consumers, but, in Philip Brooke Manville's phrase: 'Shareholders in a corporation whose profits are moral excellence'.

Close to this, lies *philotimia,* literally love of honour, but in ancient Athens it was conceived as the individual honour essential for the good of the community: the pride of athletes winning honours for their country, the pride of international recognition for individual achievement of all kinds, scientific, literary, cinematic, academic, artistic. The love of honour for one's country's sake, as well as one's own.

8. There are several other keywords that flesh out the qualities of democracy: *aidos,* a reverent respect for the judgement of others; *graphi paranomon,* the prohibition against proposing laws that would be against the good of the citizens; *euthynai,* a legal process for the examination of the conduct of anyone who held public office, and for the audit of their accounts, i.e. accountability.

Perhaps the concept that draws us even closer to the theatre, however, is that of *hubris* – defined by Victor Ehrenburg as 'the overbearing attitude of man both towards the gods and his fellow men'. A whole society can commit *hubris,* just as much as an individual.

Castoriadis: the Social Imaginary

One of the most thoughtful and helpful of the interfaces between democracy and the creative, the concept of the Social Imaginary, comes from the work of Castoriadis, a Greek thinker who died in Paris recently. If I may, I'll cite his work for the illumination he throws:[96]

First, on the role of socialisation in human history:

> I hold that human history – therefore also the various forms of society we have known in history – is in its essence defined by imaginary creation. In this context, 'imaginary' obviously does not signify the 'fictive', the 'illusory', the 'specular', but rather the creation of new forms. This creation is not determined, but rather determining; it is an unmotivated creation that no causal, functional, or even rational explanation can account for . . .
>
> Each society creates its own forms. These forms in turn bring into being a world in which this society sees itself and gives itself a place. It is by means of them that society constitutes a system of norms, institutions in the broadest sense of the term, values, orientations, and goals of collective life as well as of individual life. At their core are to be found in each instance social imaginary significations, which also are created by each society and which are embodied in its institutions.

Clearly the role of a public theatre in the processes of socialisation is vital. But a theatre dedicated to a critical challenge to its society can play a much more important role in the creation of a genuine theatre.

'Philosophical interrogation' – and I would add, theatrical questioning – 'does not halt before any postulate presented as ultimate and unchallengeable.' Here Castoriadis makes a remarkable leap:

> The same thing goes for democracy. In its genuine signification, democracy consists in this, viz., that society does not halt before a conception, given once and for all, of what is just, equal, or free, but rather institutes itself in such a way that the question of freedom, of justice, of equity, and of equality might always be posed anew within the framework of the 'normal' functioning of society . . .
>
> I will say that a society is autonomous not only if it knows that it makes its laws but also if it is up to the task of putting them into question.

Just as the individual has to rely on him/herself for salvation, so society can look for no help from God, revealed truth, or any outside agency:

> There were in the ancient world no 'constitutions' in the proper sense. Once one exits from a sacred world, from the imaginary signification of a transcendent foundation for the law re God and an extra-social norm for social norms, the crucial problem of self-limitation arises. Democracy is quite evidently a regime that knows no external norms; it has to create its own norms, and it has to create them without being able to lean on another norm for support. In this sense, democracy is certainly a tragic regime, subject to *hubris*, as it was known and was seen in the second half of the fifth century BC at Athens; it had to confront the issue of its own self-limitation.

Then he makes the connection between authentic democracy and theatre very plain:

> Finally – and unfortunately I cannot dwell on this immense theme – there is tragedy. Although its many different significations can by no means be reduced simply to a political aspect, tragedy also possessed a very clear political signification: the constant reminder of self-limitation. For tragedy was also and especially the exhibition of the effects of *hubris,* and the demonstration that contrary reasons can coexist (this was one of the 'lessons' of

the tragedy *Antigone)* and that it is not in obstinately persisting in one's own reasons *(monos phronein)* that it becomes possible to solve the grave problems that may be encountered in collective life (which has nothing to do with the watery consensus of contemporary times). Above all else, however, tragedy was democratic in this, that it was a constant reminder of mortality, that is, of the radical limitation of human beings. What is specific to *hubris* is that there are no marked boundaries; no one knows at what moment *hubris* begins, yet there is a moment when one is in *hubris* and that is when the gods or things intervene to crush you.

I'm sorry to have quoted the good Cornelius at such length, but in my discussions with him, I felt nothing but admiration for and almost total agreement with his profound and humane perception, his ability to connect the individual and society through the 'social imaginary,' and so to express what I feel passionately theatre ought to be doing in a society calling itself a democracy.

In all areas central to the working of a democracy, theatre has its role to play:

In celebrating and scrutinising the values within the borders of the *demos*;
In contesting these borders, external and internal;
In giving a voice to the excluded;
In giving a voice to the minority;
In constantly guarding against the tyranny of the majority;
In demanding the right to speak publicly, to criticise without fear;
In giving a voice to the oppositional;
In seeking true and balanced information;
In combating the distorting and anti-democratic powers of the mass media;
In questioning the role of large corporations, national and transnational, to influence both the law and the government of the day;
In defining and redefining freedoms for the age;
In questioning the borders of freedom;
In giving a voice to the less equal;
In demanding impartial justice and equality of all citizens before the law, rich or poor.

It may well be argued, for reasons both honourable and dishonourable, that theatre exists in the realm of Art, and these tasks for democracy operate in the realm of politics. To which I would reply in two ways: one, theatre, of all the arts, surely works at the interface between the creative and the political, calling together audiences of citizens to contemplate their society or its ways; and two, the theatre can only renew itself for audiences and for theatre-makers if it is part of the times it lives in. Pure Art there has never been, least of all 'pure' theatre.

But let us turn now to the less tangible role of *paedia*, the formation of the democratic personality, the inculcation of values, the renewal of ideologies and ways of thinking.

The Formation of the Democratic Personality

Castoriadis rightly draws attention to the relevance of tragedy to the democratic ethos. The *hubris* or excess of classical tragic heroes is directly related to the very openness, the constant questioning of human and social limits as imposed by the consensus of any society. We have only to look at Euripides' heroes and heroines to find a group of people who wittingly or unwittingly went too far ahead of the norms of society to survive.

In the modern theatre, it is often the playwright who assumes this tragic, going-too-far role. Wedekind, for example, in *Spring Awakening*, Büchner, Ibsen, Strindberg, O'Casey, Arden, all pushed the boundaries of their society's acceptable nexus to an unacceptable extent. All became hate-figures in their societies, and were punished in various ways for their *hubris*.

Perhaps it is a function of the transition from classical collective values to modern individual values that the heroic actions are not so much looked at objectively on the stage, as embodied in the creative heroism of the individual author.

Whether the *hubris* is presented in its context on the stage, or is an act of creative defiance by the playwright, its effectiveness as part of a learning *paedia* or Socialisation process, is related to two main features:

1. Its *accuracy:* the audience must recognise and accept the emotional and social veracity of what is happening on stage, must identify with the core situation, whatever style may be used to present it; and

2. Its *relevance:* the core situation must reflect the central, most profound realities of its time, must speak to its audiences about a truth that matters in their lives, whether social, moral, political, emotional or individual. Needless to say, the theatre must use all possible means to reach every citizen in the *demos,* and not itself act as an excluding agency, whether by the price of its tickets, the manner of its box-office staff, its location or its impenetrability.

Theatre Today

The combined Arts Councils can clearly be seen by their actions as agents for the Security Forces, a kind of MI6 of the imagination, determined to crush all oppositional theatre, to insist on what Castoriadis called the 'closure of the social imaginary', to stifle the dialectic of history, in fact to bring about the ultimate wet dream of the politician in power with dictatorial tendencies, to bring about the end of history.

The subsidised theatre, towards which one could once look for adventure, now has been taught that it must embrace the values of the commercial theatre, indeed become a major contributor to the West End by selecting for its productions only shows that will, or could, make money when transferred into the West End's electronic arcade.

So let us look at the values of this commercial theatre, which dominates now as in the 1950s. The huge successes, the multi-million pound Really Useful businesses, are the musicals of one, Andrew Lloyd Webber, or imitations of them. Their storylines are slender, and either whimsical or mildly melodramatic. They are packed every night with citizens seeking not recognisable relevant *hubris* but a fawning, flattering escape from reality. We must pause and ask why these musical escapades are the most triumphant pieces of theatre of the 1990s? Why their titillating sexism, their bland 'moralisms', their refusal to question anything, fit so well with the ideology of our so-called socialist society?

But let's look outside London, at what used to be called 'the provinces' but are now known as 'the regions'. Most of the brave bold questioning theatres have either been closed down by Arts Council decision – like the Liverpool Everyman – or are now run by administrators, the management experts, the New Realists, who know a safe bet when they see one, and are not given to punting on long odds.

But here and there, rather like the readers and dissidents in *Fahrenheit 451* or *Brave New World,* small, heroic groups still huddle together trying to 'get away with' genuine theatre-making, with creative thinking, with playing a tiny but significant role in the democratic process. Jude Kelly's work in the West Yorkshire Playhouse; small touring companies in Newcastle and Nottingham; there are still a few out there, trying to break the intellectual and imaginative closure on our society imposed by Jim Callaghan, Margaret Thatcher, John Major and Tony Blair.

The rest would rather like to be a touch bolder, but prudence and managerial expertise forbids.

The Future

I can't end there. Apart from being a ridiculous optimist, I embrace Ernst Bloch's Principle of Hope, and believe the dialectic of society can never be stopped or suppressed for too long. There is in every human being, as well as a proclivity to passive authoritarianism, a spark of perception, of self-interest, of anger at injustice, of the desire that Blake saw in every mortal, that will not allow the human spirit to be finally broken.

I would propose that theatre today would regain its role, dignity and audience if it were to take as its project the responsible drive towards what Castoriadis calls 'authentic' democracy, if it once again saw its role as setting in motion the major forces, the conflicting ideologies, the central realities of our time, as finding the theatrical images and characters, style and language for such setting in motion, as the fearless pursuit of the consequences of such setting in motion, as struggling to extend the limits of our thinking about our society, as breaking out of the closure and complacency of much western civilisation, as risking the *hubris* of the personal and political, as becoming an excellent part of the socialising process, the *paedia* of our demos, and as making its work available to the whole of our society, not to the few.

On another level, to return to Brecht's wonderful *Anachronistic Procession*, the creation of a genuine comedy form for our times with a coherent basis in philosophy as well as a talent to entertain on a random basis, would be more possible if it were to explore the difference between authentic democracy and the state of bad-faith pseudo-democracy we live in. There are enough yawning gaps between our pretensions to social equality, equality before the law, freedom of all kinds, to motivate a million comedies. There is a need for a sharp, satirical theatre to scrutinise our values, to contest the borders of our democracy, to give a voice to the excluded, to the minorities, to guard against the tyranny of the majority, to criticise without fear, to seek true and multifaceted information, to combat the distorting power of the mass media, to define and re-define freedom for our age, to demand the equality of all citizens for the short time we have on this earth before we die.

From all of this you may detect that I am brooding on a new play. I have always argued that a writer needs to reinvent the theatre every time he or she writes a play. I hope you will wish me luck in this daunting task, and in the most difficult task of all, making all the levels of thought, imagination, perception, research and analysis, characterisation, style, language, a way to engage the audience, the work with the actors, the designer, the musicians, all work together as theatre: the most thrilling and important social event ever invented by humanity.

NOTES

NOTES

1   Unpublished manuscript, undated.
2   *Isis*, 29 April 1959, p. 12–13.
3   *Isis*, 6 May 1959, p. 20–21.
4   *Isis*, 13 May 1959, p. 16–17.
5   *Isis*, 17 June 1959, p. 18–20.
6   *Isis*, 10 June 1959, p. 16–17.
7   'Better a Bad Night in Bootle', *Theatre Quarterly*, No. 19, Sept–Nov 1975, p. 39–54.
8   *Encore*, May–June 1960, p. 40–41.
9   *Encore*, July–August 1960, p. 20–26.
10 'Better a Bad Night in Bootle', op. cit.
11 *New Statesman*, 25 August 1967, p. 238–9.
12 'Clap, Clap, Clap', *New Statesman*, 1 September 1967, p. 266–7.
13 'Murky Depths', *New Statesman*, 8 September 1967, p. 298–9.
14 'Better a Bad Night in Bootle', op. cit.
15 Unpublished manuscript, undated.
16 *Scottish International*, October 1971, p. 10–15.
17 *A Good Night Out*, 2nd ed., London: Nick Hern Books, 1996, p. 46–49.
18 *Black Dwarf*, 12 June 1970.
19 *Anti-Apartheid News*, June 1968, p. 6–13.
20 *A Good Night Out*, 2nd ed., p. 50–53.
21 Introduction to text, London: Pluto Press, 1977.
22 Unpublished manuscript, 10 January 1972, 7:84 England Archive, Cambridge University Library (C.U.L.).
23 Unpublished interview with Clive Barker, 1974.
24 Letter to Sir Hugh Willatt, Secretary General, The Arts Council, 9 October 1972.
25 *Writers News*, April 1972, p. 7.
26 *Plays and Players*, Vol. 21, No. 5, Feb 1974; and Introduction to text of *The Cheviot*, Methuen, 1981.
27 *A Good Night Out*, 2nd ed., p. 71–77.
28 *New Edinburgh Review*, No. 30, August 1975, p. 9–10.
29 Memo to the New Drama Committee, 16 September 1974.
30 Introduction to text, London: Pluto Press, 1977.
31 Extract from company document, 4 March 1975, 7:84 England Archive (C.U.L.).

32 Unpublished interview with Colin Mortimer, 27 March 1980.
33 Introduction to text, London: Pluto Press, 1978.
34 Mortimer interview, op. cit.
35 Company document, 1 October 1976, 7:84 England Archive (C.U.L.).
36 Mortimer interview, op. cit.
37 Programme note.
38 Unpublished manuscript, undated.
39 *History Workshop*, Spring 1978, p. 234–237.
40 Mortimer interview, op. cit.
41 *Theatre Quarterly*, Vol. 9, No. 35, 1979 p. 43–54.
42 Programme note.
43 *The Guardian*, 16 October 1981, p. 11.
44 *A Good Night Out*, 2nd ed., p. 54–60.
45 Paper delivered at *The Future of the Arts in Edinburgh* conference, 18 August 1984.
46 Introduction to text, 7:84 Publications and Aberdeen People's Press, 1979.
47 Introduction to text, *Two Plays for the Eighties*, 7:84 Publications and Aberdeen People's Press, 1981.
48 Ibid.
49 Programme note.
50 Submission to Scottish Arts Council, May 1982.
51 *The Bone Won't Break*, London: Methuen, 1990, p. 100–104.
52 Programme note.
53 Company document extract, 7:84 England Archive (C.U.L.).
54 Unpublished interview with Sandy Craig, 13 September 1982.
55 Programme note.
56 *The Guardian*, 5 October 1984, p. 19.
57 *The Bone Won't Break*, p. 44–50.
58 Programme note.
59 Policy Document, July 1984.
60 Film and television production company founded by McGrath in 1982.
61 Report to 7:84 Board, 1 December 1987.
62 Internal memo, 26 March 1988.
63 Unpublished interview with Robert Dawson Scott, 1993.
64 Dawson Scott interview, op. cit.
65 *The Bone Won't Break*, p. 3–16.
66 Extracts from 'Theatre in Thatcher's Britain: Organising the Opposition', *New Theatre Quarterly*, Vol. 5, No. 18, p. 113–123.
67 *Discourse*, Spring 1988, p. 20–23.
68 Unpublished manuscript, undated.
69 Unpublished interview with Nadine Holdsworth, 23 May 1999.

70 *The Weekend Guardian*, 1–2 April 1989, p. 2–3.

71 *Glasgow Herald*, 12 March 1989, p. 12.

72 Holdsworth interview, op. cit.

73 Programme note.

74 Review of *The Cheviot*, 20 August 1991.

75 Paper delivered at 'The Writings of Thomas Carnduff', an event organised by Tinderbox Theatre Company, The Old Museum Arts Centre, Belfast, 24 March 1991.

76 Programme note.

77 Holdsworth interview, op. cit.

78 Programme note.

79 *Artworks*, BBC, 20 July 1992.

80 Extracts from an interview with Janice Forsyth, 'The Usual Suspects', BBC Radio Scotland, 13 March 1995.

81 Cited in John Peters, 'Harold Pinter: The Poet of No Man's land', *The Sunday Times*, 7 October 1990, p. 13, 16.

82 'National Stages', Birmingham Theatre Conference, 2–4 April 1993.

83 'Beauty and the Beasts: European Policy to Rescue Cinema from the Jaws of Hollywood', Royal Museum of Scotland, 6 November 1998.

84 'A Hop, Skip and a Jump from Reality', *The Scotsman*, 28 January 1997, p. 15.

85 Unpublished manuscript, 2000.

86 Holdsworth interview, op. cit.

87 'Reaching the Stage of Optimism', *The Scotsman*, 4 September 1996, p. 13.

88 'The Last Twitch of a Dying Dogma', *The Scotsman*, 1 October 1997, p. 16.

89 Holdsworth interview, op. cit.

90 Keynote address, 'European Theatre, Justice and Morality', University of London, June 1999.

91 See John Willett, ed., Bertolt Brecht, *Poems 1913–1956*, 2nd ed., London: Methuen, 1979, p. 409–414.

92 I am indebted to Michael Kustow for introducing me to Castoriadis and his work. For further information, see Cornelius Castoriadis, *The Imaginary Institution of Society: Creativity and Autonomy in the Social-Historical World*, Cambridge: Polity Press, 1997, and *The Castoriadis Reader*, ed. David Curtis, Oxford: Blackwell, 1997.

93 I am deeply grateful to Eleni Cubitt for providing me with a list of these keywords – which proved not only helpful but illuminated the whole area.

94 Castoriadis, quoted from McGrath's notebooks.

95 Ibid.

96 Ibid.

CHRONOLOGY OF PLAYS

CHRONOLOGY OF PLAYS

Year Title   **Company/Theatre (first production)**

1958   *A Man Has Two Fathers* (a play in two acts)
                                    Oxford University Drama Society

1958   *The Tent* (a one-act play)   Royal Court

1959   *Why the Chicken?* (a play in two acts)
                                      Oxford University Theatre Group

1960   *Tell Me, Tell Me* (short sketch)   Live New Departures
                              Institute of Contemporary Arts

1960   *Take It* (short sketch)   Live New Departures
                              Institute of Contemporary Arts

1960   *Jack* (a play with songs)   Unperformed
       (music by Dudley Moore)

1963   *Basement in Bangkok* (a play with songs)   Student Group, Bristol
       (music by Dudley Moore)

1966   *Events While Guarding the Bofors Gun* (a play in two acts)
                                        Hampstead Theatre

1968   *Bakke's Night of Fame* (an adaptation)   Hampstead Theatre
       (based on William Butler's novel *The Danish Gambit*)

1969   *Comrade Jacob* (an adaptation)   Gardner Arts Centre
       (based on the novel by David Caute)

1970   *Random Happenings in the Hebrides* (a play in two acts)
                                      Edinburgh Lyceum

1970   *Sharpeville Crackers* (a multi-media collage)
                                    Lyceum Theatre, London

1971	*Unruly Elements* (six one-act plays) (renamed *Plugged Into History*)	Liverpool Everyman
1971	*Trees in the Wind* (a play with songs)	7:84
1971	*Soft or a Girl* (a rock musical) (renamed *My Pal and Me*)	Liverpool Everyman
1972	*Plugged into History* (six one-act plays)	7:84
1972	*Out of Sight* (a one-act play)	7:84
1972	*Underneath* (a play with songs)	7:84
1972	*Serjeant Musgrave Dances On* (an adaptation) (based on John Arden's *Serjeant Musgrave's Dance*)	7:84
1972	*Fish in the Sea* (a play with music)	Liverpool Everyman
1973	*The Cheviot, the Stag and the Black, Black Oil* (a *ceilidh* play)	7:84 Scotland
1974	*The Game's a Bogey* (a variety show)	7:84 Scotland
1974	*Boom* (a musical play)	7:84 Scotland
1975	*My Pal and Me* (a rock musical)	7:84 Scotland
1975	*Lay Off* (a play with songs)	7:84 England
1975	*Little Red Hen* (a play with music)	7:84 Scotland
1975	*Yobbo Nowt* (a musical play)	7:84 England
1975	*Oranges and Lemons* (a one-act play)	John Bett & Jenny Stoller
1976	*Out of Our Heads* (a play with songs)	7:84 Scotland
1976	*The Rat Trap* (a political allegory with songs)	7:84 England
1977	*Trembling Giant* (a pantomime for children of all ages, with songs)	7:84 England

1977   *Joe of England* (a play with songs)   7:84 England

1979   *Joe's Drum* (a play with songs)   7:84 Scotland

1979   *Big Square Fields* (a play with songs)   7:84 England

1979   *Bitter Apples* (a musical)   7:84 England

1979   *If You Want to Know the Time* (satire)
                    Blair Peach Memorial Event, Royal Court

1980   *Swings and Roundabouts* (a comedy with songs)   7:84 Scotland

1980   *Blood Red Roses* (a play with songs)   7:84 Scotland

1981   *The Catch or Red Herrings in the Minch* (a play with songs)
                                         7:84 Scotland

1981   *Nightclass* (a play with songs)   7:84 England

1982   *Rejoice!* (a play with songs)   7:84 England

1983   *On the Pig's Back* (street theatre)   7:84 Scotland/Wildcat
       (written with David MacLennan)

1983   *The Woman of the Dunes* (a community play)   Ijmuiden, Holland

1983   *Women in Power* (a musical play)   General Gathering
       (adapted from *Thesmophoriadzusae* by Aristophanes)

1984   *The Baby and the Bathwater* (a one-person play with music)
                                         7:84 Scotland

1984   *Six Men of Dorset* (a documentary play)
       (adapted from the play by Miles Malleson and Harry Brooks)
                                         7:84 England

1985   *The Albannach* (a play with songs)   7:84 Scotland
       (adapted from the novel by Fionn MacColla)

1985   *All the Fun of the Fair* (carnival theatre)   7:84 England

1986   *There is a Happy Land*
        (a concert on the entire history of the Gaels)   7:84 Scotland

1987   *Mairi Mhor – the Woman from Skye*
        (a play with songs)   7:84 Scotland

1989   *Border Warfare* (an historical pageant with songs)
                                                        Wildcat/Freeway Films

1990   *John Brown's Body*
        (an historical pageant with songs)   Wildcat/Freeway Films

1992   *The Wicked Old Man* (a black comedy)   West Yorkshire Playhouse

1992   *Watching for Dolphins* (a one-person play)   Freeway Stage

1994   *The Silver Darlings* (an adaptation)   Wildcat
        (based on the novel by Neil Gunn)

1994   *Half the Picture* (a documentary play)   Tricycle Theatre
        (written with Richard Norton Taylor)

1994   *Reading Rigoberta* (a one-person play)   Freeway Stage

1996   *The Last of the MacEachans* (a one-person comedy)
                                                            Freeway Stage

1996   *A Satire of the Fourth Estaite* (a satire)   Wildcat
        (based on Sir David Lindsay's *Ane Satyre of the Thrie Estaitis*)

1996   *Media Star* (a play for schools)   Theatre Workshop, Edinburgh

1997   *Worksong* (a play for schools)   TAG [Theatre About Glasgow]

2000   *The Road to Mandalay* (a musical play for schools)
                                            Bryn Celynnog School, Pontypridd

2001   *HyperLynx* (a one-person play)   Freeway Stage

INDEX OF NAMES

INDEX OF NAMES

INDEX OF NAMES